Quantum Transformational Healing

Dear Suzy!
Wishing you
Love Blessing
and Miracle

Jann Sturgis, Ph.D.

Ellara Archturya, Ph.D.

outskirtspress
DENVER, COLORADO

Outskirts Press, Inc.
http://www.outskirtspress.com

ISBN: 978-1-4787-1966-3

Outskirts Press and the "OP" logo are trademarks belonging to Outskirts Press, Inc.

PRINTED IN THE UNITED STATES OF AMERICA

Dedication

This book is dedicated to:

My parents – for giving me a strong foundation,

My friends – for supporting me along the way,

My clients – for inspiring me and giving me the opportunity
to create and develop Quantum Transformational Healing!

Acknowledgements

I would like to thank first the Creator, God/Goddess for being the ultimate Source and inspiration for the creation of this book. My eternal gratitude goes to beloved Master Jesus, for his love and the integration of my own Christ Self; Archangel Michael for his powerful protection and assistance in spirit release work; St. Germain for the gift and teachings of the use of the Violet Transmutational Flame; Serapis Bey, my main master teacher, for the keys to Ascension and the "Detaching from Outcomes to Receive Clear Inner Guidance" process; Mother Mary and Kuan Yin, as expressions of the Divine Feminine, and blessing me with their gifts of love, compassion, forgiveness, mercy and healing; Voltar, for psychospiritual integration on theoretical, conceptual and practical levels; and the Heavenly Hosts of Ascended Masters, Angels, Archangels, Elohim, Christed Extraterrestrial and Cosmic Masters for assisting me in my personal, and our collective planetary ascension.

I would like to thank the following people who have blessed my life with their friendship, support, love, healing, inspiration and assistance in my spiritual evolution: Michael Lindsey, for being a dedicated spiritual disciple of the Ascended Masters, and facilitating my spiritual awakening; Patricia Murphy for her love, friendship and intuitive support through my darkest hours of karma clearing, spiritual initiations, trials and tribulations; Michael Simpson – as a model of a high level of poetic and spiritual intellectual integration and transformational language; Rick and Colleen Parlee – for their friendship and support, and for being like my brother and sister in Hawaii; Genie Joseph and Kirk Rector for their spiritual friendship and introducing me to Holodynamics; Cynthia Chu - for being a spiritual teacher and healer, and bringing the Goddess energy into my life, and especially the energy and presence of Kuan Yin; Wally Minto - for the gift of his inspirational speaking and writing skills; Donald Baird, David Ostler, and Yon Herbert for assisting me with karma clearing, and being an inspiration to do personal and planetary healing; and Ernest Alatan for his friendship, support and encouragement.

I would like to express my thanks to Bennett Marks and Marissa Iannuzzi for deciphering and transcribing my handwritten notes, and to Marissa for persevering in the final rounds of edits. I want to thank Lori Chaffin for her support, encouragement, and referrals; Worth Grace James for her editorial expertise and her support and encouragement through the publication process, Leslie Fisher for doing a great job on the cover design, and the entire staff at Outskirts Press for their publication and promotional support of this book.

Preface

Since I have received the information and inspiration for this book through activation of my Spiritual Self, Ellara Archturya, I therefore have used my spiritual name as the author.

I believe there is no new information in the universe, but the information may be re-organized in new, more evolved forms or expressions of truth. I hope that you, the reader, will approach this book with an open mind, and find this book to be a practical expression of spiritual truths, concepts, tools and techniques for your spiritual self mastery, transformational healing, and Ascension.

I have endeavored to credit the various authors of previous original, unique ideas or works. As is the case with the evolution of mass consciousness or paradigm shifts, what may be considered impossible, false, heretical or unscientific in one period, may later be found to be possible, true, ingenious and scientifically sound.

August 2012
Ellara Archturya, Ph.D.
aka Laura M. Sturgis, Ph.D.
www.DrLauraSturgis.com

Table of Contents

CHAPTER 1

Integrating Eastern and Western Models of Psychology and Spiritual Evolution

An ever increasing number of individuals, many with a predominantly Christian religious background, have over the past four decades begun exploring the limits of human potential and investigating Eastern religions (primarily Buddhism and Hinduism), as well as mysticism, esoteric spiritual studies, and meditation. This human potential movement and integrative religious orientation constitutes an evolutionary renaissance and global spiritual awakening of consciousness. This awakening and transformation has, in large part, arisen out of the growing perception of emptiness of a life focused on the selfishness of personal material gain and narcissistic sensual gratification, which has resulted in a shift in values from "doing" and "having" to "being." As early as 1975, Gopi Krishna stated: "At a critical state in the development of the human mind the unanswered 'Riddle of life' attains an urgency which no treasure on earth can counteract. This is the state of mind of millions of disillusioned young people of the world today." He goes on to state that modern psychology is absolutely dead to one of the most powerful impulses in the psychic makeup of man, namely the search for the true meaning and purpose of human existence.

Western psychological theories of human nature have been linked to the study of the human "ego" or personality and have defined diagnostic categories of pathology that include adjustment disorders, neurosis, depression and bipolar disorder, along with personality disorders and increasing levels of psychopathology (including psychotic states and schizophrenia). Mainstream psychology has no coherent psychological model representing increasing levels of integration or wholeness. Normality is defined as the absence of mental illness and is considered the highest or optimal state of human evolution.

Beliefs in the supremacy of intellectual analysis, logic and reason, as well as linear cause and effect models of science, coupled with the illusion of scientific objectivity, have seriously limited the efforts of Western psychologists to account for psycho-spiritual phenomena that cannot be explained by the prevailing scientific models of objective reality and western psychological theories. Awareness of the process of spiritual awakening among traditional Western, typically Christian, mental health practitioners is extremely limited. Thus, attempts by Western psychologists and psychiatrists to move beyond the limitation of intellectual elitism and the illusion of scientific objectivity have resulted in egregious categorical errors, often pathologizing critical states of psychic opening and spiritual and kundalini awakenings. This has resulted in what Kuhn (1996) in "The Structure of Scientific Revolutions" calls a "paradigm clash."

From Eastern wisdom gleaned from centuries old religious and spiritual philosophy, tradition and discipline, the normal state of consciousness is not only considered sub-optimal, but dreamlike and illusory (Walsh, Elgin, Vaughan and Wilber, 1981). The normal, healthy individual is considered to be asleep, in a dormant state of smug self-complacency and contentment, as well as material and ego attachment. Typical beliefs of the human ego or personality self include statements such as: "I am my body," "Intellect is superior to intuition," "Material acquisition is the measure of success," and "Death is the end of life as we know it." These are all based on conceptual models or paradigms that are devoid of spiritual dimensions of reality and anchored in Western scientific and materialistic values which are distorted. Charles Tart (1983), an early pioneer in the study of consciousness, has noted the reluctance of Western psychologists and psychiatrists to apply the concept of maya or samsara to themselves, and he considers the possibility that their psychological models of reality may be seriously flawed. However, this is simply due to a lack of experience with meditation, higher or paranormal states of consciousness, and the spiritual science of enlightenment, traditionally associated with Eastern religious beliefs and practices (e.g. Buddhism and Hinduism).

In order for higher states of consciousness to be known, they must be directly experienced, since one does not miss (or understand) what is outside the realm of personal experience. The solution, proposed by William James (1966) is to remain open to the idea that there is always more, to allow us to outgrow the limitations of our present paradigms of psychological reality. The leap of faith in exploration of meditation and the higher reaches of human consciousness requires great courage, since it can ultimately engender a radical transformation and upheaval in the personality, and an altered understanding of the meaning of life and human experience then leads to experiential states of awareness that can include a newly developed sense of profound humility and shifts in values. Then, a pluralistic or integrative understanding and acceptance of both scientific and spiritual viewpoints becomes available as a coherent frame of reference.

Ken Wilber (1980, 1981), one of the major contributors in the field of transpersonal psychology, has described a spectrum of consciousness evolution, which includes three transpersonal levels integrating elements found within ancient Eastern religions and modern Western studies. He specifically delineates three realms of the transpersonal – the Subtle realm, the Causal realm, and the Atman realm.

At the Low-Subtle realm, one experiences seeing auras, traveling out-of-body and witnessing psychic phenomena, including clairvoyance, clairaudience, clairsentience, precognition, telepathy, healing through "laying on of hands," etc. At the High-Subtle realm, one experiences symbolic visions, as well as spiritual illumination through experiences of auditory/visual synthesis that can encompass sensations of being filled with white light, or other colors of light. Additionally, one experiences direct intuitive communication with one's guides, higher spiritual teachers, and angelic beings. Proof of Subtle experience is characterized by an emotionally felt appreciation of the universe as an integrated whole and one's unity with all levels of creation.

At the Low-Causal level, one's identification with the self and sense of ego-imposed boundaries as the dualistic split between self and God collapses entirely. One's consciousness expands further at the High-Causal realm to the knowing of formlessness, and the "ecstasy of the void," with feelings of great peace and joy predominating. On the personality level, integration at the High-Causal level is manifested when a person experiences the equivalence or equal valuing of pain and pleasure, with an internalized self-discipline, inner peace and altruistic rather than egotistical orientation. At the Causal level, this sense of unity and mutual interdependence will frequently be evidenced at a deeper level of behavioral integration, which is often illustrated as an expressed sense of service and dedication to personal, social, environmental and global transformation.

The final state of Ultimate Unity or Atman is defined by Wilber (1980) as the perfect integration of all prior levels - gross, Subtle, and Causal, which continue to arise spontaneously in the moment in an iridescent play of consciousness. Thus, one sometimes experiences rapid shifting of levels, dimensions, or planes of consciousness while simultaneously experiencing the reality, validity or "suchness" of all states as an integrated interactive process. This is what I call the experience of multi-dimensional simultaneous truth.

Joshua David Stone (1994) has also delineated a more detailed cartography of spiritual evolution, and he identifies seven levels of spiritual initiation to achieve planetary ascension: physical, emotional (astral), mental, Intuitional/ Buddhic or Christ, Spiritual or Atmic, Monadic, and Logoic.

Kundalini Awakening

Kundalini, which means "coiled," is a Hindu concept referring to the dormant evolutionary spiritual energy that resides in all humans. It originates at the base of the spine, and when activated, travels up through the seven main chakras, (or "wheels" in Sanskrit) up to the top of the head. Light and energy move up the physical body from the root chakra (at the base of the spine), through the Ida, or feminine nerve channel, and weaves primarily up the left side of the spine. It moves simultaneously through the Pingala, or masculine nerve channel, which weaves predominantly on the right (masculine) side of the spine, as well as the central nerve channel (Sushumna in Sanskrit). All three channels open to the crown chakra at the top of the head (Stone, 1995).

Kundalini activation creates the opening up and clearing out of all of the chakras, albeit in a somewhat idiosyncratic fashion, depending on the individual. Perhaps the most important chakras to open are the Heart Chakra (to activate the Christ Consciousness), and the Third Eye Chakra, (to see with the so called "3rd eye"), and the crown chakra, to be able to connect with one's Higher, Spiritual Self and Source. There are a broad range of Kundalini "symptoms" or signs of awakening of this powerful energy, which typically occurs from doing meditation or breathing practices.

Research Studies on Meditation and Spiritual Evolution

Relatively few investigators have conducted phenomenological research studies to examine the experience of kundalini awakening and transformation via meditation or other spiritual practices (Brown (1981), Joy (1979), Kornfield (1979), Sannella (1987). During the process of meditation, certain common physical, emotional, mental and spiritual correlates have been described which transcend personal and cultural differences. Some slight variations, however, have been suggested based on the type of meditation technique used; e.g. Zen Buddhist, Tibetan Buddhist, Hindu Yogic, etc.

From these studies, the process of meditation does not appear to lead to a linear upward learning curve, although the overall course represents a positive growth pattern. It is characterized by advancement, possible plateauing, and mild regression during periods when disintegrated, unhealed or unconscious issues are being worked through. This is then followed by restructuring of awareness, reintegration at a higher level of functioning, and resumption of growth. The periodic fluctuations affecting mental, emotional and social behavior are highly variable and idiosyncratic, occurring over days, months or years (Kornfield, 1979). It is important to note that persons working at advanced levels of psychotherapy, self-actualizers, as well as meditators may experience the same process of growth.

In meditative or contemplative, relaxed states of consciousness, the process of turning one's attention inward in deep self-exploration typically results in a variety of unusual sensory experiences. Typical inner sensory phenomena include seeing visions of colors and/or patterns, hearing ringing or buzzing sounds, feeling tactile or proprioceptive sensations in skin, muscles, or internal organ tissues, and unexplained tastes or smells.

An exemplary phenomenological study of psycho-physiological alterations occurring concurrent with intensive meditative practice, in this case, Theravadan Buddhist insight meditation, is a study by Kornfield (1979). Insight meditation commences with concentrating one's attention on the breath to quiet the mind. Later, it is followed by concentration exercises to cultivate a detached, non-reactive awareness, observation and appreciation of experience, whether it be internal events (breath, body sensations, thoughts, feelings) or experiences derived from the 5 senses (external stimuli). A total of 22 categories of experience were gleaned from Kornfield's data pool of over 1000 questionnaires from Buddhist insight meditation students engaging in intensive 2-week or 3-month retreats.

In the category of spontaneous movement, for example, subjects described the following experiences: body twitching, involuntary jerks, violent shaking and tension release, and spontaneous hand, arm and body movements (flapping, dancing, stretching). These have been interpreted as signs of kundalini awakening, or also as bodily energy releases of deeply held tissue memories of unpleasant experiences (Lowen, 1994); or unstressing responses similar in description to changes secondary to autogenic training (Schultz and Luthe, 1990). Alterations in body image include sensations of floating, heaviness, expansion or reduction in the size of the torso and/or limbs, and sensations of pain in the head or various body parts, experiences also frequently seen in deeply relaxed or hypnotized individuals.

Unusual visual perceptual experiences (eyes open) included: flashes and changes of light and color, clearer, brighter, improved vision, still objects moving, seeing imaginary objects, visual after-images, and luminous energy fields (auras) emanating from the body. With the eyes closed, the following visual alterations were noted: seeing various colors of light (especially white light), seeing the Buddha or Christ, or other religious imagery of gurus, masters, etc., and seeing mental pictures – moving and still. Additional experiences of spontaneous visions of violent, aggressive or lustful sexual imagery with strong emotional catharses were also reported (Kornfield, 1979). The latter I would interpret as spontaneous release (via inner imagery) of repressed or unhealed psychological material. Auditory perceptual changes reported by experienced meditators include: ringing, buzzing, and high pitched sounds, hearing one's inner voice or the voice of one's guide, guru, or divine beings, including God. Other sensory-perceptual alterations may include increased sensitivity to or awareness of inner-sensory or "imaginary" odors and tastes, although these experiences are less frequent than the kinesthetic, proprioceptive, visual and auditory phenomena mentioned earlier.

It is easy to imagine the possible misinterpretation of such phenomena by the clinician or client who is unaware of the probable relation of similar symptoms to meditative transformation or spiritual awakening. For mental health practitioners trained in psycho- diagnostics, the close similarity of the experiences aforementioned to signposts of schizophrenia and schizotypal personality disorder is readily evident.

Report of strong emotional experiences and mood swings included: intense "roller-coaster rides" of emotions of anger, love, fear, sadness, and joy, with blissful highs and very depressed lows; experiences of flatness and boredom, feeling like one is an open cut, raw, exposed and very sensitive. Additional symptoms include violent crying, depression or anxiety that passes away, then stillness. Barring prior significant affective illness (cyclothymic or bipolar illness), these intense and labile shifts in mood states require clinical explanation and interpretation as normal experiences of clearing out blocks, inhibitions, traumas, and mental/emotional patterns on the path of healing, as self-mastery leads to detached, peaceful awareness.

Other changes include fluctuations in sleep and eating patterns, with usually marked decreases during periods of intense meditation retreats. It is postulated that in an alert, balanced and non-reactive state, less stress and tension are accumulated, thus requiring less sleep. Similarly, such a state would require less energy for daily tasks, resulting in decreased food consumption.

Other Life Events that Facilitate Spiritual Awakening

There are other precipitants to spiritual awakening and/or crisis besides intensive meditative and spiritual practice previously mentioned (Bragdon, 1988). States of physical distress from intensive physical workouts where ecstatic levels of transcendence, euphoria and one-pointedness are reached, near death experiences, surgery, or pregnancy and childbirth may precipitate intense spiritual experiences and insights. An existential crisis in material/spiritual values, or another life crisis (dark night of the soul) may catapult others into spiritual self-discovery. Intense emotional distress from life transitions associated with death, serious illness, and loss or separation from loved ones or loved jobs, can also stimulate spiritual insight and transformation.

Intense sexual experiences modeling the archetype of the sacred marriage of male and female energies, as in Tantric yoga practices, may result in spiritual experiences from the Subtle to the Atman levels. Substance use/abuse, specifically of psychedelics, and empathogens or designer drugs, can initiate an opening to spiritual experience and facilitate integration if used in the appropriate dosage and setting (Grof, 1989). Recovering from alcohol and drug use may also stimulate spiritual transformation with or without spiritually based treatment approaches such as AA and NA.

Cycles of Transformation

The process of spiritual evolution occurs in irregular waves, or cycles of active clearing (contraction) manifested as physical, emotional, mental or spiritual "symptoms" followed by a period of rest and stabilization at a higher vibrational frequency in the more light filled, expanded state.

During times that denser energies are intensely experienced as uncomfortable symptoms, it is paramount to remember in "our darkest hours" that this too shall pass. It is therefore critical to not avoid, block, deny or suppress the thoughts, feelings and memories that arise, but to lovingly embrace (accept) this phase as part of the normal process of human spiritual evolution.

Additional differential diagnostic and treatment considerations with individuals who are experiencing spiritual awakening, kundalini activation, or other signs of spiritual transformation, will be discussed in the final chapter 13.

In the next chapter, I will present some tools and techniques to facilitate spiritual self-development, which address some of the important needs and considerations that arise in the course of spiritual awakening and evolution.

CHAPTER 2
Spiritual Self Development

In order to become enlightened and progress spiritually, one literally needs to increase his/her light quotient or integrate a greater amount of light in the physical, emotional, mental, and spiritual bodies. The two most basic methods of increasing one's light quotient and vibrational frequency are through the use of 1) visualization of light or color rays and 2) vocalization of sacred sounds, words or mantras. Visualizing colors is a more universally acceptable method of clearing and balancing one's energy bodies, since it is non-language based, which is why I prefer this specific technique over sound and language based methods. Visualization of colored light fields in and around the body activates the specific qualities of that color ray. Clear crystalline, diamond white light is the highest frequency of white light. Similarly, the highest vibrational frequency of the various color rays (red through violet, etc.) have an underlying diamond, crystalline transparency (vs. more opaque or translucent colors). Interestingly, society's integration of this higher spiritual truth is reflected in the fact that greater monetary value is placed on precious gems (diamond, ruby, sapphire, emerald, etc.), which are clear and appear as colored diamonds, whereas semi-precious rocks and minerals are translucent or opaque.

The following meditation or guided imagery process, which I call the Spiritual Alignment, Christ Integration, Transmutation and Protection Process (or meditation) is a four step process adapted from the *Chart of the I AM Self* (Prophet, 2004). In the first step, golden white light is visualized as projected from the Divine I AM (God/dess) Self, down through the Inner Christ Self, and into the human body, to form a cocoon of light around the spiritual disciple, or initiate.

Golden, diamond white light is considered by many spiritual groups and individuals to be more powerful than the pure crystalline white light alone. Gold is the color of wisdom and illumination. This is the same color of the halos around the heads of Jesus and the saints depicted in Christian, Renaissance and medieval art!

The second step involves visualizing a triune, or three-fold flame of intertwining pink (love), gold (wisdom) and blue (power) in the heart center, which is also known as the Christ Consciousness Flame (Prophet 1997). The importance of the three-fold flame will be discussed in greater length in Chapter 3.

The third step is to visualize violet light, which is the most powerful healing ray in our visible light spectrum. When violet light is effectively visualized by a powerful meditator, it will clear and transmute negative or discordant energies, emotions, thought forms, etc. into pure light energy, which leaves a void or vacuum. Since "nature abhors a void," it is important to seal the energetic field of the person by first visualizing golden-white (gw) light, or another pure color of light in the rainbow spectrum, in order to fully surround and interpenetrate the area filled with violet light. The reason for this is to prevent unwanted, negative energies from entering the void that was created by the violet light. Hence, we first visualize a golden-white cocoon of light, and then inside it, visualize a smaller cocoon of violet light nested within.

In the fourth step, blue-silver, silver or platinum (the highest frequency of silver) light is visualized for spiritual protection on the outside of the golden-white cocoon. Blue is traditionally the color ray of power and protection and silver is an even more powerful ray of Divine Grace and protection. Interestingly, silver is the color of mirrors, and the silver ray can deflect, or reflect back any negative energies, and/or transmute them by the Law Of Grace!

This meditation is recommended to be used on a daily basis in order to safely progress and minimize excessive emotional upheaval, which can lead to mental and emotional overwhelm, depression, anxiety, or even psychotic symptoms, especially during intense periods of clearing and healing. It addresses the typical problems or crises in psycho-spiritual transformation, including: inadequate grounding, lack of psychological/spiritual boundaries and/or protection, and mental/emotional overwhelm as layers of repressed, unconscious material surfaces in conscious awareness, and one becomes increasingly aware of subtle energies, inner blocks, and develops spontaneous psychic, or "inner sense" abilities.

The "Spiritual Alignment, Christ Integration, Transmutation and Protection," meditation is a multi-purpose meditation, which includes use of specific color-ray visualizations that cover several important facets of spiritual development including: 1) the enhancement of one's spiritual connection or alignment and grounding of higher spiritual energies using the golden (wisdom, illumination) and white (purity) rays; 2) integration of the Christ Consciousness through visualization and balancing of the three-fold flame of love (pink), gold (wisdom), and blue (power) in the heart center, to minimize the creation of karma; 3) clearing, transmuting and healing energies or karmic patterns that are continuously surfacing or being brought up during ones transformational process through use of the violet ray, which is the most powerful transmutational healing color; and 4) spiritual protection from unwanted "negative" thoughts, emotions, energies or entities outside of your physical, emotional, mental and spiritual bodies through use of the blue/silver or silver ray of power and protection.

Spiritual Alignment, Christ Integration, Spiritual Transmutation and Spiritual Protection

Spiritual Alignment

Sit upright with your spine straight and head balanced above your shoulders, with your arms and legs uncrossed. Close your eyes, relax and breathe deeply. Visualize a golden white sun or sphere above your head (symbol of the Great Central Sun and the Christ Light), about the size of a basketball or larger. See it streaming brilliant golden white (gw) rays of divine illumination in through the top of your head (crown). Breathe in the gw light, and intensify the color each time you inhale. As you exhale, breathe out and expand the gw light above your head. Next, allow the gw sphere to descend into the middle of your head. Inhale, using your powers of focused concentration to visualize deepening and intensifying the gw color in your head; and exhale, expanding the gw color all around your head. Visualize the gw sphere descending progressively down through the middle of your body, and filling each area with the gw light. See the sphere now descend into your neck and shoulders…and breathe the gw light down through your arms and hands … into your heart … through your back and chest area…and down through your stomach and abdomen. Next, breathe and visualize the gw light moving down from your hips into your thighs, down through your legs, to your feet. Just go at your own pace, taking all the time you need to visualize to the best of your ability the gw light filling your entire body from head to toe… and when that is complete, have the sphere or sun rest below your feet. After the sun is resting below your feet, then see the sun spiraling upward and around your body in a clockwise direction (from left to right) filling your aura or the space around your body about 2-3 feet in all directions with gw light, creating a cocoon of gw light all around your body, until the gw sun spirals upward and rests above your head. Now visualize a gw or silver cord about 1 ½" in diameter from the top of your head extending upwards into the higher dimensions, connecting to your Higher Christ Self and continuing upwards to Divine Creator Source. Breathe in, and then exhale while simultaneously visualizing the gw or silver cord going higher and higher. When you feel a greater sense of peace and higher connection to Source, then breathe this energy back down the cord, all the way down into your head. Then, extend a grounding cord of gw or silver light from the top of your head down the center of your body to your heart, down your torso and down through the base of your spine, breathing it down into the earth. Continue to visualize this gw or silver cord going down deeper and deeper into the earth until you feel yourself firmly anchored deeply within the earth. (N.B.

you will feel your buttocks pressing down onto the surface on which you are sitting when you have effectively visualized this grounding cord. Also, grounding cords can additionally be projected down from the soles of both feet).

Christ Integration

2. Next, I'd like you to visualize the three-fold flame in your heart, a flame of three intertwining colors: pink (divine love), gold (divine wisdom), and blue (divine power), of equal height. At first, the flame may only be about an inch or so in height. As you breathe in, continue to expand the flame in your heart even higher. Breathe new life into the flame until it is about five inches in height.

As you bask in the radiance of your own being, you will see yourself now enfolded in an oval or cocoon of golden white light extending about two to three feet out from your body. In your heart center is the three-fold flame of Divine Love, Wisdom and Power with intertwining flames of pink, gold, and blue.

Spiritual Transmutation

3. Now, visualize a sphere of violet (purple and pink) light around your head about the size of a basketball. See this violet sun radiating clear violet light, like a violet diamond, filling your entire head. Then, imagine the violet sun descending through your body, filling your neck, chest and middle torso with radiant, sparkling, crystalline violet light. See the violet light next moving down through your body into your pelvic region and legs, all the way down to your toes. After you have completely filled your entire body with violet light from head to toe, allow the violet sun to rest below your feet.

Then imagine the violet sun spiraling upwards in a clockwise direction (from left to right), until it fills your aura or the area around your body about one foot in all directions with violet light. Breathe up the spiraling violet sun until it has rotated and filled the area around your body about one foot in all directions with violet light, from below your feet to above your head. Then allow the violet sun to return to a resting place in your heart center. If you would now imagine looking at yourself from above, your body would be filled and surrounded by an ovoid (or cocoon) of violet light about one foot out in all directions, with the three-fold flame in your heart center, and golden white light filling your entire body, extending out about two to three feet in all directions.

Spiritual Protection

4. Now I'd like you to visualize a brilliant blue-silver or silver sun above the gw sun over your head. See this blue-silver sun radiating rays of blue-silver protection all around you. Then, imagine the blue-silver sun spiraling downward in a clockwise direction all around the outside of the gw light cocoon, creating a blue-silver ring of protection about one foot in all directions around you.

The following is a diagram of how the color meditation fields would appear if you were looking at yourself from an external point of view.

Figure 2-1

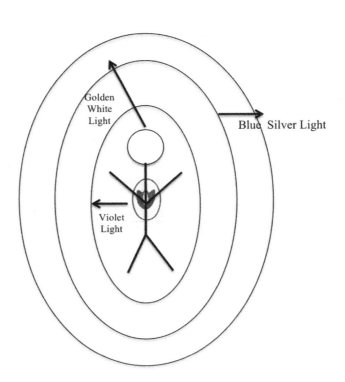

Visual Representation of the Spiritual Alignment, Christ Integration, Transmutation and Protection Meditation

5. Now affirm "I AM the golden white light of Divine Wisdom and Illumination healing every atom, molecule, cell and organ in my physical body. I AM the balanced three-fold flame of pink (Divine Love), gold (Divine Wisdom), and blue (Divine

Power), blazing and expanding in my heart chakra and encompassing my entire body. I AM my Inner Christ Self and integrated Divine "I AM" Self in action and service. My personal will is in full alignment with Divine Will and Purpose in this lifetime. I AM God's Will in Action here. I AM the perfected balance of love, wisdom, and power in the fullness of my individualized expression of my spiritual mission. I AM the fulfillment of my divine Plan in full expression now. I AM the violet light transforming all negative energies into pure light, clearing karma and transmuting my genetic structure and DNA into my Divine Blueprint. I AM the blue silver ring of Divine Protection and Grace, instantaneously protecting me from all negative energy, emotions and thought forms outside myself. THROUGH THE WISDOM OF DIVINITY ALL NEGATIVE ENERGY FORMS ARE EITHER INSTANTLY REFLECTED BACK TO THEIR SOURCE OR TRANSMUTED BY THE LAW OF GRACE AS THEY CONTACT MY BLUE-SILVER FIELD OF PROTECTION. I AM THAT I AM.

N.B. The affirmation to have all negative energies either 1) transmuted on contact with the blue-silver shield of protection, or 2) reflected back to their source, is important, because sometimes it is in the highest and best interests of oneself and significant other(s) to have the negative energies instantaneously cleared and transmuted (silver is an even more powerful transmutational color ray than violet). In other instances, it is in the highest and best interests of oneself and the person (or negative entity) that projected the negative energy to have the energy sent back to them. In this instance, he or she feels the impact of what they are projecting to others.

For example if someone sends out verbally critical, angry energy, and it is reflected back to them (either verbally or energetically), they feel the impact of the negativity (and get a taste of their own medicine so to speak) which can be the catalyst that is needed to get them to stop doing it! Leaving the choice of which option is best to the Divine is the best course of action since it removes the "ego" or human personality self from the opportunity to react from a lower level of consciousness!

Chakra Clearing & Balancing Meditation

Another foundational spiritual meditation practice is to visualize the seven main energy centers, also known as the chakras (wheels), as spheres of the corresponding colors from red to violet, also known as ROYGBIV.

Figure 2-2

Colors		Chakras
Violet	7th	Crown
Indigo	6th	Third Eye
Blue	5th	Throat
Green	4th	Heart
Yellow	3rd	Solar Plexus
Orange	2nd	Sacrum/Navel
Red	1st	Base of Spine

The Seven Chakras and The Color Rays

This sequence is often called the Rainbow Bridge Meditation.

An enhanced or improved version is to follow these steps: 1) visualize a cocoon of golden-white light to create a light shield around the body; 2) use the violet light to clear the chakras, which are often partially closed down, blocked, or filled with muddied or unclear colors if seen from a clairvoyant perspective; 3) activate the Rainbow Bridge Meditation by visualizing the red through violet colors in the appropriate chakras.

Here is a script for doing the Chakra Clearing and Balancing Meditation:

1. Follow steps one and three (Spiritual Alignment and Transmutation) from the four step process outlined in the *Spiritual Alignment, Christ Integration, Transmutation and Protection Meditation*. Now, visualize a sphere of clear bright crystalline red light (the color of a ruby) at the base of your spine (perineal area), about three inches in diameter. See it shimmering and radiating brilliant red light, and as you inhale, intensify the color even more. Pause, then exhale, and expand the sphere of red light. Repeat the cycle by first inhaling and intensifying the color, then exhaling and expanding the color sphere for another three breath cycles.

   If you sense blockage in any chakra or see dark or muddied colors, visualize a sphere of bright violet (purple and pink) light to clear and transmute the unclear color energies, before proceeding with the desired color for that specific chakra or energy center.

2. Visualize a three inch diameter sphere of brilliant orange light centered at your navel. Repeat three breath cycles focusing on inhaling and intensifying the color, then exhaling to expand the orange sphere.

3. Visualize a bright yellow sphere in the solar plexus (stomach) chakra for three breath cycles (as above).
4. Visualize a brilliant green sphere in the heart-center chakra for three breath cycles.
5. Visualize a bright blue sphere in the throat-center chakra for three breath cycles.
6. Visualize a brilliant indigo (blue and purple) sphere in the third eye center (above the bridge of the nose in the middle of the forehead) for three breath cycles.
7. Visualize a bright violet sphere (purple and pink) in the crown chakra (top of the head) for three breath cycles.

A more advanced higher octave version of the Rainbow Bridge Meditation has been called the "New Age Bridge." Various spiritual teachers including Montgomery (1993) also add the Thymus Chakra, otherwise known as the "Higher Heart," which represents the integration of energies of love from the heart, connecting the thymus (unconditional love) and the throat (creative communication) in unconditional, loving communication. Additionally, the transpersonal point (above the crown) is added, which connects the person to his/her soul and divine I AM Self (Aeoliah, 1992).

The following is the Higher Octave Color Bridge Meditation, which includes the thymus and transpersonal chakras or centers (adapted and integrated from Aeoliah (1992) and Montgomery (1993).

Figure 2-3

Chakra / Energy Center	Color
1. Root	Diamond White
2. Sacral / Navel	Violet
3. Solar Plexus / Stomach	Ruby / Gold
4. Heart	Pink
5. Thymus (half way between Heart & Throat)	Turquoise / Silver
6. Throat	Cobalt Blue
7. Third Eye	Emerald / Indigo
8. Crown	Gold
9. Above the Crown (Transpersonal Point)	Mother of Pearl

The 9 Chakras and Higher Octave Color Bridge Meditation

For the Higher Octave Color Bridge Meditation, follow the same basic process as the Chakra Clearing and Balancing Meditation, visualizing a cocoon of golden white light, then a violet cocoon nested within the golden white cocoon. This is followed by sequentially visualizing spheres of light in the following order: crystal, violet, ruby-gold, pink, turquoise-silver, cobalt blue, emerald-indigo, gold, and then iridescent mother of pearl in the corresponding chakras or energy centers from one to nine.

Developing Your Inner Sense Abilities

Just as we have five "outer" sense abilities (sight, sound, touch, smell, and taste), we also have corresponding "inner sense abilities," more often referred to in the popular literature as intuitive or psychic abilities. In Neuro-Linguistic Programming (NLP), there are three main outer sensory modalities we use to gather data about the world: visual, auditory, and kinesthetic (feelings and movement) (Bandler, 1998). From my experience, there seems to be a correlation between outer and inner sensory modality strengths, or preferences.

The following questionnaire can be used to determine your current Inner Sense Abilities (ISA). In order to prevent potential bias, it's best to take the self-assessment questionnaire prior to reading further about the four different types of inner sense abilities.

Inner Sense Abilities Questionnaire

For each question, rank from one (most likely) to four (least likely) how you would respond in each situation. Place your number value in front of the letter item.

1. **Your present job has ended. To find a new job and further your career, you:**
   _____ A. Systematically buy several papers and analyze every ad, then choose which ones are the most logical ones to apply for.
   _____ B. Picture yourself in several different jobs, and then search for the one that fits your mental pictures.
   _____ C. Answer only the want ads that instantly strike you and feel confident the right job will come along.
   _____ D. Choose a job because you felt comfortable with the people you met when you were interviewed.

2. **You are single and have reached a time in your life when you are ready for a new love relationship. To go about choosing a new partner, you:**

_____ A. First form a mental picture of what your partner should look like.

_____ B. You are less concerned about how he/she looks, or his/her qualities, and care primarily about how you feel when you are with him or her.

_____ C. Make a list of all the qualities you want in a partner, then set out to find someone who fits your list.

_____ D. Go by instinct, knowing you will be led to the right person at the right time.

3. **When you are ready to purchase a new home, you:**

_____ A. Interview several real estate brokers, identify the most competent one, and then review every home listed in your price range.

_____ B. Find a broker with whom you feel comfortable and trust him or her to locate the ideal home for you.

_____ C. Drive around the neighborhood you'd like to live in, find houses that look good to you, and set up an appointment to view them.

_____ D. Simply know that the right place for you will turn up if you stay open and aware.

4. **It's vacation time. You choose to go:**

_____ A. To an isolated spa on the Florida coast where you can enjoy the mud baths, massages, ocean and warm sunshine.

_____ B. On a working Windjammer cruise, spending a week as part of the crew.

_____ C. Traveling in Europe, visiting as many major cities as you can in your two-week trip.

_____ D. On a photographic tour of the Grand Canyon and other nearby scenic wonders.

5. **When you are going to purchase a car, you:**

_____ A. Trust your intuition to guide you to the right car for you, regardless of the seller, the type, the location, etc.

_____ B. Visit car dealerships advertising the makes and models you find attractive in terms of design and color.

_____ C. Examine the newspaper ads for good buys, review all cars listed in your price range, and talk to car sales people you know.

_____ D. Pick the car that feels the most comfortable and handles well when you are driving it.

Adapted from Sanders Jr., Pete A. (1989) "You Are Psychic!"

ISA Questionnaire Scoring Key

CODE:
CS = Clairsentience = clear feeling
CV = Clairvoyance = clear seeing
CA = Clairaudience = clear hearing
CO = Clairomniscience = clear knowing

First, transfer the number you gave for each item in the space after each code.

1. A. CA = _____
   B. CV = _____
   C. CO = _____
   D. CS = _____

2. A. CV = _____
   B. CS = _____
   C. CA = _____
   D. CO = _____

3. A. CA = _____
   B. CS = _____
   C. CV = _____
   D. CO = _____

4. A. CS = _____
   B. CA = _____
   C. CO = _____
   D. CV = _____

5. A. CO = _____
   B. CV = _____
   C. CA = _____
   D. CS = _____

Next, fill in the score key box below by placing the number you assigned to each code in the corresponding category spaces (CS, CV, CA, or CO).

Example: If your answers for question #1 were:

1. A. CA = 4
    B. CV = 2
    C. CO = 1
    D. CS = 3

You would complete the question #1 score key box as follows:

	CS	CV	CA	CO
1.	3	2	4	1

SCORE KEY BOX				
	CS	CV	CA	CO
1.				
2.				
3.				
4.				
5.				
Total				

Figure 2-4

Now, to determine your Inner Sense Abilities (ISAs) from your most preferred (strength) to least preferred (weakness), fill in the score key boxes above, and then sum up the totals for the four Inner Sense Abilities of CS, CV, CA, and CO.

Finally, list your scores from lowest to highest, which represents your strongest, most preferred inner sense ability to your weakest, least preferred ISA.

Most preferred 1. _____ 2. _____ 3. _____ 4. _____ Least Preferred

Characteristics of the 4 Types of Inner Sense Abilities Personalities

The four types of Inner Sense Abilities are: clear inner knowing (clairomniscience), clear inner seeing (clairvoyance), clear inner hearing (clairaudience), and clear inner feeling (clairsentience). The top of the head or crown chakra is the center for clairomniscience, the third eye corresponds to the center for clairvoyance, the clairaudient centers are in the right and left temples, and the clairsentience center is in the navel (Sanders,1989).

The following descriptions of the characteristics (strengths and weaknesses) of the four Inner Sense Abilities personalities are adapted from the book, *You Are Psychic,* (1989) by Pete Sanders, Jr.

The person who is predominantly a CO or clairomniscient personality receives clear information, knowledge or wisdom as a direct "knowingness," (without actually hearing words as in clairaudience), and with a deep sense of certainty that the information is correct. It is knowingness without reason or supporting information, with information coming in through the crown chakra. It represents a multi-sensory integration of condensed information or synesthesia. Such a person gets instant insights and awareness, is precognitive and prophetic, and knows what the future will bring. COs are quick to think and act, and they tend to be in the right place at the right time. They function at an accelerated pace, are spontaneous, flexible and adapt quickly to changes. They tend to be complex, quick minded and can multi-task well. They tend to worry the least of the 4 types. On the negative side, if they become flooded with thoughts and ideas, they may be tangential in conversation and not finish their sentences. This is the most frequently encountered psychic or Inner Sense Ability strength.

The CA, or clairaudient type, receives information via direct words, sounds or even songs. The center for inner hearing is located in the temple area of both sides of the head. This person can more readily hear the inner voice of his or her own I/H Self or Guides, when they are clearly connected to their own superconscious spiritual self or spiritual guides. At times however, the voice of their Inner/Higher Self or Guides may be confused with their (lower) conscious mind's self-talk, and they need to learn how to discern whether information is emerging as clear spirit guidance detached from ego (desires or fears). Clairaudient individuals may come on strong verbally or energetically. They take words literally and may need lots of data. This inner sense ability type is good for getting keywords or phrases, and they can excel with specific answers to questions. They may have trouble trusting feelings or intuition and in some respects are considered the least sensitive to psychic subtleties because of being more literal, logical and left-brained. Clairaudience is the least frequently developed inner sensory ability.

The clairvoyant (CV) person can receive pictures, images and visual impressions easily. The area of the body for inner vision is the third eye (above the bridge of the nose in the frontal (forehead) region). Clairvoyants tend to be visionaries who need to see the "big picture" in order to proceed, and these individuals see things symbolically. They are good advance planners, and have excellent visual and spatial skills (interior and exterior design, finding directions, map reading, etc.) Clairvoyant types may have a resistance to change even to the point of rigidity if asked to change their plans. The key is to give them the idea and let them sleep on it, so they can visualize a way to integrate the changes into the total picture. These individuals can also be some of the best worriers, since they have an ability to visualize everything that can go wrong in a series of events.

The clairsentient (CS) is the feeling type that functions according to gut feelings or instincts. The center for inner feeling is in the navel. Clairsentient people are natural empaths, who can sense when others are troubled, and they can easily read other people emotionally to know what is being felt or thought. They lack a sense of time, trust their feelings and not logic, and they may get their feelings easily hurt. Since they are caring and empathic, they need to guard against picking up negativity from others in environments, because they magnify it. They may find it hard to turn off their inner feeling sense and detach from others' emotions, and they can become overwhelmed and overloaded by the feelings of others. The CS ability is the most natural and easiest to develop.

Excessive focus on the development of one's Inner Sense Abilities to the exclusion of broader spiritual self-development is discouraged in traditional Buddhist or Hindu teachings, because it can lead to becoming overwhelmed or overloaded with inner sensory information. Also, development of these abilities, which is usually considered "paranormal," can lead to ego inflation in persons with low self-esteem or imbalanced personalities. Specifically, a person may tend toward feelings of being special, or psychically gifted, which can occur when there are significant over-compensatory underlying inferiority feelings or unhealed, unresolved (conscious or unconscious) facets of the personality. Notwithstanding the above, the following meditation can be used to open and clear the energetic centers to enhance clairsentient, clairaudient, clairvoyant and clairomniscient Inner Sense Abilities. By using this technique, a person can become more proficient at doing the inner healing work of Quantum Transformational Healing to be described in chapter five.

Meditation to Open Inner Sensory Energy Centers

First, use the Spiritual Alignment Meditation to visualize golden-white light in and around your body, forming a cocoon or oval of golden-white light.

Open Clairsentience

Visualize a violet sphere of light in the navel (clairsentient center) about three inches in diameter. Breathe into the violet sphere, with each inhalation brightening and intensifying the violet light (which is purple, pink, and diamond white combined) and exhale out the violet light through the front of the navel. Visualize the light opening and expanding that center (chakra). Repeat for several breath cycles of inhaling and exhaling, until you experience a sense of clearing or opening.

Open Clairaudience

Next, visualize a violet sphere in your left temple, (about three inches in diameter). Inhale into the violet sphere, intensifying and expanding the violet light, and exhale out through the left temple. Repeat for several breath cycles. Do the same visualization for the right temple.

Open Clairvoyance

Now, visualize a violet sphere about 3" across in the center of your forehead (third eye) just above the bridge of your nose. Inhale, expanding the violet light, and then exhale out through the third eye. Continue breathing for several cycles, visualizing this center opening and expanding.

Open Clairomniscience

Finally, focus on visualizing a sphere at the very top and center of your head (crown chakra). Repeat the inhalation/exhalation sequence, breathing out violet light through the crown until you sense it opening.

For additional protection, visualize a shell of blue-silver or silver light around your cocoon of golden white light to "seal your field" or aura to prevent any outside, unwanted thought, emotional, or energy forms from entering.

An understanding of the location of the Inner Sensory centers combined with the use of golden-white and violet light to open and expand these centers is helpful when one wishes to enhance his/her ability to clairaudiently hear, or through the crown telepathically receive, direct communication from one's Inner /Higher Self or Spiritual Guides and Teachers, which is the subject of the next section. Visualizing light is also useful to unblock these inner sensory centers as one seeks to receive clear guidance and healing in the process of Quantum Transformational Healing.

Connecting With Your Inner/Higher Self and/or Spiritual Guides

Connecting with and integrating your Inner/Higher/Christ or Spiritual Self, or your spiritual guides or teachers, is an important aspect of raising one's vibratory frequency. This process allows one to receive clear inner guidance and healing when feeling disconnected, confused, unclear, blocked, or in need of healing.

In this guided imagery process, you will be guided to your own Inner Spiritual Place of Peace where you are connected with your own Inner/Higher Self, or your spiritual guide or teacher, in order to receive inner guidance and healing.

1. Do steps one and three from the Spiritual Alignment, Christ Integration, Transmutation and Protection Meditation.
2. Next, focus your attention on finding an Inner Spiritual Place of Peace (or use Temple of Healing, Sacred Space, Spiritual Sanctuary, or whatever name you prefer). Your Inner Spiritual Place of Peace (ISPOP) can be anywhere in the universe, a place you have been before, a place you create with your active imagination, or a combination of both. There is no right or wrong place, just the place that seems right for you today. When you have found your ISPOP, allow yourself to be fully immersed in the sights, sounds, smells and feelings of being there right now. As you look around you, see the sights, the colors and shapes… and hear the sounds with more clarity and definition. Breathe deeply and sense any smells…as you feel the peace and serenity, and whatever other feelings you may have. Just focus on your inner sensory experience to be fully and deeply present in that place right now.
3. As you continue to enjoy relaxing in your ISPOP, shift your attention and focus on calling from your heart for your Inner /Higher Self (I/HS), Inner Christ Self, Divine "I AM" Self or Full Potential Self (use the name you prefer), or one of your Spiritual Guides, Teachers or Healers, Ascended Masters, Angels and/or Celestial Guardians to come and be with you there in your own ISPOP. This is for the purpose of making a deeper connection with your own spiritual self or one of your spiritual teachers. Ask your I/HS (or the preferred name of your Spiritual aspect) or your spiritual guide or teacher to make itself visible in front of you in a form you can recognize. Please note that since spirit energies are not densified into matter, they can take many forms: human, angelic, light body

(usually spherical or oval shaped) animal (as in shamanic journeying with an animal/guide/teacher), or symbolic.

Optional – If you have difficulty with step 3:

Open your inner vision by breathing clear crystal light up from the base of your spine. See a clear crystalline diamond white sphere at the base of your spine, breathing it up and through your body and into your head. Fill your head with clear white light (or violet light for transmutation), and then breathe it out through the middle of your forehead (third eye) between your eyebrows.

Continue to make a sincere, heart-felt call for your Spiritual Self aspect or guide to make its presence visible in a form you can recognize. Just keep your mind open, like a blank TV screen, and allow any images (which at first may be fleeting or unclear) to appear, and watch as they take shape. Please note: this is a passive receptive process of receiving pictures from your subconscious or superconscious mind. Do not try to actively imagine something, just passively observe whatever is happening.

If you do not see or connect by feeling the presence (or hearing the voice) of your I/HS or Spirit guide, go back and repeat through steps one, two and three again in order to go deeper into a meditative state, and become more detached. If this process does not work after the 2nd time, then you are probably not ready to connect with your inner spiritual Self or guides at the present time, which may be due to not feeling worthy, an inadequate activation of your Spiritual Self, or it could also be a lack of sincere intent.

4. Notice what your I/HS or Guide looks like. Send love energetically from your heart (and/or visualize pink light streaming from your heart) to this spirit. Ask this spirit telepathically if it will talk with you (it always will). Please understand that in the event this spirit looks, feels, or sounds as if it is not a clear, higher spiritual teacher or healer, it is probably a discarnate astral or other spirit appearing because it wants to be released into the Light. Ask the spirit if it is aligned with the Christ Consciousness, God, or the forces of Light. If it does not give you a clear "yes" answer, ask it lovingly but firmly to leave, and call again for a clear spiritual guide to appear in your ISPOP.

5. At this point, you may ask any questions or for healing of a specific problem, but the best procedure is to ask Spirit, "What is the most important issue or problem for me to receive guidance or healing on today?" When Spirit tells you what the most important issue is, you can then ask additional questions about the nature of (and solutions to) the problem. Continue to carry on an inner dialogue with your spirit until you feel complete for that session. Ask for "homework

assignments" about how to advance your spiritual evolution.

6. Finally, allow your I/HS to fully merge with you, to anchor in the higher frequencies of spiritual love, compassion, wisdom, and power.

Detaching from Outcomes to Receive Clear Inner Guidance

The process of detaching from outcomes to receive clear inner guidance is premised on abiding by the two Cosmic or Universal Laws of Love and Free Will, the latter being related to the Law of Detachment. In order to abide by the Law of Free Will, we need to DETACH from our personal wants, needs, or selfish desires, and choose not to misuse power if our power in a particular area (intellectual, spiritual, physical, financial, etc.) is greater than that of other(s) involved.

In order to receive clear inner guidance, we need to release our desires or attachments to having certain outcomes. This next guided imagery process teaches you a technique to know when you are in a CLEAR state to receive spiritual guidance and how to know when you are NOT CLEAR. You are clear when you are ready to hear or accept any of the three possible answers to a question that can be answered with a *yes, no* or *maybe/ undecided response*, representing the range of possibilities, which means you are not attached to a certain answer or outcome.

If we do not accept the full range of possibilities, it means even if our superconscious, or Inner/Higher Self indicated a correct answer, we would block or not hear it, or perhaps even fool ourselves into thinking we are getting clear guidance. This is because WE ONLY HEAR WHAT WE WANT TO HEAR when we are in a state of ego attachment (vs. detachment).

In reality, if our unconscious, conscious and superconscious minds are all aligned with the answer that is in the highest and best interests of our self and significant others, we cannot possibly err, and we always receive clear inner guidance.

Generally speaking, our unconscious (representing our needs, wants, fears and unresolved, unhealed problems or issues), is usually "running the show" in most people, and is often a dominant force in the personality. To be dominated by our unconscious nature means that our unhealed or unresolved issues are keeping us stuck in "negative" thoughts, feelings and behavior patterns.

If a person is dominated by their conscious mind, they will use their personal will or ego, and mental and imaginal powers to create or manifest the outcome that he or she desires. Karma is created when one misuses personal power (will) to the exclusion of incorporating and abiding by the Laws of Love and Free Will with equal regard for the well being of others.

Here is a real life example of how conscious and unconscious blocks can interfere in our life and create problems by not allowing us to detach from outcomes to receive clear inner guidance (and subsequently create karma with our self and others). Let's say you have been offered a promotion at your job. The promotion would enable you to make more money, receive more acclaim or recognition in your chosen field, or achieve more of your full potential. However, it would involve longer hours at work, and it would result in more stress and fatigue, and so your health and your family relationships would suffer. What you want to do at this point is to focus on accepting the range of possibilities, which is expressed by being willing to accept a "yes", "no" or "maybe/ undecided" answer to your question: "Is it in the highest and best interests of myself and significant others for me to accept the promotion at work?" In order to receive clear guidance, we need to detach from our ego's wants or fears. Then, we need to remove any blocks or barriers to following our guidance on that particular issue. When you accept these three "choice-points", you are creating polarity integration, which then allows you to transcend polarity/duality, moving toward Divine Oneness!

If you have a *conscious* (ego) attachment to receiving more money, acclaim or recognition, you would tend to be biased in favor of a "yes" answer to accepting the promotion, with a potential tendency to block or not accept a "no" answer. You also may not want to hear a maybe/undecided answer either, because you can't wait, and you know the boss needs a decision the very next day. In order to get clear inner guidance, you would need to detach your conscious ego's desire for a "yes" answer, and open up to accept a "no" or "maybe/ undecided" answer to what is in the highest and best interest of yourself, as well as significant others. If you used your ego to make the decision to accept the promotion, you would also be creating karma with yourself and family (significant others).

Using the same situational example, let's say you were offered the promotion and you had an *unconscious* block to accepting the job promotion because of a fear of success. In this case you would be biased in favor of a "no" answer to "Is it in the highest and best interests of myself and significant others to accept the job promotion?" Your unconscious tendency (possibly from low-self esteem, fear of misuse of money, power, or the attachment to the glamour of acclaim/fame) would be to only accept the "no" answer, and possibly the "maybe/undecided" answer if you weren't too afraid of the greater success the promotion represented.

The process of detaching from a particular answer or outcome is a very valuable guided imagery process that you can use to check if you are ready to receive clear guidance for making important decisions in any and all areas of your life. Use it often to see what is in yours and others, "highest and best interests" in any given situation, and then follow your clear inner guidance!

Here is the *Detaching from Outcomes to Receive Clear Inner Guidance* technique:

1. Align yourself with your Inner/Higher Self using whatever meditation techniques work for you. Or, use the Spiritual Alignment and Christ Integration Meditation.
2. Then do steps two through four from "Connecting With Your Inner/Higher Self or Spiritual Guides."
3. Ask Spirit, "What is the correct question regarding the _____(name of the particular problem or issue)?" To test for clarity of detachment, ask Spirit for a question, which can be answered as *yes, no* or *maybe/undecided.*
4. After you receive or know the correct question, visualize 3 categories of answers such as "Yes," "No," and "Maybe/Undecided," each at the end of a straight line extending out in front of you in space. For example, "Yes," can be visualized in front of you to your left, "No" straight out in front of you, and "Maybe/ Undecided," to your right.

Figure 2-5

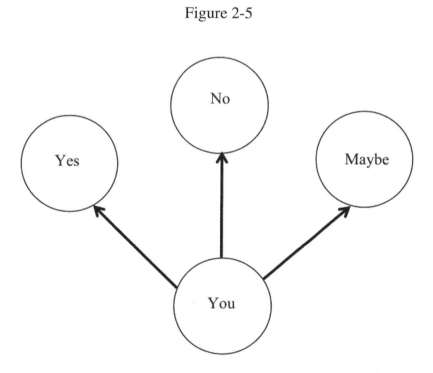

The 3 "Choice Points" to Test One's Detachment

5. Next is the key step in the process where you check whether or not you are open to receive each of the three possible "choice points" or answers to your question. It is imperative that you be *totally emotionally honest* with yourself. Notice any resistance or blocks to receiving any of the three answers. The hardest person to receive clear guidance about is *yourself*, and the hardest issues to become clear and detached about are those we have strong emotional feelings of attachment, or preferences for particular answers or outcomes!

    Say silently or aloud in a single, unbroken question to yourself: "Will I accept a "yes," answer to _____ (then say the question)?"

    Ex: If the question is "Is it my highest and best interest to move into a new living situation in the next month?" Then ask yourself "Will I accept a Yes answer to: Is it in the highest and best interests of myself and significant others to move into a new living situation in the next month?"

    If you will NOT accept a "yes" answer, then go back to the beginning of this meditation and repeat Steps 1 through 5. Then check again to determine if you are detached enough to accept the 3 choice points or answers to the question. If after a second attempt, you are unable to achieve sufficient clarity and detachment, then take a break, and use another technique (such as the Spiritual Alignment and Transmutation Meditation steps) to incorporate use of the violet transmutational flame to create greater clearing, transformation and transmutation.

    If you will accept a "yes", then ask if you will accept the next choice point, which is a "no" answer to the question "Is it in the highest and best interests of myself and significant others to move into a new living situation in the next month?" If you will not accept a "no", then go back to the beginning of the meditation and repeat Steps 1 through 5. If you will accept a "no", then proceed to check if you will accept a "maybe/undecided" answer to "Is it in the highest and best interests of myself and significant others for me to move into a new living situation in the next month?" If you will accept the "maybe/undecided" answer to the question, then you are sufficiently detached to proceed to the next step.

6. Finally, ask your Inner/Higher Self or Spiritual Guide the original correct question after you are in a clear state of detachment (demonstrated by accepting all of the three main answers – yes, no, and maybe/undecided) as choice-points in the range of possibilities.

    Ex. Ask, "Is it in the highest and best interests of myself and significant others to move into a new living situation in the next month?" Generally, you will HEAR a clear answer.

Alternate Visual Strategy

If you feel you are nonetheless clearly connected with Spirit, but you cannot hear a response, place a door at each end of the three choice points (*Yes, No and Maybe/ Undecided*) in front of you. Ask Spirit to have the doorway light up and brighten to the correct answer.

Alternate Kinesthetic Strategy

If you cannot hear or see the answer using the previous two auditory or visual strategies, just ask spirit to give you a feeling (kinesthetic) sense of the correct answer by checking the three lines of energy going to the three possible answers, to feel the strongest, clearest line of energy going to the answer which is in the highest and best interests of yourself and significant others.

Again, it is highly recommended to use the "Detaching from Outcomes to Receive Clear Inner Guidance" technique whenever you are needing to make an important decision in any key area of your life – personal, financial, relationships, business, spiritual, etc. to detach from your ego's desires or wants. This detachment allows the Divine Play of Freedom to unfold at its highest level, in accordance with the Universal Laws of Love and Free Will.

After practicing the Detaching From Outcomes to Receive Clear Inner Guidance Meditation, write down your answers, and follow through with your clear inner guidance. When you come out of your clear and detached state, and you return to your normal state of consciousness, it is very typical to experience resistance or blocks to following the guidance you receive. Then it is important to do additional clearing work, in order to be able to follow through with your clear guidance. Use whatever clearing, healing or meditation technique works best for you, or you can use Quantum Transformational Healing (QTH), to be presented in chapter five.

CHAPTER 3
Christ Consciousness Integration, Mastery and Ascension

The True Story of the Lost Years of Jesus

The true story of the life and teachings of the Ascended Master Jesus the Christ has been the subject of great controversy since the time of his birth. It has been well established by several authors that many books in the Bible, which contained the original teachings of Jesus, were either deleted or burned by the church forefathers in the 4th and 6th centuries A.D. (Prophet, 1994). Additionally, a large portion of what Jesus said in public and private teachings, and in the initiations he taught and entrusted to his disciples, have been lost or destroyed, (Prophet, 1988).

Specifically, in 325 A.D., the Emperor Constantine called together the first Council of Nicea, which amended the Biblical scriptures with numerous deletions and additions, establishing Jesus as the only begotten Son of God, so that gnosis (knowledge) could only be obtained through the Church hierarchy (the Popes, Bishops, and priests), which became (and still is) the hallmark of orthodox patriarchal Catholicism today. In 389 A.D., the Catholic Church put to fire large numbers of manuscripts in the greatest repository of ancient mystery teachings and spiritual knowledge in the libraries of Alexandria, Egypt.

Finally, in the last great wave of destruction, in 553 A.D., the Emperor Justinian II in the 2nd Council of Nicea in Constantinople deleted all direct references to reincarnation from *The Bible*, and *The Book of Enoch*, which contains the story of Archangels Michael and Lucifer, as well as the story of the fallen angels on earth. Additional critical information pertaining to Jesus' whereabouts during the so-called "lost years" from ages 12-30, when he traveled to India, Tibet and Egypt, before returning to the Holy Land, was also deleted. Preserving information in the Bible about the fact that Jesus studied sacred texts with spiritual masters of Hinduism and Buddhism would have created a unified body of truth and integrated spiritual wisdom from the three main world religions of Christianity, Buddhism and Hinduism.

The first rediscovery of evidence about Jesus' travels to the East during his so called "lost years" from age twelve when he left the temple and mysteriously disappeared from Biblical references until his return to Palestine at age thirty, was made by Nicholas Notovich, a Russian journalist who journeyed to Ladakh in Tibet in 1887. Notovich discovered ancient Buddhist scrolls in the Pali language at a monastery in Himis, Tibet, which stated that Jesus, who was called Issa or St. Issa, visited India and Tibet during those so-called lost years, at which time he became a master of Buddhist and Hindu teachings (Notovich, 2006). His findings were later denounced by Russian and Christian political and religious leaders as "pure fiction" and a "forgery."

In 1922, Swami Abhedananda visited the same Tibetan monastery in Himis to either verify Notovitch's findings or expose him as a fraud. He too found the same manuscripts, which confirmed the route that Jesus took during the 18 years after he left Palestine.

In 1925, Nicholas Roerich visited the Himis monastery and reported his accounts, which paralleled Notovitch's and Swami Abhedananda's findings, in his two books *Altai Himalaya* (2001) and *Heart of Asia* (1990). Finally, in 1939 without any prior knowledge of historical records of Jesus in Tibet, Madame Elizabeth Caspari was shown three books from the library at Himis confirming that Jesus (Issa) was there (Bock, 2007).

At age fourteen, Jesus had crossed the Indus River and spent time in northern India in the region of the Singh, and later in the cities of Jagganath and Benares. He studied with the Brahmin priests, becoming a master of the teachings contained in the Vedas and Upanishads, although he chose to live with the lower classes and preach that all people were equal in the eyes of the One God, a doctrine which ran counter to the Indian caste system and infuriated the Brahmin priests to the point Jesus had to flee for his own safety (Yogananda, 2007). He then went to Tibet and studied the Pali and Tibetan Buddhist scriptures, and mastered the Sutras. At age twenty six, after spending twelve years in India and Tibet, he journeyed back through the ancient land of Persia, staying in Persepolis then moving on to Athens, Greece, and finally traveling to Alexandria, Egypt, to study the teachings of the Egyptian mystery schools and secrets of the Great Pyramids and ascension. At age thirty, he returned to Palestine to fulfill his destiny.

Jesus As a Model of Ascension

What is the significance of the fact that Jesus integrated spiritual and religious beliefs and practices from the two major world religions of the East, Hinduism and Buddhism? Obviously, he demonstrated a path of eclectic spiritual integration for mankind! Jesus the Christ, a Jewish Essene (Hebrew), had studied and mastered Buddhism, Hinduism, Zoroastrianism, and the Egyptian Mysteries, and ultimately became the inspiration for the new world religion, founded on Christ Consciousness Integration, namely Christianity.

He was able to demonstrate various siddhis (Sanskrit for "powers") to perform many miracles, including exorcising demons, healing the sick, and raising the dead. These miracles were attributed by Buddhist and Hindu scholars to high accomplishments as a yogic adept in the science of Raja Yoga. He said, "I and My Father are one," and "I of myself can do nothing," referring to the Individualized God or "I AM" presence working through him; and "These things I have done, ye shall do also, and greater works than this shall ye do." Thus, Jesus inspired through example and taught us and his disciples that by following in his footsteps (integrating the Christ Consciousness and fulfilling his mission of teaching and ministry) that one's God-Self, or "I AM" self could be activated to perform the same miracles. It has been said that Jesus is the man, and Christ is the consciousness; the word Christ from the Greek, "Christos," meaning "anointed." He anointed his twelve apostles as well as many of his close friends and associates, including his mother Mary, Mary Magdalene, and other holy men and women.

Christianity has distorted the message of the life of Jesus, focusing on the crucifixion, and glorifying him as a martyr (victim), or Savior who died for our sins, so that we could be free. At a higher level of truth, he was a model of Self-Mastery, and his greatest message and teaching (by example) was how to complete the ascension, being freed from the cycle of death and rebirth by sufficiently clearing one's karma and fulfilling one's dharma or individual mission, or completing service work as requirements for ascension. He taught his disciples (the word means *one who is self-disciplined*) that the path of ascension was not easy, and their faith and strength in the spirit would be tested with many initiations.

As previously mentioned, Jesus preached a pro-egalitarian spiritual doctrine of equality and embodied a gylanic feminist and integrative view of human relations. As a model of embodying the feminine virtues of love, compassion, gentleness and mutual responsibility, he rejected the dogma that the high-ranking men of his day - priests, nobles, rich men and kings - were the favorites of God. Jesus violated the androcratic custom of talking openly to women, and he had female disciples (such as the woman known as Tabitha or Dorcas). In all four of the official gospels there is mention of his close relationship to Mary Magdalene, to whom he first appeared (prior to the Apostles) with instructions to inform the others that he was going to ascend.

After writing his Apocalypse, the Apostle John founded a secret order of

"Christed" Tibetan Monks called "The Ishayas" (named after Issa, the name the Tibetans gave Jesus), and ordered them to keep the teachings secret until the dawn of the new millennium (MSI, 1995). These ascension techniques are a progressive series of attitudes, each with a specific positive affirmation and point of focus to direct the consciousness on that attitude. The first four attitudes are the fundamental techniques to correct core negative erroneous and judgmental beliefs. They are: 1) praise, 2) gratitude, 3) love, and 4) compassion. These four basic attitudes create a positive mental-emotional, integrative unitary consciousness of loving connectedness within one's self and all forms of creation, leading to harmlessness (ahimsa) and the loving, wise use of power.

The Ishaya's ascension techniques transcend any particular religious belief. As such, they have a broad appeal as a modern day course in achieving enlightenment and Christ Consciousness that can be accepted by open-minded individuals of any faith or spiritual belief system seeking a system of further advancement in spiritual evolution.

Christ Consciousness Integration and Spiritual Evolution

Does one need to believe in Jesus to be saved? It is a distortion in Christian thinking to assume that all of the non-Christian world population cannot achieve salvation or eternal life (freedom from sin or karma). The following Biblical quotes provide examples of Jesus' teachings on the subject.

When Jesus was asked, "What must I do to inherit eternal life?" he answered, "Love the Lord your God with all your heart, and with all your soul, and with all your mind; and Love your neighbor as yourself" (Luke 10:25-28). Jesus did not explicitly state that one must follow him to be saved. In John 14:6, he said, "I AM" the way, the truth and the life. No man comes to the Father except through me." In the Aramaic Bible, "I" is ena-ena referring to the "cosmic I" also known as the Divine "I AM" self, or the God Self. Thus translated, the hidden esoteric meaning can be interpreted as the way to the Father (God) is through integration of one's God Self, or Divine "I AM Self." The Inner Christ Self is the intermediary integration between God and man.

In the "Chart of Your Divine Self" (King,1989; Luk,1996; Prophet, 2004) there are three figures representing the human spiritual disciple (lower figure), the Higher Christ Self (consciousness) also known as the Christed Oversoul Self (middle figure), and the God Self, also known as the Divine "I AM" Self (upper figure). A silver or crystal cord descends from the individualized Divine I AM Self through the Christ Self, to the human self.

Furthermore, in Luke 9:49-50, Jesus said unto him "Forbid him not: for he that is not against us is for us." Therefore, all those who are not explicitly against Jesus, which is the entire non-Christian world population, who may not believe in Jesus specifically, but embody and live a "Christed" lifestyle of love, compassion, and goodwill toward others, will also be able to attain eternal life in the heavenly realms (free of the cycle of death/rebirth).

How can we reconcile the great ancient spiritual philosophies and practices of Hinduism and Buddhism, which predated the birth of Christ and advent of Christianity, with Christ Consciousness integration in a more synthesized modern day approach to spiritual evolution?

Let's begin by examining the core goals, models and techniques of Eastern vs. Western religious traditions.

Integrating Eastern & Western Paradigms of Spiritual Evolution

In the spiritual teachings of the East, predominantly Hinduism and Buddhism, the goal is enlightenment, transcending the human personality self (ego) and its desires (attachments) that lead to suffering. The Eastern model of enlightenment represents the ascent of matter into spirit, traditionally described in the model of kundalini awakening where the dormant life energy literally rises up from the base of the spine (root chakra) to the top of the head (crown chakra). This is symbolized by the upward pointing (masculine) triangle.

The next stage of spiritual evolution according to Sananda, (2004) is the Christ Consciousness integration, which is the descent of spirit into matter, symbolized by the downward (female) pointing triangle. In the western Christian model, the focus is on attaining salvation and eternal life as the result of forgiveness of one's sins (similar to clearing one's karma in the East). This is achieved through prayers, and devotion to Jesus the Christ (as the intermediary to God consciousness).

Jesus speaks of this process of integration in *"The Gospel of the Holy Twelve"* (2005) as follows: "By involution and evolution shall the salvation of the world be accomplished, by the descent of spirit into matter, and ascent of matter into spirit, through the ages."

Thus, the Eastern and Western models of spiritual evolution can be depicted symbolically as the integration of the two triangles in Figure 3-1.

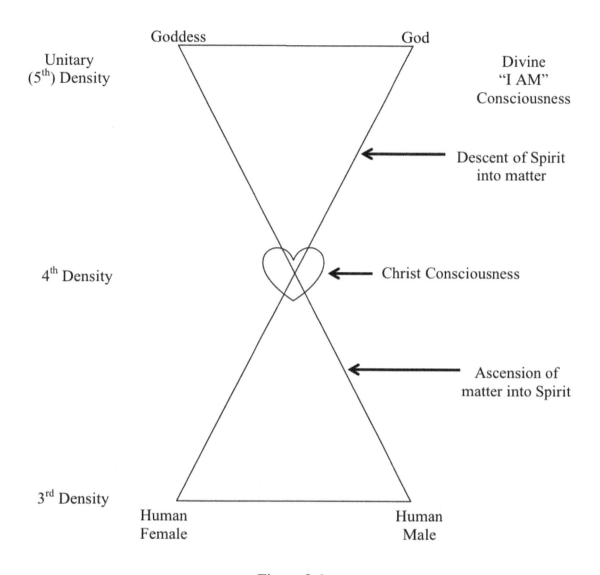

Figure 3-1

As the Descent of Spirit into Matter occurs, coupled with full Christ and Goddess Consciousness, the "Star of David" is formed, which is a two dimensional model of the three dimensional Star Tetrahedron, which is the sacred symbol of G-O-D, or Geometry of Divinity. The Christ Consciousness represents the opening of the Heart Chakra as 4th density (intermediary) consciousness (see Figure 3-2).

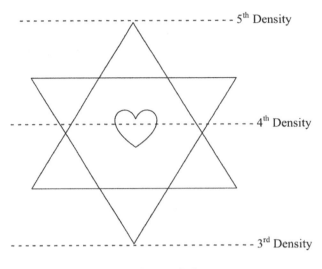

Figure 3-2

When kundalini awakening occurs without Christ Consciousness integration (and without more balanced love, wisdom, and power), the person is often left feeling empty or void, as a result of detachment from one's human ego or personality self. This has been referred to as "biological kundalini" (Sananda, 2004), which describes kundalini awakening that occurs without a higher spiritual focus and integration, and often results in more extreme physical, emotional, mental and spiritual integration problems, or psychological symptoms of spiritual emergency, as discussed in chapter one.

When spiritual evolution includes the opening of the heart chakra and integrates energy of the Holy Christed Spiritual self, (or includes other beings at the Christ consciousness or Ascended Master level), one can access states of consciousness that bring increasing acceptance, inner peace, love, wisdom, spiritual guidance, and inspiration, and greater love and forgiveness of self and others. The Christed Oversoul Self integration is necessary to be able to process effectively the repressed (unconscious) or suppressed (subconscious), unhealed material from this or other lifetimes that literally emerges and is brought to our attention through physical or emotional dis-ease symptoms. Often, understanding kundalini or other ascension symptoms, and loving acceptance of the emergence of the unhealed psychic material as part of the process of becoming truly Hu-man (literally God-man), can make the critical difference in whether one becomes depressed, fearful or anxious, and/or deteriorates into a chronic state of internal chaos from continual fear, resistance, avoidance, or suppression of the release of cellular memory during the process of transformation and as spiritual evolution is activated.

The divine attributes of love and wisdom from the integration of the Christed / Holy Spiritual Self need to be applied in greater measure for healing of the self, which includes compassion, mercy and forgiveness of both self and others for all "sins" (or karmic acts) of omission or commission.

The Three-Fold Flame of Christ Consciousness Integration

One of the meditation techniques for activation of the Christ Consciousness is the visualization and expansion of the Three-Fold Flame, which is composed of intertwining flames of pink (Divine Love), gold (Divine Wisdom), and blue (Divine Power) (Prophet, 1997). When we visualize the Three-Fold Flame in perfect balance in the heart chakra and focus on generating a spiraling action to encompass the entire physical body as well as the aura, which encompasses the emotional, mental and spiritual (etheric) bodies, this action balances and aligns the chakras or energy centers of the body, and assists the spiritual initiate in activating his/her Inner Christ /Higher Self aspect.

What is the hidden significance behind the Three-Fold Flame? The energy of the number three represents the Trinity, which is the three-in-one God, or Geometry of Divinity (G-O-D). If we superimpose the Divine Attributes of the Three-Fold Flame on the upward pointing triangle, correlated with the male and female polarities, it would be most appropriately represented as follows:

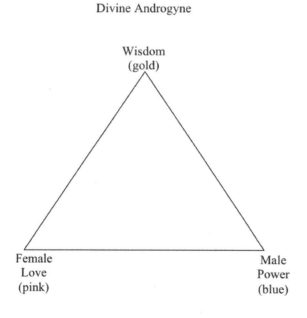

Figure 3-3
The 3 Fold Flame of Christ Consciousness Integration

The Three-Fold Flame is the very spark of the Creator's Divinity within man, and its balanced expansion is a key to advancing one's spiritual evolution. How is that possible? Just think about how a person who had perfectly balanced levels of love, wisdom and power would think, feel and behave. If one is <u>equally</u> loving, wise and powerful, one would not be able to create any new karma (or sin, in the Christian sense) involving self or others. Meditation on the Three Divine Attributes of Love, Wisdom, and Power and visualizing the Three-Fold Flame in perfect balance, combined with using the affirmation: "I AM perfectly balanced love, wisdom, and power," is a powerful and effective way to create greater integration of your Inner Christ Self.

Next, I will present three common examples of patterns of imbalance in the Three-fold Flame.

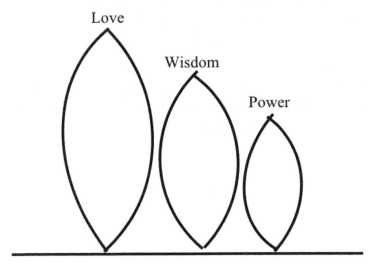

Figure 3-4

In the above example, the spiritual disciple is very loving, but lacks a matching level of wisdom (discernment), which may tend to create lessons around being excessively loving and giving to others or being overly trusting (poor judgment), leading to feeling victimized, used or abused by others, or betrayed. The least developed or shortest flame of power would result in the avoidance or fear of taking initiative and action for the benefit of self and others and to fulfill one's mission. This pattern can be likened to that of a loving, abused, victimized or "martyr" role, which leads to feelings of disempowerment and a lack of accomplishment. Karma would be created with oneself for lack of protection of the self, and also typically through "sins of omission;" i.e. lack of taking positive action in the highest and best interests of self and others, when the situation or "call to action" occurs.

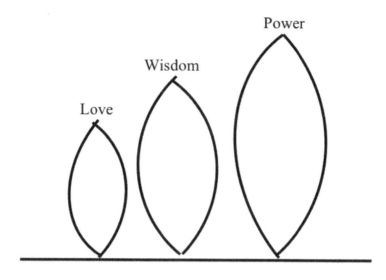

Figure 3-5

In the opposite flame pattern above, where the power ray or flame is in excess of the pink love flame, the person is likely to initiate selfish actions or significantly misuse their power through "sins of commission" because they lack the balanced levels of love and wisdom to exercise their will (power) appropriately. This pattern can be described as that of an unloving, victimizer, or abuser role. Karma would be created most likely with others, due to having and exercising power which is in excess of one's love and wisdom.

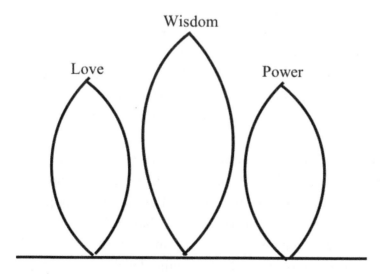

Figure 3-6

In the third pattern in Figure 3-6, (which is less frequently seen), the wisdom flame is the highest relative to lower levels of the love and power rays. This is a pattern of a person who is spiritually wise, but excessively detached and disengaged from the world. The imbalance in the relative lack of both love (and service orientation) and power (initiation and action) would lead to the inability to initiate and sustain the drive to complete one's mission. Karma (or sin) would arise mostly from errors of omission (toward self and others).

The Six Initiations to Self-Mastery and Planetary Ascension

In addition to the opening of the heart and Christ consciousness integration, there are six initiations or levels of increasing spiritual self-mastery leading up to the goal of planetary ascension. I consider Dr. Joshua David Stone to be the clearest and most comprehensive voice on the ascension process. He has elucidated the actual initiations and signposts of the steps to planetary ascension. In his two books, *The Complete Ascension Manual (1994b)* and *Beyond Ascension (1995),* he outlines and describes the six initiations to achieve 5th density integration, which is the lowest level of unitary consciousness beyond karma and polarity/duality. The following briefly describes Dr. Stone's outline of the ascension process.

Generally speaking, the spiritual initiate is given instruction predominantly during the sleep state. Only those spiritual disciples who have a sincere desire to be of selfless service to others are accepted on this probationary path. The progress of the spiritual initiate is measured by the magnitude of his/her light quotient, including the rate of vibration of their four bodies, and the purity of tone and clarity of color of the aura. In order to achieve planetary ascension (6th initiation), the spiritual disciple must have at least an eighty percent Light Quotient, and only fifty one percent of their Karma needs to be cleared, which is a Divine Dispensation of karmic grace established by Sanat Kumara, the Planetary Logos for planet Earth. All initiations occur on the Inner planes and are very subtle, as most people will not even be consciously aware of completing them.

The First Initiation is focused on mastery of the physical body, which is the densest of the four lower bodies. At this beginning level, one gains control over any "sins" or excesses of the flesh. As such, a beginning level of mastery is required to be developed over one's appetites for food and drink, sexual behavior, and sleep habits, etc.

The Second Initiation involves beginning mastery of the second densest vehicle, which is the emotional (or astral) body. Beginning levels of mastery are developed over the desires and emotions. Material desires begin to be transformed into a strong desire to achieve spiritual liberation and God realization. Conscious control via detachment from desire, and the release of core fear, as well as a corresponding release of other negative emotional patterns (along with integration of higher levels of loving energies toward self and others) occurs at this stage.

In the Third Initiation, one develops a certain level of mastery of the mental body, the 3rd densest vehicle. To pass this initiation, one must develop a significant beginning level of self-mastery over one's thoughts and release judgmental thinking (mental judgment) at this point.

It is at the third level of Initiation, which represents basic mastery over the physical, emotional, and mental vehicles, that the human personality self becomes merged in with the Spiritual Inner/Higher Self or Soul. The Soul is the intermediary between the incarnate human personality and the monad, or Divine God/dess Self. This initiation in the Life of Jesus was referred to as the transfiguration. Mastery of the 1st three initiations (pertaining to the physical, emotional (astral) and mental bodies) leading to integration of the lower human (personality) self with the higher or Soul Self, results in a desire to be loving, forgiving and of service to others in order to clear one's karma and be liberated from the wheel of death and rebirth.

In the Fourth Initiation, *The Rainbow Bridge* (Two Disciples, 1982), also known as the *Antakarana*, has been successfully connected with the soul in the spiritual Triad (Trinity) and the monad. This level represents the renunciation and/or the initiation of crucifixion, involves release (renunciation) of all attachments, as necessary - including family, friends, money, reputation, character, status and even life itself. At this level, the soul or causal body is at the Buddhic (or Christed) level of consciousness where the spiritual initiate is fully aligned with his/her spiritual service work or mission. The person is considered a master of wisdom and compassion and is referred to as an arhat after passing the 4th initiation.

In the Fifth Initiation, one begins the merge in consciousness with the Divine I AM Self or monad (aka monadic merge). In Christian terminology, it is referred to as the resurrection. It is a merge with the Atmic plane of consciousness. To complete the 5th initiation, one needs to have a 70% Light Quotient.

The final initiation to complete the planetary ascension experience is the 6th Initiation. In the past, most people who took the 6th Initiation left their bodies and passed on to the spiritual plane. On rare occasions, they were able to dematerialize their physical bodies as Jesus had done when he demonstrated the actual resurrection and ascension of his physical body to his disciples, and reappearance three days later. At the present time, the goal of the Spiritual Hierarchy and Sanat Kumara, the Planetary Logos for Planet Earth, is to have as many people ascend and continue to remain in their physical bodies, to be of service in bringing in the start of the Golden Age of Enlightenment which, according to many ancient prophesies, began on December 21, 2012.

The sixth Initiation of Ascension represents the full Monadic merger with the Divine I AM Self, and represents movement into the 5th density (unitary consciousness transcending duality/polarity distinctions). A 6th level initiate is typically doing planetary service work. Since the two key signposts or requirements for planetary ascension are 1) to balance fifty one percent of your karma (from all incarnations), and 2) have a Light Quotient of eighty to eighty-three percent, one does not have to be one hundred percent clear on physical, emotional, mental and spiritual levels to attain planetary ascension. There are usually unresolved emotional or mental issues, and the disciple can be in less than perfect physical health and still achieve ascension.

I would highly recommend reading Dr. Joshua David Stone's three major books - *Soul Psychology (1994a), The Complete Ascension Manual (1994b) and Beyond Ascension, (1995),* if you are seriously focused on maximizing your spiritual evolution and attaining planetary ascension in this lifetime.

CHAPTER 4

Integration: The Key to Transformation and Spiritual Evolution

In this chapter, the importance of integrating the two energies of polarity (or duality) which are (1) light/dark, and (2) male/female, will be discussed from biological/ scientific, cultural, linguistic and spiritual perspectives. Next, I will address the importance of integrating the three levels of mind: unconscious, conscious and super-conscious, and their integration from spiritual, psychological and Hawaiian perspectives. Then, the importance of integrating and balancing the four bodies: physical, emotional, mental, and spiritual, will be presented. Finally, I will elucidate the five density levels, especially 4th and 5th density, as they relate to consciousness integration and human evolution.

The Two Energies of Polarity/Duality

In order to understand the process of spiritual evolution, it is important to begin by re-examining the story of creation. Although there are many cultural and mythological versions of the genesis of the Hu-man (God-man) race, one common denominator is that we originated from a single unified consciousness field, also known as God/dess Creator, Source, All that Is, Universal Mind, etc. From the undifferentiated Source symbolized by a point of light emanating from the void (darkness), the most primary (and primordial) polarity is that of light and dark, often depicted as the Taoist Yin/Yang symbol.

Yin/Yang Symbol
Figure 4-1

Dark and Light

According to the Big Bang theory of the creation of the universe, and research in areas of quantum physics, we understand that even within quantum space, there is light within the darkness and that quanta, or discrete subatomic units of energy, particularly photons, have both wave (female) and particle (male) properties. The term quantum, as coined by Max Planck and Albert Einstein at the turn of the century, refers to various subatomic particles, including photons or light particles (Talbot, 1988). They were puzzled when they tried to account for the instability of atoms while studying black holes. Later, in 1974, Stephen Hawking (by combining the mathematics of quantum theory with the physics of black holes) announced the spectacular discovery that black holes are cloaked in a veil of heat radiation now known as Hawking radiation. Thus light, and its usual by-product, heat, co-exist within the dark (black holes) in so-called "empty" space. This to me confirms that the primordial forces of creator/source energy contain both dualities/polarities of light and dark (which is really the absence of light).

Interestingly, the macrocosm of the universe, with the myriad of stellar bodies, suns, planets, nebulae and galaxies, etc., lighting up the darkness of intergalactic space, has its microcosmic mirror in the atom, with the subatomic particles of photons, electrons, neutrons, etc. being separated by more than 99.99% empty space. The proportion of matter (solids) vs. non-material substance (light, pure energy) comprising the void is similarly represented throughout the many forms and kingdoms of creation.

Male and Female

Through the course of history, major civilizations have varied in their interpretation of which gender was created first, although the predominance of patriarchal or androcratic civilizations and cultures in the last 2000+ years have resulted in primarily his-tories of genesis or stories of the initial creation of the male first, and then the female. As Riane Eisler points out in *The Chalice and the Blade* (1988), even within the first chapter of Genesis of *The Bible*, there is an internal inconsistency and contradiction which states that both woman and man were simultaneous divine creatures, but the more promulgated and elaborate is the second version, which describes that the woman (Eve) was created from the rib of the man (Adam). Although it is not of critical importance which gender was actually created first, the epigenesis from a purely biological or scientific viewpoint is that the zygote (embryo) is created first as a female, and then differentiated as male. As such, the basic blueprint of a species is and remains female.

In the book *The Gnostic Gospels* (Pagels, 1989), Source (Goddess) Consciousness is described in "The Invisible Perfect Spirit" as the Divine Mother/Father (Matropater) of all things in the Jewish writings of Nag Hammadi Library (NHL). In the Apocalypse of Adam (NHL), the Creative Spirit is described as a feminine power who creates her own immaculate conception from the image of thought. And the image of thought (ennoia) is feminine, since it is the power of conception. In the Trimorphic Protennoia (literally the Triple-formed primal thought) the voice of Protennoia as a Divine Feminine aspect of thought and intelligence speaks, "I am androgynous," and "I AM both Mother and Father, and I AM the womb that gives shape to the all." As such, the creation story appears to have been anthropomorphized, e.g., ascribing human (male and female) characteristics to a non-human form, in this case, the Creator, or Source, which is neither male or female, but an androgynous integration of both genders.

Also, I find it interesting that if we examine the etymological roots of gender related words in the English language, which is linguistically considered to be a balanced composite of vowel (female) and consonant (male) sounds, we notice that many of the female gender related nouns and pronouns encompass or include the male. For example, the words: (fe)male, s(he), wo(man) and God(dess) all reflect this higher spiritual truth that the feminine encompasses and includes the corresponding masculine noun or pronoun.

However, female (yin) gender qualities or personality characteristics have been typically categorized as negative or dark. From a more enlightened perspective on the evolution of the dominant Eastern and Western socio-political-cultural and religious systems, this has simply been an artifact of misogyny rooted in fear of woman's power.

As feminist authors such as Eisler (1988) have postulated, this phenomena is due to higher value being placed on stereotypical "male" attributes, with male qualities being ascribed as "positive." In actuality, "male" stereotypical characteristics are inherently no more positive (or negative) than those considered female, and vice-versa. However, one only needs to take a cursory look at the recorded history of the planet in so called civilized androcratic/autocratic societies, by predominantly male authors to see the bias in favor of recording both the famous and infamous achievements of men (vs. women), due to the fact that the fuller expression of personal power (for both good and evil) has been afforded to men throughout most of recorded history.

This explains, for example, that despite females and males performing equally well on measures of general intelligence, males have attained greater positions of social and historical prominence (both good and evil) and achievement of success in extra-familiar environments, due to the fact that avenues of achievement for women outside of the roles of being a wife and mother have either not been sanctioned, or been overtly and covertly blocked via transmission of societal norms, values, and laws in almost all societies, cultures and nations for much of human history.

For most of recorded human history, Freud's phrase "biology is destiny" has been the case, as women did not have any reliable means of birth control, and most of their energies and achievements were focused on child rearing. In order to achieve balance both individually and collectively as a society and culture, we need to place equal value on the positive attributes stereotypically ascribed to both genders, moving toward true balance, developing and integrating positive female and male personality attributes or qualities, in order to re-create the original undivided androgynous God/dess consciousness prior to our descent into matter.

The concept of androgyny has been shrouded in mystery, misperceptions, fear and prejudice, being originally associated with the Greek word hermaphrodite, which referred to the bisexual offspring of the Greek Gods Hermes and Aphrodite. A distinction needs to be made between biological androgyny (having reproductive organs of both sexes) vs. psychological androgyny, which is having high levels of personality characteristics of both genders.

Models of divine androgyny have existed in the religions of both pre-Christian Hinduism and Buddhism. The Indian androgyne, for example, is half Shiva (male) and half Shakti (female), symbolizing the original cosmic union of both sexes, before their primordial separation literally gave birth to the two genders (Van Lysabeth, 1995).

Researchers Sandra Bem (1976) of Stanford University and her husband Daryl Bem studied psychological androgyny and found that persons who possessed high levels of BOTH male and female characteristics were more psychologically well-adjusted than those who had less well-developed characteristics of both genders. That is because in order to realize the fullness of our human and divine potential, we need to integrate the positive characteristics of both genders.

Integrating the Two Polarity Distinctions

Thus, combining the spiritual, scientific, biological and gylanic social-cultural theories, we find a convergence of support for the Divine Creative Source being described as an undifferentiated combination of both light and dark, both male and female, prior to the split of the Divine Monad (the single unit of individualized God/Goddess divine consciousness), into two parts.

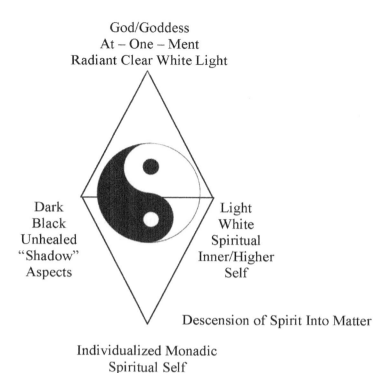

Figure 4-2

From the top of the chart downward, the Creator Source energy, which is pure diamond white light, is stepped down and densified into the opaque black and white light symbolized by the yin/yang symbol. Then, the individualized Divine Hu-Man is created by Source as a Monadic spark of light.

This Divine Monadic spiritual spark of light can be conceptualized as a vertical line descending into matter, which creates the four bodies – spiritual, mental, emotional and physical.

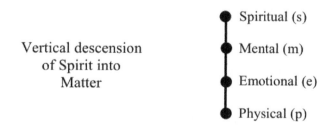

Figure 4-3

Then we have the horizontal split into the polarities of female and male in the material plane.

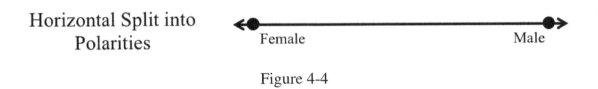

Horizontal Split into Polarities

Female   Male

Figure 4-4

Finally, here is a simplified graphic model of the Descended Master -Spirit into Matter, then a Return to Wholeness (Holiness) through Heart Integration and Healing, which leads to the Ascended Master – Matter returns to Spirit, and then the Reintegration into Divine Oneness and Ascension.

Integrating the above 4 figures and conceptual models, we have the following:

Simple Sacred Geometries of the Ascension Process

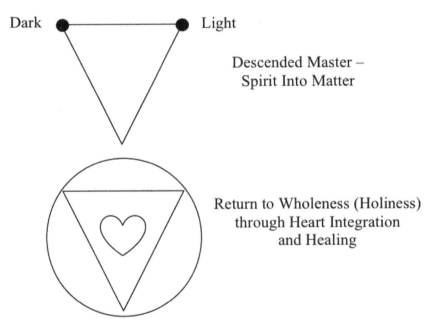

Dark   Light

Descended Master –
Spirit Into Matter

Return to Wholeness (Holiness)
through Heart Integration
and Healing

Figure 4-5a

Simple Sacred Geometries of the Ascension Process

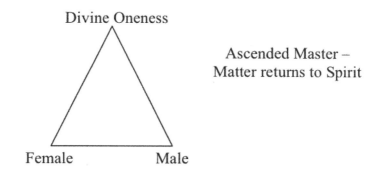

Ascended Master –
Matter returns to Spirit

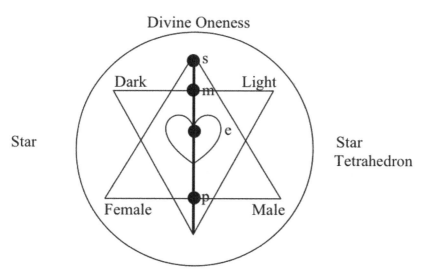

Reintegration into Divine Oneness and Ascension

Figure 4-5b

Integrating the previous 5 Figures and conceptual models, we have the following:

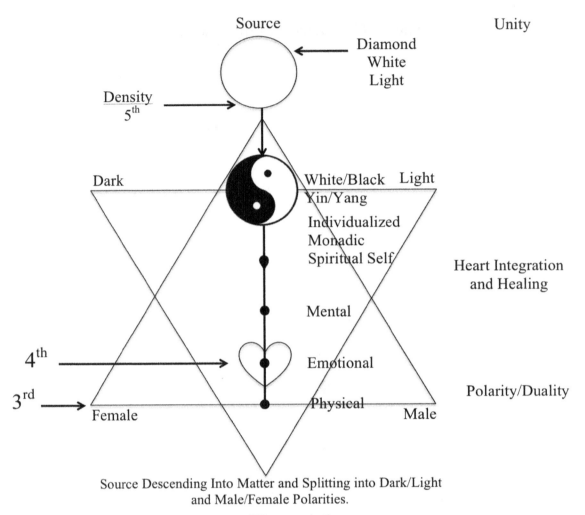

Source Descending Into Matter and Splitting into Dark/Light
and Male/Female Polarities.

Figure 4-6

We have explored how seeding of spirit into matter resulted in the primary, or primordial split into the polarity or duality of light and dark. The second duality distinction, that of female and male, should not be "hyperpolarized" or assigned characteristics of being exclusively light or dark, as both females and males have stereotypical positive (light) and negative (dark) human characteristics.

These two types of energies have been alternately described by various authors from spiritual, psychological and scientific perspectives, which are synthesized below in the following chart. Of course these energies exist on a continuum or spectrum.

Spectrum of Polarities		
Primary Polarity	Dark	Light
	Evil	Good
	Negative	Positive
Emotions	Fear	Love
Quantum Physics	Disintegrative	Integrative
	Incoherent	Coherent
	Disorganized	Organized
	Chaotic	Orderly
Freudian Psychology	Death	Life
	Mortido	Libido
	Thanatos	Eros
Evolutionary Progression	De-evolutionary	Evolutionary
Human Social	Malevolent	Benevolent
	Controlling	Detached
	Dominating	Non-Dominating
	Aggressive/Warlike	Peaceful
	Separatist	Integrationist
Eisler	Androcratic	Gylanic
Thought Patterns	Elitist and Superior/Inferior	Equal
	Hierarchical	Egalitarian
Capra	Egological	Ecological
Power	Having Power over Others	Sharing Power with Others
Rotational Movement	Counterclockwise Movement	Clockwise Movement
Values	Personal Gain	Mutual Gain
	Selfish	Selflessness
Karma	Negative	Positive

Table 4-1

The Two Governing Laws of Polarity:
The Law of Similars and The Law of Opposites

Two primary natural laws governing the energetic relationships of the polarities are "like attracts like," also known as the Law of Similars, and "opposites attract," also known as the Law of Opposites. As such, we will tend to attract persons and situations which reflect both the same or similar characteristics and qualities, as well as those from the opposite polarity, as part of our spiritual evolutionary process. For example, owned (similar) or disowned (opposite) thought, emotional energies and behavioral patterns of selfish, fear-based manipulation and control will tend to attract persons with similar qualities as lovers, friends or associates. Our Inner/Higher Spiritual Self inherently knows these are not desirable qualities, and will also attract those who embody opposite characteristics of being selfless, loving, and accepting as we become more aligned with these positive characteristics. When we embrace our negative, disowned, disintegrated qualities (which we find ourselves indulging in), or we become emotionally upset/ unbalanced when we see these traits in others, we integrate through love and acceptance our shadow aspects via connection with our Spiritual, Inner/Higher Self. As we continue integrating our individual polarity expressions of Light and Dark, this enables us to transcend these dualities and return to At-One-Ment. Thus, atoning for our sins (Christianity) or clearing our karma (Hinduism/Buddhism) leads to atonement or At-One-Ment, the hidden root meaning of this word. Ken Page, author of *The Hidden Side of The Soul* (1991), also describes the integration or reunification of polarities as the key to healing. The manifestation of the place of balance is clear light.

How do we reconcile these opposites in a return to Divine Oneness? By first moving out of denial and consciously accepting our unconscious dark/shadow or unhealed aspects, and releasing resistance, fear, and judgment, to embrace these aspects within others or ourselves as part of the whole, or pure potentiality of Source.

We lead this process by anchoring in our own Spiritual Inner/Higher Self, also known as the Full Potential Self, True Self, Inner Christ Self, or Divine "I AM' or God/dess Self. We align with the part of ourselves that is Divine: all-loving, wise, and powerful, the aspect within that knows what is in the highest and best interests of oneself as well as others in order to receive clear inner guidance and healing. By connecting with our superconscious, we can then uncover the hidden unconscious shadow aspects, and ultimately bring them into conscious awareness for integration, transformation, and healing.

The process of Quantum Transformational Healing, which is described fully in chapter five, is based on the principles of integrating the dark or "shadow" aspects into the light by connecting with our Inner/Higher Spiritual Self, creating integrity which is synonymous with wholeness, which is necessary to transcend duality and return to our God given state of Holiness. That is how consciousness Integration leads to Integrity, which is synonymous with Wholeness, which then leads to Holiness or spiritual purity.

Here is a depiction of that progressive continuum.

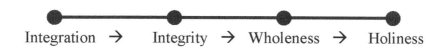

Integration → Integrity → Wholeness → Holiness

Ego Integration

We do not surrender or eradicate the ego, as that is what I call a half-truth, or partial truth, from Buddhist and Hindu spiritual teachings. We simply align and integrate our human ego, the individualized personality aspect, with our Inner/Higher or Inner/Self Christ as an intermediary, to connect with our Individualized God Self, our Divine "I AM" Presence, to actualize our spiritual evolution and ascension in the light.

With the wisdom and guidance of the I/H Self, we can choose to integrate our unconscious aspects from this lifetime - the unhealed, Shadow aspects from our childhood or adulthood as disowned, dis-integrated parts of the human personality self, (also known as multiple ego states, sub-personalities, or rarely, multiple personalities). Then other aspects of the unhealed self, e.g. past/parallel future lives, attached spirits/entities, spiritual implants, etc. need to be integrated, healed, transformed, and/or released.

Consciousness Integration and Spiritual Evolution

The Three Levels of Mind or Consciousness

In studying a variety of spiritual and psychological systems of human consciousness, a convergence of similarities becomes apparent as we find consciousness partitioned into three main categories, or a tri-partite consciousness model.

Quantum Transformational Healing
Tripartite Consciousness Systems Integration Model

DIVINE (Spiritual)	"I AM" SELF Inner/Higher Self	Super Conscious	Superego	Aumakua	Parent
Human (mental emotional)	Human Self (Personality)	Conscious	Ego	Uhane	Adult
Animal (physical instinctual)	Shadow Self (immature unhealed self)	Unconscious (subcon- scious)	Id	Unihipili	Child

Spiritual	Psychological	Hawaiian

Chart 4-1

Let's examine these various three part models, which represent similar qualities or characteristics across the horizontal spectrum.

First, we all recognize that biologically, we are mammalian animals with neuro-hormonal systems and instinctual drives governing survival as a species, such as to procure food and water, and for protection and procreation. Our particular human faculties, at a more evolved neurological level, enable us to experience more complexity and a greater range of feelings and thoughts than our mammalian animal counterparts, and to reflect upon and change our conscious mental and emotional patterns. Since we are created in God's likeness and image, we also possess a divine counterpart - the Human or God-man, representing our connection to Source and fulfillment of our highest evolutionary potential which is to reunite with our Inner/Higher or Christ Self as the bridge to our Divine "I AM" Self or God/dess Self.

The animal- human - Divine spectrum also represents moving from (1) group (species) consciousness to (2) greater individual consciousness and differentiation in the human realm, to (3) a Unitary God/dess consciousness of Oneness.

As such, Ontogeny recapitulates Phylogeny; e.g., the maturational development of the individual from infancy, toddler, preschool, school-age, and adolescence into adulthood, is repeated or recapitulated in the evolutionary development of the group or species. Thus, both the individual and the human species evolve from behavior based primarily on animal or instinctual drives, to higher cortical development, to language and human emotional-mental development, to integration of our spiritual Divine God/dess consciousness.

For the typical person who has not developed her own *superconscious* Divine "I AM" spiritual, Inner/Higher Self, the shadow aspects of the self, which represent all immmature, unhealed aspects, are not typically known consciously, and they remain (for the most part) in the *unconscious*. Nonetheless, the unconscious exerts a significant influence over the person's thoughts, feelings, and behavior. The Human Self, with its unique individual personality traits based on genetic and environmental - family, racial, societal and national, etc. influences, evolves as the *conscious* governing self aspect overriding many of the more primitive animal drives and instincts of the shadow, or unhealed self.

Here are the triangulation models of Spiritual Consciousness Integration:

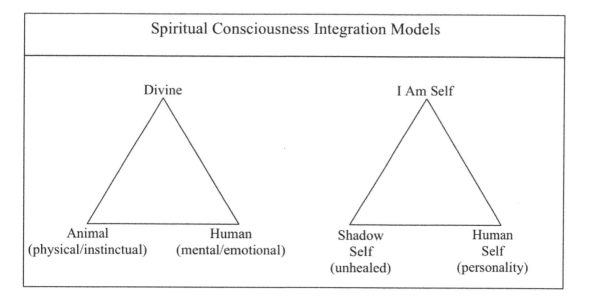

Figure 4-7

Freud's three levels of consciousness is the most predominant Western psychological model of the mind. From a Freudian psychological perspective, the three parts of the psyche are the id, ego, and superego (Hall, 1999). The id, governed by the pleasure principle, is driven to obtain satisfaction of instinctual needs and avoid pain or tension, and it has an infantile character that is demanding, impulsive, irrational, asocial, selfish and desires immediate gratification. The id corresponds to the unconscious mind.

The ego, which corresponds to the conscious mind, is the executor of the personality. It uses logic and reason, and is governed by the reality principle. The ego strives to maintain functioning in the external world in the interest of the total personality. The ego has mastery over instinctual drives and impulses, acts as a complex filtering agent and organizer, and strives toward goal achievement.

The superego is governed by the principle of the ideal, rather than the reality principle, as it strives for moral perfection. The superego, according to Freud, is made up of two subsystems - the ego-ideal and the conscience. The ego-ideal represents the internalized conception of what is considered morally good thoughts, feelings, and behaviors according to parental and societal, etc. norms and values. One's conscience, or knowledge of what is accepted as "good" or "bad," is developed by the experience of being rewarded or punished for one's expressions of values, thoughts, words, or behaviors. The superego corresponds to the superconscious mind.

Here are the triangulation models of Psychological Consciousness Integration:

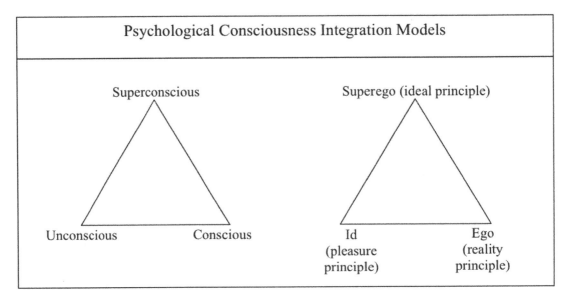

Figure 4-8

In the ancient Hawaiian system of Huna, the mind was similarly divided into the Aumakua (Parent) also known as the Higher Self; Uhane (Adult) or Middle Self; and Unihipili (Child) or Lower Self (Hoffman 1991). The Aumakua represents the highest vibrational frequency, receives pure mana (life energy) from the Divine Creator, and functions in a loving, parental manner to guide and protect the individual. The Uhane exercises logic and reasoning power to discriminate, make choices and express the individual will and power. It also acts as a teacher or guide to the Unihipili, as the conscious reasoning mind may exercise its will to override the instinctual inner child self of the Unihipili. The Unihipili represents the computer memory bank of the individual, recording and storing all sense impressions, feelings, attitudes, thoughts and behavior, and vibrates at the lowest frequency of the three selves.

A person was considered to be in unity, balance, and harmony when the Aumakua, Uhane, and Unihipili are acting in a single integrated unit. Congruent with other psycho-spiritual systems, the three selves or minds are linked from the Aumakua (superconscious mind), to the Uhane (conscious mind), to the Unihipili (subconscious mind).

Here are the integration triangles corresponding to the three levels of consciousness in the Hawaiian Huna System.

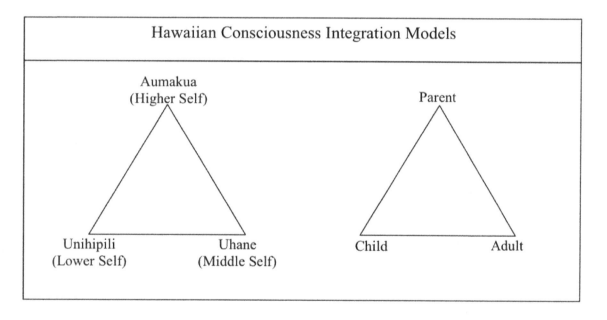

Figure 4-9

The Four Bodies

Most spiritual systems describe four basic bodies: the physical body, the emotional (astral) body, the mental body, and the spiritual (etheric and/or causal) body. In actuality, there are multiple spiritual bodies in ascending order beyond the causal, including the Buddhic, Atmic, Monadic, Logoic, etc., up to the Cosmic consciousness level (Stone, 1994b, 1995).

Balancing the Four Bodies

In order to achieve the ultimate goal of ascension, the four bodies must be balanced and integrated in daily life on the Earth plane in service to God and one's mission. Taking care of our four bodies as aspects or vehicles of the Self, is a way to be in a healthy service to the self, which is distinct from being selfish. We can only serve and care for others to the extent that we love and care for our self and our four bodies. The majority of people over identify with one or two of their bodies, most often the emotional body.

For example, a person can be excessively focused on being run by his subconscious mind, correlated with their emotional needs for validation, love, or support. A person dominated by his physical body might do a wonderful job at maintaining a healthy diet, exercise, rest, etc., but pay little attention to emotional-social, mental (intellectual) or spiritual balance and self-development. A person overly focused on her intellectual (mental) body may be preoccupied with accumulating knowledge or expertise, but neglects her physical, social, or spiritual needs. Finally, a person whose primary focus is on spiritual self-development may engage in excessive contemplative prayer, meditation, or spiritual studies, and neglect to take care of his financial needs, diet and exercise (physical needs), socio-emotional needs, etc.

The Physical Body

The physical body is a vehicle for the integration of the higher emotional, mental, and spiritual energies, and is the densest or lowest vibrating body. When we take care of our physical temple, several simple basic tenets apply. It is important to eat a natural (preferably organic), healthy diet, with lots of fresh fruits and vegetables, whole grains, and healthy fats. If meat is eaten, it should be organic. We should also eat foods that are low in salt, sugar and saturated fat, and avoid processed and refined foods cooked with artificial chemicals and food additives. If possible, we should minimize or avoid alcohol, as well as prescription or recreational drugs due to the toxic load on the liver and other organs.

According to the diathesis – stress theory of physical illness or disease, accumulating excess toxins in the body (combined with individual biochemical imbalances and constitutional or genetic, hereditary weaknesses in various organ systems) will lead to illness or dis-ease in the most vulnerable, weakest organ(s). Depletion of our soil from lack of fertilizer and adequate natural soil supplementation over the past fifty years, coupled with contamination from use of pesticides and herbicides, has resulted in grain, vegetable, and fruit products that are significantly depleted of their vitamins and mineral content. The combined effects of excessive pollution of our air, water, and food with additional toxic ingredients in our personal care and household products, results in the average person continuously absorbing, ingesting or inhaling a broad spectrum of toxins on a daily basis.

Therefore it is important to take a multi-vitamin and mineral supplement, along with antioxidants as well as other nutritional supplements to correct dietary or genetic/organ weakness. Drinking lots of pure water is recommended to keep the body hydrated and allow the body to cleanse itself of metabolic waste and toxins. Regular, aerobic exercise is suggested at least several times per week to oxygenate the body, keep the muscles toned and strong, and normalize neuro-hormonal and endocrine gland functioning. And finally, getting adequate sleep (6-8 hrs./night) is another well-known basic cornerstone of good physical health.

Here is the integration triangle for the physical body:

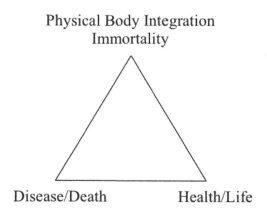

Figure 4-10

The Emotional Body

The emotional body, also known as the astral body, pertains to feelings, desires and fears. When we are able to release or eliminate fears (wanting to avoid something) and desires (wanting to have something) we are in a state of emotional detachment, which allows our higher spiritual and soul energies to inspire us with positive emotions of love, inner peace and tranquility. Everyone has unhealed negative emotions stemming from past experiences which need to be accepted (not ignored, denied, or continuously repressed). If these emotions are not expressed, individuals will develop psychological (emotional-mental) problems, or if ignored long enough, physical dis-ease will appear in the body.

It is a common psycho-spiritual tenet that the most basic primary positive emotion is love (which is integrative, unitary, and coherent energy on subatomic to cosmic levels). Its primary polar opposite is fear (which is the emotional equivalent to dis-integrated, separated, and incoherent). In the book *A Course in Miracles* (Schucman, 2007), which is a book of Christ consciousness inspired truths, there are only two basic emotions: love and fear. All positive emotions are considered to be "variants" of the original coherent, magnetic (attracting) force of love. And since fear is the absence of love, just as darkness is the absence of light, we need to increase our "love quotient" on the emotional level, and release and heal all core complexes of fear and "its cousins," which are all other negative emotions.

Here is the integration triangle for the emotional body:

Figure 4-11

The Mental Body

The purpose of the mental body is to consciously gather information, knowledge, and wisdom from experience. The challenge is to do so without judgment, e.g. mental judging. The tendency to judge a person, situation or experience as "bad" represents getting trapped in polarity thinking. By going within, meditating on the hidden positive intention, function or purpose, we can see the "higher" reason for having that person or situation in our life.

When we see a part that we judge in others, it is always a "mirror" of our own self-judgment and lack of acceptance. As such, all judgment is self- judgment. If we find ourselves judging another, we are either: 1) actually judging ourselves for how we were in the past, or 2) judging ourselves because we have the same trait now, or 3) projecting judgment on ourselves if we might be that way in the future.

As we learn from "negative" experiences, we can then simply choose to not engage in the situation; e.g., we learn discernment. Just as we learn to not touch a hot burner on a stove, we can also learn discernment and choose to not allow ourselves to become involved with others who would manipulate, control, or mistreat us.

Here is the integration triangle for the mental body:

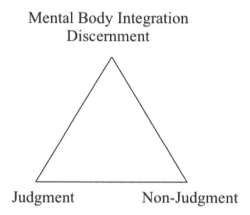

Figure 4-12

The Spiritual Body

The spiritual (etheric) body can be sub-divided into the causal, Buddhic, Atmic, Monadic, Logoic, and Cosmic light bodies (Stone, 1994a, 1995).

One progresses through to these increasingly higher levels of spiritual body integration by experiencing spiritual or kundalini awakening, opening and balancing the chakras, and the 4 lower bodies – spiritual, mental, emotional and physical. It is especially important to open the heart center (chakra), to increase love and forgiveness, prior to opening the higher chakras (the throat, 3rd eye, and crown) to be able to speak, see and receive clear, loving and detached inner guidance. The opening and expansion of the heart chakra, integrating the Higher Christ Self and balancing the Three-Fold Flame of Christ Consciousness (Love, Wisdom, and Power), clearing one's karma, raising one's light quotient, and fulfilling the unfolding levels of one's spiritual mission, facilitate the progression through the stages of spiritual initiation, mastery and ascension outlined by Joshua David Stone (1994a, 1995) previously described in greater detail in chapter three.

Here is the integration triangle for the spiritual body:

Spiritual Body Integration
Divine "I AM Self"

Shadow Self   Inner/Higher
                     Christ Self

Figure 4-13

Below is a chart of how the two polarities of positive (light) vs. negative (dark) express in the spiritual, mental, emotional, and physical bodies.

Chart 4-2

	Positive State	Negative State
	Ideal Health	Dis-Ease
Physical Body	Energy Optimal Health Healing/Reversal of Aging Process	Fatigue Illness Disease Death
Emotional Body	Inner Peace Calmness Optimism Love	Worry Anxiety/Depression Pessimism Fear
Mental Body	Non-Judgmental	Judgmental
Spiritual Body	Connection with God and one's Spiritual (Inner/Higher) Self	Lack of Connection with God and one's Spiritual (Inner/Higher) Self

The 4 bodies & the 2 Polarities of Positive (Light) vs. Negative (Dark)

Species Evolution and Vibrational Frequencies

In order to understand the spiritual evolutionary progression of consciousness and see where QTH (as well as other therapeutic processes) fit in, a brief description of the first five density levels is appropriate. The following description of density levels is primarily derived from the book *The Prism of Lyra* (Royal and Priest, 1989).

Density refers to a vibrational frequency. It is distinct from "dimension," with which it is often confused, as there are multiple dimensions existing within a given density or vibrational level. Since matter is vibrational energy solidified or densified into physical form, these vibrational frequencies basically reflect the Kingdoms of Creation, in ascending order from 1st Density - rocks, minerals, and elemental substance (earth, water, air, fire, etc.); 2nd Density - plants and animals; 3rd Density – humans; 4th Density – human integration of love and forgiveness, and Christ Consciousness Integration, and upwards into 5th density – the lowest level of Unitary Consciousness.

First Density - Physical Matter:

(Elements) Awareness as a point. Examples of first density are rocks and minerals, and the elements of earth, air and water, which are all operating from this most basic level of vibrational frequency.

Second Density - Biological Matter:

(Plants and Most Animals) Awareness as a line (two points). At the 2nd density level, group or species consciousness or identity develops. The ability to be self aware and self-reflective, as well as having an ego or identity, is not yet developed.

Third Density - Human Consciousness and Cetaceans:

(Humans, Dolphins and Whales) Development of ego, individualized consciousness, identity, and volumetric awareness. This is the primarily "Human" level of density where individuated self-awareness, conceptual thought, and the ability to experience linear time (past, present, and future) emerge as well as mental faculties of judgment (good-bad) and awareness of polarized or dualistic thinking and behavior occurs. However, evolved mammals such as the cetaceans (dolphins and whales) and some primates display characteristics of third density consciousness, such as language acquisition.

In humans, this vibratory frequency creates the greatest relative loss of group identification. There is a sense of being separated (distinct) from the group (species), as well as other kingdoms and species-rocks and minerals, plants, animals, and higher consciousness spirit energies, such as angels, or extra-terrestrial (off planetary) beings. This density is where the spiritually un-awakened humans are attached to ego, power, and control.

Fourth Density - Superconscious Awareness:

At this level there is a reintegration of group identity without loss of ego identity. This is the transitional density that many humans are experiencing as spiritual awakening, which is reflected in the many rapid changes that the human race is undergoing to move forward in conscious evolution from a separatist, ego-centric perspective, to a view of our common humanity and with respect for all lower kingdoms and life forms, replacing "negative" judgment of self and others with unconditional love, to create inner (personal) and outer (societal and world) peace.

I call this the level of "Heart Integration," where opening of the higher chakras (most importantly the heart center), and also the third eye (6th chakra) and crown (7th chakra) occur. At this stage of human species evolution, the vibrational frequency increase leads to emergence of one's unhealed issues, so the need for opening the heart (4th chakra), becomes paramount for the integration and healing of one's shadow aspects, and clearing and balancing one's karma. This represents an activation of the Inner/Higher Self, with the opening of the crown and transpersonal (7th and 8th chakras), respectively, and retrieval of soul memory (previously lodged in the unconsciousness or cellular memory). Typically, many people begin to have dreams (subconscious) or waking (conscious) recall of other lifetimes or embodiments, which necessitates greater levels of unconditional love, and forgiveness of self and others, as one releases fear (the polar opposite of love) and all its negative emotions and judgmental attitudes.

The 4th density level is often very intense, with many trials, tribulations, upheavals and initiations related to gaining greater self-mastery. The first five levels of initiation described by Dr. Joshua David Stone in *The Complete Ascension Manual* (1994b) and *Beyond Ascension* (1995) are all taken as one is transitioning through the 4th density level.

The first Initiation, as per Dr. Joshua David Stone, is mastery of the physical body and it's appetites and requirements, including overcoming addictions to food, alcohol, drugs, sex, and sleep habits. The 2nd initiation requires mastery over the emotional, or astral body, and involves the relinquishing of selfish or ego based emotional desires and transforming them into the desire for soul liberation and God realization. The third initiation is realized when one gains self-control and mastery over the mental body; i.e. thoughts. The ability to originate and co-create one's reality through the power of thought (charged with the magnetic force of unselfish desire to be of higher service) is understood and developed. This level of initiation is also referred to as the soul merge, as the spiritual disciple's human self merges with the Inner/Higher Self to become a soul-infused personality.

In the 4th initiation, which has been esoterically referred to as the initiation of renunciation, there is a letting go or release of all attachments to the material world, including fame, fortune, power, people, family and/or friends if they no longer serve one's spiritual evolution. The 4th initiation occurs on the Buddhic plane and represents an integration of the Buddha Consciousness (enlightenment) as well as the Christ Consciousness (balanced love, wisdom, and power) and commitment to one's spiritual service to self and others. That is why those passing through the 4th density vibrational frequency level may undergo dramatic and even traumatic losses or changes of jobs, material possessions, and relationships in the process of spiritual alignment with their soul purpose and mission dharma, as it is all part of clearing and releasing karma, or learning detachment.

During the 5th initiation, the I/H Self or Soul progressively merges with the monadic, or Divine Self, also known as the Divine "I AM" Self, or Mighty I AM Presence, creating greater levels of unconditional love, joy, inner peace and bliss.

The QTH process is a spiritual evolutionary and ascension tool, which allows for the continuous soul progression from 3rd to 5th density by facilitating connection with one's I/H Self and Higher Spiritual Guides, to receive clear inner guidance and transformational healing of the range of unhealed physical, emotional, mental, and spiritual problems or issues.

Fifth Density – Experiential Awareness of the merger of the Self with the Whole (Group) or Unitary Consciousness:

In a fifth density consciousness frequency, one is in a state of having transcended the polarities of dark and light and male/female into Divine Oneness (or the Divine I AM Self), and he/she abides by the Cosmic laws of Love and Free Will, and is known as an Ascended Master. At this level, one has the choice to ascend with one's physical body or remain on earth to be of service. Most people who have passed the 6th initiation of planetary ascension and achieved 5th density unitary consciousness are choosing to stay to further assist others and planet Earth in achieving ascension.

Characteristics of 4th Density Integration

Fourth density consciousness integration occurs when one is actively clearing and healing the myriad of unresolved childhood and adult issues, from this and other lifetimes, and releasing negative entities and implants, etc.

When one is in the process of actively integrating and healing, fluctuating levels of physical, emotional, and mental symptoms are commonplace. There are often periods of intensified symptoms (regression in service of the ego, as per Freud), followed by relief, improvement, and then plateauing, with overall stabilization at a higher level of vibration and healthier functioning.

Opening of the heart chakra (including Christ Consciousness integration) occurs at this level in order to accept, integrate, love, and forgive all facets of the self and experiences with others.

Some characteristics of 4th density processing include:

- re-processing or re-experiencing negative physical, emotional, mental or spiritual energy patterns or complexes expressed as physical dis-ease symptoms (health issues).
- Clearing negative emotional complexes such as fear, anxiety, resentment, anger, remorse, shame, guilt, depression, jealousy, and pride (hubris), and mental or attitudinal patterns of inferiority/superiority, victim/abuser.
- integrating your Inner/Higher Self and Christ Consciousness to facilitate clear inner guidance and healing.

Living in the 4th density can be intense, dramatic and even traumatic as one is clearing and balancing karma, and typically one may attract persons or situations representing disowned/disintegrated aspects of the self from this (or other lifetimes) in order to integrate and heal these issues. There can be much turmoil, upheaval, and dramatic change in relationships, occupation, lifestyle, residence, etc.

Kundalini awakening (activation and opening of the dormant energy centers or chakras in the body), with increased sensitivity and "paranormal" perceptual abilities, occurs within the realm of 4th density experience.

Quantum Transformational Healing is essentially a "4th Density" spiritual evolutionary guided imagery process which allows one to progressively integrate, heal and transcend the various categories of shadow aspects, including: child or adult neglect, abuse and other dysfunctional relationship dynamics/patterns; physical, emotional, mental or spiritual problems or issues; past/parallel/future life issues, and the release of spiritual entities and implants, etc.

Characteristics of 5th Density Integration

As previously mentioned, 5th density is the beginning, albeit the lowest level, of Unitary Consciousness. In this level of vibrational awareness, there is no duality consciousness, i.e. viewing things as good or bad, light or dark (two polarities). Everyone and everything "just is," and all is viewed as energy or experience, without judgment (i.e. mental judging), as part of the Divine order.

In 5th density the healed Inner Child Self (or Imago Dei, as John Bradshaw (1990) refers to it) emerges as your free-spirited, spontaneous and creative True Self. This integration is expressed as being childlike (having the positive qualities of children), distinct from being childish (immature).

As a prerequisite of 5th density integration, one has integrated the three divine attributes of love, wisdom, and power in perfect balance aka the Christ Consciousness integration, regardless of one's spiritual or religious affiliation or practices. This is because when the three fold flame is in perfect balance no new sin or karma is or can be created.

On the physical level, one experiences physical health and increased energy and vitality, often with resolution of previous disease issues, and sometimes miraculous healing of past ailments or illnesses.

In the financial arena, one experiences prosperity and abundance (at the relative level of one's choosing) with freedom from concerns about meeting basic survival needs of food, clothing and shelter.

In the area of career/work, one is in alignment with his/her spiritual purpose and mission and is engaged in productive self-expression of his/her talents and gifts.

On the level of relationships, one attracts and is involved with friends in healthy, interdependent, mutually rewarding, beneficial and supportive relationships. Relationships with family members are similarly supportive, or at least stabilized with healthy limits and boundaries, and forgiveness for all past issues. Romantic partners are soul-mates (persons you have known or loved in other lifetimes) with whom you have a harmonious relationship (karma/drama is cleared or no longer present). As one further evolves, many people are reunited with their twin flame (monadic mate), as the penultimate of Divine Union and twin soul integration of the Divine "I AM" God and Goddess self.

In 5th density consciousness, one feels continuously safe and secure with an incredible sense of peace, and increasing experiences of ecstasy, joy and bliss. There are increasing levels of understanding, love and compassion for all life forms and aspects of creation. You experience increasing ability to control your thoughts and feelings unaffected by "negative" persons or your surrounding environment, staying centered in positivity, and able to focus on creating and manifesting your reality or world based on loving focus on what is in the highest and best interests of self and others. In 5th density, one lives "in the flow" with minimal effort, with frequent synchronicity and serendipity, and with relatively less effort to achieve one's dreams and desires that are in alignment with the highest good of self and others.

Life is experienced with a greater appreciation for simple pleasures and a simpler (less complicated, achievement focused or materially acquisitive) lifestyle. The psychic abilities (also know as siddhis) naturally develop as an expression of the individual's unique soul expression, with "inner sense abilities," of clairsentience, clairaudience, clairvoyance and clairomniscience emerging, as well as telepathy, psychokinesis, teleportation, the ability to heal oneself or others, or the capacity to release attached spirits.

A person can be actively clearing and transitioning (4th density) in certain areas of their life, and simultaneously be already cleared and stabilized in 5th density in other areas. For example, one can be in a period of upheaval, struggle and strife (4th density) in the area of work/finances/career, while simultaneously stabilized in healthy interpersonal relationships (love and friendship), representing a 5th density level integration.

One only has to closely examine what is manifesting in his/her own, or another person's life, in the key areas of physical health, financial abundance, interpersonal relationships, work/career, intellectual, creative and spiritual self development to determine which areas are at a 4th density (actively integrating and healing) level vs. a 5th density (balanced and stabilized) level.

CHAPTER 5
Quantum Transformational Healing

The choice of the name for this spiritual evolutionary guided imagery or hypnotic healing process is Quantum Transformational Healing, or QTH. Each of the three words was chosen for its particular individual and combined significance.

Quantum, as in "quantum leap," refers to a sudden and significant change in a system. Rapid and significant positive changes in thoughts, feelings and behaviors can and have occurred using QTH, which is based on the principle and process of integrating and healing the disowned, unhealed, unconscious "shadow" aspects of the human personality or psyche.

"Quantum," also refers to discrete subatomic particles or quanta - photons, electrons, etc., originally described by Max Planck and Albert Einstein at the turn of the century (Talbot, 1988). Quantum particles, like all matter, were later found to have both particle (singular, discrete) or wave (unitary) properties, based on whether they were viewed from a linear cause and effect model vs. a holographic or unitary view of reality, dependent on the observer and also the substance they interacted with. Particle functions are perceived when reality is viewed from a logical, linear, analytical or rational (primarily left brain) thought process. Wave functions are perceived by intuitive (primarily right brain) thought processes which are non-linear, creative, and holistic. In scientific research (as in life), one's perspective or worldview shapes the experimental design and interpretation of the findings or events.

QTH is premised on a holographic model of reality. In the classical example of the holographic or unitary model of quantum physics, we need to understand how a hologram is created. A hologram is a three dimensional photograph made with the aid of three lasers (Talbot, 1988). To create a hologram, scientists first shine a laser beam on an object, and then project a second laser beam off the reflected light of the first. This results in an interference pattern, which looks like a meaningless swirl of light and dark lines. But when the developed film is illuminated by a third laser beam, a three-dimensional image of the original object appears. Extraordinarily, other than simply being three dimensional, a holographic image cut in half and then illuminated by a laser, will still contain the entire image of the original hologram! Thus, each part contains all the information processed by the whole. This holographic model runs contrary to our typical mechanistic cause-effect scientific thinking. Viewing reality from a holographic model of the universe is the equivalent of a unitary, fifth density perspective, which is beyond duality (light-dark) and contains the "Implicate Order", a term coined by David Bohm (Bohm and Peat, 1987) in which all of the potentialities exist in multi-dimensional simultaneity, beyond linear time (past-present-future) and space (distance).

David Bohm, a world renowned physicist, developed a new paradigm of scientific synthesis called the "Holographic Model of the Universe," based on findings of the research team of Alain Aspect in 1982, which showed that certain quanta (subatomic particles) could travel faster than the speed of light and instantaneously communicate with each other regardless of the distance separating them. According to Bohm, the properties of these subatomic particles, also known as tachyon energy (which in Greek means traveling faster than the speed of light), reflect that at deeper (higher) levels of reality, all things are interconnected and indivisible.

Dr. V. Vernon Woolf developed *Holodynamics* (1990), a therapeutic model based on a holographic model of the mind. QTH was developed using some of the same "tracking" steps utilized in Holodynamics.

Viewed from a holographic perspective, the process of self-healing takes on new possibilities as our consciousness therefore creates the holographic projection of the physical body. Holographic theory thus leads to "quantum healing" based on an integrated mind-body medicine described by Deepak Chopra (1990). Research on spontaneous cures of cancer, for example, are typically preceded by a dramatic (quantum) shift in consciousness of the dis-eased person to a higher state of consciousness in which they become hopeful, courageous and positive with a renewed will and certainty that they will be healed and live.

Dis-ease, or lack-of-ease, in the physical body is the result of accumulated densification of unhealthy "dis-eased" thought and emotional complexes or patterns, which have been repressed, denied or ignored. Dr. Bernie Siegel (1986), author of *Love, Medicine and Miracles*, describes all disease, at its most basic level, to be a result of lack of unconditional love of self and others. Although this may seem oversimplified, the underlying energy of love represents the magnetic, cohesive, integrating power, which results in wholeness, harmony and health, from the body tissues, organs and glands, to the cells and atoms, all the way down to the subatomic particles. The oft-heard phrases "God is Love," and that "Love is the greatest healing power there is," are reflections of Siegel's simple but profound truth. So, by unconditionally loving (accepting and integrating) the "shadow" aspects of our personality that we resist, fear, or judge the most, we open the door to deep cellular transformation and healing from the physical body up through the emotional, mental, and etheric (spiritual) levels or bodies.

Thus, the words "transformational healing" in the QTH process refer to literally changing the form of thoughts, feelings, and behavior, which leads to dramatic positive changes in the personality. When we connect to our Inner/Higher Self and bridge our consciousness to the unitary source beyond polarities, beyond pain and suffering, we create the wholeness and activate our own spiritual Higher Self and Creator-Creative consciousness, which allows us to re-create our human physical, emotional, mental and spiritual self. When we are in union with the Divine Co-Creative energies of Source, we are able to change all aspects or our life expression, including being able to change the form of physical matter, since energies can neither be created or destroyed, but can change form! Thus, cancer or other chronic mutated or dis-eased cells can be transformed, transmuted and restored to healthy, vibrant functioning by our shift in consciousness. Spontaneous healing can occur by connecting our physical (unconscious), emotional and mental (conscious), with our spiritual (superconscious), which is most typically achieved through meditation (in the Buddhist, or Hindu tradition) or prayer (Christian tradition), but is also central to the consciousness integration of QTH.

Integration is the Key to Spiritual Evolution

By using QTH we can connect with a source of higher consciousness, our own Inner/Higher Self or Guides, for specific inner guidance to be directed to the healing solution for a particular problem or issue.

Transformational Healing can thus be conceptualized as a continuum based on integration, which leads to integrity, which is synonymous with wholeness and leads to holiness. Consciousness integration, as previously described at length in chapter four, involves integration of the two polarities (dark/light, male/female), the three levels of mind (unconscious, conscious, superconscious) and the four bodies (physical, emotional, mental, and spiritual).

The Continuum From Integration to Holiness

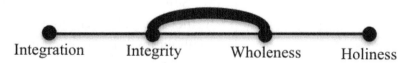

Integration   Integrity   Wholeness   Holiness

Figure 5-1

The vibrational frequency where spiritual awakening, integration, transformation, and evolution occurs is at the Fourth Density level. Below is a chart of the vibrational frequency levels and the corresponding evolutionary levels.

Vibrational Frequency Levels		
	Chakra	Evolution
First Density	1	Awareness as a point; physical matter; ex. atoms, minerals, water
Second Density	2	Awareness as a line; biological matter; group or species identity; ex. plants and animals
Third Density – Consciousness Emerges	3	Linear time and space awareness; individual identity or ego development; loss of group identity; duality consciousness; ex. Humans
Fourth Density – Superconciousness Emerges	4-7	Spiritual awakening and transitional awareness and reintegration of group identity without loss of individual identity; reality of time and space; perception of past, present and future begins to reintegrate multidimensionally; Christ consciousness integration occurs with love and forgiveness of self and others as keys to re-integration, healing and return to wholeness; intense clearing of karma and raising of one's vibratory rate; living by Universal Laws of Love and Free Will
Fifth Density - Lowest Level of Unitary Consciousness	8	Remembrance and integration of Divinity; "I AM" Self or Unitary God/dess consciousness; further integration of group consciousness without loss of individual consciousness

Chart 5-1

* Adapted and amended from *The Prisma of Lyra* (1989) by Lyssa Royal.

Introduction to QTH

The subconscious or unconscious mind, with the help of the superconscious (I/H Self or Guides) can uncover both the source of the client's problems as well as the solutions. Neither the therapist nor the client needs to consciously believe in some of the information held within the unconscious, such as past or parallel lives, attached spirits, or spiritual implants, for them to be revealed and transformed using the guided imagery process of QTH. However, both the therapist and the client need to have an open-minded, heuristic attitude, as well as a willingness to experience the truth of the underlying cause or source of the client's problems. The therapist simply encourages the client to trust his/her own inner perceptions, in the form of visual images, feelings, thoughts and words that come to mind during the QTH process. There is no scientific way to unequivocally "prove" the validity of what emerges.
The following is the QTH basic script and outlines the process in full:

Quantum Transformational Healing

1. Spiritual Alignment and Clearing

A. Physical Relaxation and Spiritual Alignment

Sit upright in a comfortable chair, with your spine straight and head balanced above your shoulders, and with your arms and legs uncrossed. Close your eyes, and focus on your body sensations. Now, breath deeply from your abdomen (below the navel)... pushing your abdomen out and drawing the breath up, ...up to your chest and shoulders, and into your neck and head. Visualize the relaxation spreading from the top of your head all the way down to your toes. As you exhale, allow yourself to relax more and more, and release any physical tension and unwanted thoughts or feelings. Each time you inhale, breath in more life energy, love and inner peace. Each time you exhale, imagine physical tension or discomfort being released with your focused intention... using your breath to breathe out any physical tension or discomfort. Take several deep breaths, breathing up from your abdomen all the way up to the top of your head. Breathe in to the count of seven, and then out to the count of seven. Inhale one-two-three-four-five-six-seven...Exhale one-two-three-four-five-six-seven (repeat for several cycles of inhalation/exhalation).

Now, visualize a golden-white sun or sphere above your head. See it streaming brilliant golden white (GW) rays of divine illumination in through the top of your head (crown). Breathe in the GW light each time you inhale, intensifying the color. As you exhale, breathe out, and expand the GW light above your head. Next, allow the GW sphere to descend into the middle of your head. Inhale, using your powers of focused concentration to visualize deepening and intensifying the GW color in your head; exhale, expanding the GW color all around your head. Visualize the GW sphere descending progressively down through the middle of your body, filling each area with the GW light. See the sphere now descend into your heart center.....breathe the GW light into your neck and shoulders...and then breathe it down through your arms and hands... filling your chest and upper back. Then, allow the GW sphere of light to descend into your solar plexus/stomach area (repeating the inhale and exhale focus pattern).....down into the navel.......and then filling your entire lower pelvic region.... Next, breathe and visualize the GW light moving down from your hips into your thighs, down through your legs, to your feet. Just go at your own pace, taking all the time you need to visualize to the best of your ability the GW light filling your entire body from head to toe... and when that is complete, have the sphere or sun rest below your feet. After the sun is resting below your feet, then see the sun spiraling upward and around your body in a clockwise direction (from left to right) filling your aura or the space around your body about two to three feet in all directions with GW light, creating a cocoon of GW light all around your body, until the GW sun spirals upward and rests above your head. Now, visualize a GW or silver cord about one and a half inches in diameter from the top of your head extending upwards into the higher dimensions, connecting to your Higher (Christ) Self and continuing upwards to Source. Breathe in, and then exhale while simultaneously visualizing the GW or silver cord going higher and higher. When you feel a greater sense of peace and higher connection to Source, then breathe this energy back down the cord, all the way down into your head. Then, extend a grounding cord of GW or silver light from the top of your head down the center of your body to your heart, down your torso and down through the base of your spine, breathing it down into the earth. Continue to visualize this GW or silver cord going down deeper and deeper into the earth until you feel yourself firmly anchored deeply within the earth. At this point you will feel your buttocks pressing down onto the surface on which you are sitting, which is a sign you have effectively visualized this grounding cord.

B. Open Heart

Next, imagine in your heart center a flame with three colors: pink, gold and blue light intertwined. This is the Three-Fold Flame of Divine Love (pink light), Divine Wisdom (gold light), and Divine Power (blue light) in perfect balance. Visualize the three flames intertwining and perfectly balanced, about one inch high. Now, see it growing larger... and each time you inhale, see the Three-Fold Flame increasing in size until it is about five inches in height.

C. Open Inner Vision and Hearing, Clear Body and Chakras

Next, I'd like you to visualize a sphere of diamond violet light in the center of your head. Inhale…and intensify the brilliant diamond violet light….exhale…and breathe out the violet light through the 3rd eye (the center of your forehead just above the top of your nose). Continue to breathe out violet light through the center of your forehead… Now, I'd like you to focus on breathing out the diamond violet light through your left temple…(pause) and then out through your right temple…(pause).

Next, allow the violet sphere in your head to descend through the center of your body…filling your neck…and chest…breathing violet light down your arms…down through your torso…, filling your pelvic region…and then extending down your upper legs…and then through your calves…and feet. Now, your entire body should be aglow with brilliant, diamond violet light. Breathe your life energy up from your heart, up to the center of your forehead, and as you exhale, breathe the light out through the center of your forehead. Do three or more cycles of inhalations for seven seconds/exhale for seven seconds. (N.B. Use violet light after visualizing GW light if client has problems later in QTH session).

2. Locate Inner Place of Peace (IPOP)

Now allow your breathing to become normal, regular and relaxed. I'd like you to shift your attention to finding an Inner Place of Peace (Inner Place of Safety, Inner Landscape, Inner Place of Healing, etc.). Let yourself go anywhere in the universe to find the place that is just right for you today. It can be a place you've been before, a place you create with your active imagination, or a combination of both. Take all the time you need to find the IPOP that looks, or sounds, or feels the best for you today.

Use your active imagination to clearly see the shapes, hear the sounds, and feel the feelings that go with your Inner Place of Peace. I'd like you to let me know when you have found your IPOP by saying, "OK." Wait until the client says "OK". Now I'd like you to increase your inner sense perceptions by focusing on experiencing as many senses as you can, as deeply as you can so that you feel as if you are really there right now. As you look around, see the colors and shapes and hear the sounds with more clarity and definition. Breathe deeply and sense any smells that go with your IPOP, feeling the peace and serenity, and whatever other feelings you may have. Whatever you experience is just fine. Let go of your mind, and just focus on your sensory experience. When you are ready, tell me about your Inner Place of Peace and what you are experiencing.

3. Connect with Your Inner or Higher Self (I/HS), Full Potential Self (FPS) or Guides

Next, as you continue to relax in your Inner Place of Peace, I'd like you to call from your heart for your Inner Self, Higher Self, Full Potential Self or a Spiritual Guide to come and be with you in your IPOP. Ask your Inner Self or Spiritual Guide (or ask the name they prefer) to make itself visible to you, in a form you can recognize. Your Inner Self or Spiritual Guide can take many forms: human, angelic, light body (usually spherical or oval-shaped) animal, or symbol. Just open your inner vision and look in front of you to see any images, which may be fleeting or unclear, to take shape. This is a passive process of receiving the pictures from your superconscious mind. Don't try to actively imagine something, just passively observe whatever you are experiencing (pause). Can you tell me what you are experiencing or seeing? What does the I/HS or Guide look like? Send love from your heart to your I/HS or Guide and ask if it will talk to you. Then, ask for the name of your I/H Self or Guide.

4. Identify the Most Important Problem / Issue (MIPI)

Ask the I/HS or Guide, "What is the most important (or beneficial) problem or issue to integrate and heal today?"

5. Access the Problems/Issue on a Sensory Level in (or around) your Body

Ask the client "Where in your body is the _____(name of problem/issue) being held or located?"
> Visual (V) "If it had a color or shape, what would it look like?"
> Auditory (A) "Will it talk with you?"

(Optional Questions)
> Kinesthetic (K) "What does it feel like?"
> Olfactory (O) "Does it have a smell?"
> Gustatory (G) "Does it have a taste?"

6. Ask the Problem Part What It Wants at Its Highest Level of Intention and Purpose (HLIP)

Ask "What does the problem part want?" If the answer is something negative, ask "What does it want at its most positive or highest level of intention and/or purpose (HLIP) for <u>name of person?</u>"

7. Ask Who Can Give the Problem Part What It Wants at its Highest Level of Intention and Purpose(HLIP)

Ask "Can your I/HS or someone else help it to get what it really wants?" Who can help it get what it really wants at it's highest level of intention and purpose (HLIP)? If it got what it really wants, what would that look like, (feel like, be like)? Have your I/H Self or Guide go anywhere in the universe to find who can help it get what it really wants at its HLIP.

8. Ask the Problem Part if it is Willing to Accept Help

Will the _____ (name of problem part) accept help from the helper/healing part that can give it what it wants at it's HLIP?

     If yes, proceed to #9

     If no:

     A. Ask "What would it need (to have, know or feel) before it can receive help from the part that can help it get what it really wants?"

     B. Then, give the unhealed, problem aspect what it needs to receive help. Or just send love (energetically or visualize sending violet light) to the area in the body where the problem is, if the problem part will not talk.

     C. Continue to focus the violet light in the area of the body where the unhealed problem is located. Then, ask the problem part if it is now willing to receive help from the part that can give it what it really wants.

9. Is the Healing/Helper Part Ready to Give Help

Is the healing/helper part that has the solution to what it really wants at it's HLIP ready and willing to help the part with the problem?

10. Integration of the Healing/Helper Part with the Problem Part to Create the Transformation

"I'd like you to then visualize the helper and problem parts merging and absorbing all the unhealed (problem) energy." Check for complete re-integration and ask "What does this transformation look like?" Optional: "What does it sound like…or feel like?" "Can the unhealed problem part be completely integrated and healed today?" If not, "What else is needed to completely heal and transform the shadow aspect?" "When will the transformational healing be complete?"

11. Integrating the Transformation on Physical, Emotional, Mental and Spiritual Levels

A. <u>Integrate on the physical level</u> Use breathing and visualize the healing energy moving up and down the spine and through the entire body.

B. <u>Integrate on the emotional level</u> "What does this new energy (part) feel like?"

C. <u>Integrate on the mental level</u> "Does this new aspect have a new understanding, or way of thinking, messages, assignments, etc. for <u>name of person</u>, others or the world?"

D. <u>Integrate on the spiritual level</u> Is your new, more healed self, integrated and aligned with your I/H Self? "Will this new aspect abide by the principles of Love and Free Will for all beings?" "Will the new you agree to focus on the Three-Fold Flame of love, wisdom and power in perfect balance?

Next, I will discuss in more depth the process and principles of the 11 step QTH process.

Progression of Steps – In Depth Discussion

In the course of continuing to improve QTH by both simplifying the steps and increasing its effectiveness over the years of developing it, I have added, unified, and/or subtracted some elements - primarily the alignment and clearing (beginning) and integration of healing (ending) steps, although the basic steps in the process, and the underlying principles guiding them, have remained the same. By adhering to the principles, one can creatively substitute an equivalent process or technique to achieve the same result.

Let's review in more depth the underlying principles and techniques used in the eleven steps of the Basic QTH script.

1. Spiritual Alignment and Clearing

A. Physical Relaxation and Spiritual Alignment

For physical relaxation, mental calming and focus, deep abdominal breathing is used as a basic technique to relax the physical body and calm the mind, drawing the attention inward to release any physical discomfort or tension. This relaxation technique is used if the person who is going to begin a QTH session is physically tense, mentally or emotionally stressed, distractible or unfocused. If the person has difficulty relaxing physically, or is mentally unfocused or over-focused on distracting or racing thoughts, repeat the deep abdominal breathing script (or a variation of same), or use another specific relaxation or meditation technique preferred by the client, which can be ascertained by asking them if they have a favorite relaxation/meditation procedure that they have found to be effective at creating physical relaxation and mental calming. Use of progressive (passive) relaxation, which focuses on relaxing specific body parts or muscle groups in a sequence from head to toe, is often very effective at both focusing the mind (reducing distractions and quieting an overactive mind), while simultaneously creating deeper physical relaxation in the body.

For the spiritual alignment meditation, from chapter two on Spiritual Self Development, a basic guided imagery process is used, which focuses on visualizing a sphere or sun of golden white light, which represents wisdom and purity. This is visualized above the head (transpersonal point, also known as the 8th chakra) and progressively downward and outward around the body to create a cocoon of GW light. Then a cord is visualized upwards connecting to the I/H Self, or Christ Self, and Creator/Source energies, and then a grounding cord is created to allow higher spiritual energies to flow through the body down into the earth.

B. Open Heart

Here, the three fold flame of love (pink), wisdom (gold) and power (blue), which is the Christ Consciousness Integration meditation, is used to open and balance the heart center or chakra. This enhances the client's ability to connect with their own Christed Inner or Higher Self.

C. Open Inner Vision and Hearing, Clear Body and Chakras

Since the most powerful color ray for transformation, healing, and transmutation is the Violet Flame, a guided meditation to visualize a diamond violet sphere in the head, to open the inner vision center (3rd eye) and inner hearing centers in the left and right temples, is used. Then, the violet light is visualized downwards to fill the physical body and auric field with violet light. In my work developing the QTH model, I have found that violet light greatly facilitates and enhances both the emergence and healing of the unhealed shadow aspects.

2. Locate Inner Place of Peace

This is a guided imagery process to focus on creating inner detachment from *outer* reality, which allows the client to find their own relaxing, peaceful inner place of peace, instead of the therapist directly suggesting a particular place. The Inner Place of Peace serves as a background landscape, or "stage" if you will, for the inner journeying and healing process of QTH to occur.

Most often, clients will find a scene in nature, often with water... such as a beach or a mountain meadow by a flowing stream. Indoor places such as in one's bedroom or house, are often the Inner Place of Peace for clients who need to feel "safe" in an enclosed space. In fact, an Inner Place of Safety, with suggestions of feeling safe, secure and protected, can be used as an alternate term if you know that the client has significant levels of fear or anxiety prior to the session, or in general, often due to past childhood or adult unresolved abuse or trauma issues.

Other alternate names for an Inner Place of Peace, which can be used if the client prefers, are Inner Spiritual Place of Peace, Heavenly Place of Peace, Inner Landscape, Inner Sanctuary or Inner Temple of Healing.

The Inner Place of Peace (IPOP) can be a place indoors or outdoors, anywhere in the universe, on or off the planet. The IPOP will vary from one session to the next, just as we would not necessarily choose the same "Outer Place of Peace," if we asked ourselves each day where we would like to go to relax and feel peaceful.

The IPOP can be: 1) a real place the client has actually experienced, seen or heard of; 2) an imagined place created with one's active imagination; or 3) a combination of both reality and imagination. If the client is having trouble finding a specific IPOP (usually related to difficulty choosing one of the several places they may have been seeing as possibilities) encourage them to pick the one that looks, or sounds, or feels the most peaceful. Alternatively, the therapist can verbally guide the client by suggesting a specific place often chosen by many people, which is at a beautiful, tranquil place in nature, such as a beach, mountain meadow, or next to a stream or bubbling brook, etc.

Once the client indicates he has found the IPOP that he senses (can see, hear, or feel) is the most preferable, or best for him that particular day, then his inner sensory experience is deepened. Inner Sensory integration is drawn from NLP sensory sub-modality integration techniques (Bandler, 1988). We gather sensory information through our five senses: sight (visual), sounds (auditory), feelings (kinesthetic), smells (olfactory), and tastes (gustatory). Of our five senses, our visual, auditory, and kinesthetic (feeling) senses are the most frequently utilized to gather and store information about our world. Specifically, the therapist can suggest deepening of the inner visual (clairvoyant) experience by seeing the colors and shapes more clearly, zooming in to focus in more detail, then zooming out to see the "bigger picture," etc. Similarly, inner hearing (clairaudience) is intensified with the suggestion of hearing the sounds that go with their IPOP with more clarity and definition. Next, heightening of the kinesthetic sense is suggested by focusing more on the feelings of peace and tranquility, and then focusing on any scents or smells that go with the IPOP.

3. Connect with Your Inner/Higher Self (I/HS), Full Potential Self or Spiritual Guides

In order to receive clear inner guidance and facilitate transformational healing, we need to connect with our superconscious, Spiritual Self, also known as the Full Potential Self, Higher Self, Inner Self, True Self, Angelic Self, Divine I AM Self, etc. or one of our clear Spiritual guides or teachers, guardians, etc. The Spiritual Inner/ Higher Self (I/H Self) or our Spiritual Guides represent a more integrated and evolved spiritual higher consciousness aspect that is a more loving, compassionate, wise and powerful higher consciousness.

A sincere heartfelt call is made for the I/H Spiritual Self aspect or Guide(s) to join the client in their IPOP. Since spirit energies can take any form, the Inner/Higher Self or Guides may appear in a variety of forms: human, angelic, light body, spherical or ovoid (oval ball of light), or animal guides and teachers (such as in shamanic journeying – see chapter six, or symbols (including geometric forms). The Spirit aspect is asked to appear, (as they usually do anyway) in a form that the client can recognize.

Many people have their first experience connecting consciously with their Inner/ Higher Self or Guides using the QTH process. Both excessive desire, as well as anxiety or fear, may inhibit or block the client's ability to successfully connect with a source of clear spiritual guidance. Suggesting to the client that he or she gently focus on sincere, loving intention (magnetic attraction), followed by detachment (letting go of desire to have the experience), maximizes the probability of actually being able to see, hear and feel one's Inner/Higher Self or Guide(s). The process of connecting to one's Spiritual

Self or guide is a passive process of just letting go and allowing, observing in a detached manner whatever happens or does not happen. At first the images may be fleeting or unclear, but then take a clearer or more distinct form, as one perceives or receives rather than actively imagines (projects or creates with one's active imagination). Once a visual image of the spirit energy is perceived, the doorway to communication with the spirit is opened by having the client ask the spirit's name and if it will talk with him/her. Occasionally, a problem arises when an unclear or "negative" spirit may appear to the client. Even when a clear spiritual guide is called for, on occasion a dark or negative spirit that is in need of healing appears. At its highest level of intention and purpose, the dark or negative spirit wants to be released, and that is why it presents itself to ultimately be freed from the host/ess. Release of "negative" or un-evolved spirits, as well as dark, demonic spirits, are important topics that are covered in detail in chapter nine on spirit release.

However, to briefly address the topic of discerning and releasing spirit entities that are not positive or clear, use the following sequence of steps to release the spirit:

Ask the spirit if it is at the Christ Consciousness (Ascended Master) level or higher, since the objective is to clear and release all energies that would block access to connecting with a clear source of Inner Guidance. If it says no, or gives no response, ask it in a firm, but loving and respectful manner to leave. If the unwanted spirit does not leave, a higher vibrational frequency of light needs to be anchored in and around the client. Repeat step one, using Spiritual Alignment with the Golden-White light, and Spiritual Transmutation using Violet Light. Use of golden-white light (for wisdom and purity) and Violet light (which facilitates the transmutational clearing and release) will usually work to facilitate the release of the unwanted spirit. If the above are not successful at assisting the spirit to be released, use the spirit release script in chapter nine.

4. Identify the Most Important Problem or Issue

Once the communication is established with one's I/H Self or Guide, the client asks the Spiritual Self aspect or Guide what the most important problem or issue is to focus on receiving clear inner guidance and/or healing about that day. Use of this technique represents detaching both the client's and therapist's human personality self (ego) from selecting the problem or issue to focus on.

If the client (or therapist) chooses a particular problem or issue, it is often based on conscious or unconscious fear or desire. In experimenting with different techniques and variations of QTH over the years, I have found that clients often pick the issue that is foremost in their conscious awareness, which is their main concern or predominant issue that day. However, when the superconscious Spirit aspect selects the most important issue, it is often different from what the client (or therapist) would have chosen, since one's Higher Self or Guide sees the "bigger picture," and will often go to the root, or deeper core underlying issue, memory or trauma related to the current problem, or pick an entirely different problem or issue, perhaps one the client is less comfortable with on a conscious level, or a problem or issue which the client is completely unconscious of.

5. Access the Problem/Issue on a Sensory level in (or around) your Body

In order to access the inner sensory experience, we ask for clarification initially on the visual (what it looks like and if it has a shape and size) and auditory (verbal communication) levels. The client can also be asked for the kinesthetic (feeling), olfactory (smell) and, if applicable, gustatory (taste) qualities of the unhealed, shadow aspect or issue.

If the client is unable to locate the energy complex by scanning in or around the body, ask for assistance from the I/H Self or Guide. The therapist can suggest, "Re-connect with your I/H Self (or Guide) by looking into his/her eyes, (the windows to the soul), and sending a stream of love from your heart to the heart of your I/HS or Guide... then ask your I/H Self or Guide to assist you by giving you clear inner vision, just like x-ray vision...scanning your body from head to toe...to find where in or around your body, the energy of _____ (the problem or issue) is being held (pause). Breathe in white (or violet) light through your body by visualizing a sphere of white (or violet) light in your head... (pause) allow the ball of white(violet) light to slowly descend through your body...illuminating any areas of blockage or unclear energy...scanning your body and asking to be shown the color and shape of the energy of _____ (problem or issue). The use of guided imagery when calling for clear inner vision and assistance from one's I/HS or Guide, as well as a visualization of white or violet light to "enlighten" any areas of unclear energy (which may appear as black, grey, brown or muddied colors) is usually effective in successfully moving through this step.

After the client can access the shadow aspect visually, the client asks the unhealed shadow aspect if it will talk with him/her. Approximately ninety percent of the time, the Shadow Aspect will agree to talk. If it refuses to talk, it is often because the unhealed part is reluctant to express itself due anger or resentment at the person for ignoring them for so long, often for years. This is especially true for unhealed Inner Child aspects, which are often reluctant to express themselves due to both fear and resentment. Other reasons the unhealed shadow aspect may be resistant to opening up and talking is fear of invalidation, or, fear of actually being healed, as it represents change.

Attached "negative" spirits may withdraw to avoid being seen or discovered. The lowest level of intention and purpose of unhealed shadow aspects represents "negative" thought, emotional and behavioral patterns such as wanting to block, hurt, injure or kill the person they are attached to. They may also prevent the person from healing and keep them attached to fear, hurt, anger, etc. in any of a multitude of ways and from making progress on their spiritual evolutionary path. The hidden positive intention and purpose of unhealed, shadow aspects is often to protect the inner child self or adult self from further harm. Spiritual (etheric) implants or blocking devices from past lives also often have a hidden, positive function to prevent the person from misusing their power.

6. Ask the Problem Part What It Wants at Its Highest Level of Intention and Purpose (HLIP)

Usually, the shadow aspect will readily reveal it's highest level of intention and purpose. If it does not, visualizing a sphere of pink (love) and or violet (transmutational) light in and around the shadow aspect will usually solve this problem.

When the shadow aspect is surrounded with loving and/or transmutational energy, this, in effect, dissolves the "negative" emotions of fear, anger, etc., since love is the greatest healing force in the Universe and the polar opposite of fear and it's "cousins" (c.g. all other negative emotions). Violet light is the most powerful transmutational healing ray in our visible spectrum. By temporarily detaching from the desire or focus on wanting to communicate with the unhealed part, we practice the law of detachment. Always remember the principle to treat unhealed/shadow "parts" like people. If you just got introduced to a person, and he/she was afraid or reluctant to talk to you, in order to open up communication, you would need to project an "aura" of safety through loving, non-judgmental acceptance, and non-attachment to outcomes (accepting that person's choice in not wanting to communicate with you). This loving acceptance and allowance of Free Will is very effective in facilitating more open communication with the shadow aspect via detaching from outcomes.

7. Ask Who Can Give the Problem Part What It Wants at Its Highest Level of Intention and Purpose (HLIP)

Unhealed or "shadow" aspects ALWAYS have a positive, pro-evolutionary or "higher" intention and purpose. For example, so called "negative" energy complexes (thought or emotional patterns from this or another lifetime, attached spirits, implants, etc.) represent forces of oppression (blocking) that typically have a hidden positive function of preventing that person from developing their abilities and full potential self because they have not yet developed sufficient love, wisdom, patience, humility or freedom from the "glamour" of beauty, status, wealth, fame, etc. to be able to use his/her power or abilities wisely.

In this step, the dis-integrated, unhealed shadow aspect is asked to go anywhere in the universe to find who (or what) can assist it to achieve what it wants at its HLIP. The helping or healing spirit energy may be the original I/HS or Guide that is already present, another higher frequency Spiritual Guide, or sometimes even deceased relatives (ancestor spirits).

8. Ask the Problem Part if it is Willing to Accept Help

In the majority of cases, the shadow aspect is ready and willing to accept help and receive what it wants at its HLIP during that session. Occasionally, however, there may be resistance to allowing a positive change to occur. This can be due to the person's feeling unworthy, other unconscious blocks, or the problem part having other conditions which must be met prior to allowing the transformational healing to occur during that particular session. It is also possible the client needs to complete *homework assignments* to create further personality integration and self-healing.

If the shadow aspect refuses to accept assistance from the helper (healing part), the most effective remedy is again utilizing a focus of violet light (pink and purple) by visualizing a sphere of violet light in the area of the body where the unhealed shadow aspect is located. Ask the shadow aspect if it will accept the transmutational healing of the violet light (which it will in almost all cases). The therapist can then hold the focus of violet light with the client for several minutes (or as long as needed) and ask again if the shadow aspect is then willing to receive help from the helper or healing part.

9. Is the Healing/Helper Part Ready to Give Help

The Healing/Helper part can be the client's I/H Self or Guide originally accessed at the beginning of the QTH session (in step three), or it may be another spirit helper. The human or personality self of the client may also be the healing/helper part that needs to integrate new thoughts, feelings and/or behaviors in order for the personality transformation to occur. This aspect of the self may also receive homework assignments that need to be completed before the transformational healing can occur.

This step is really more of a formality of asking for readiness or permission, since the more spiritually evolved I/H Self of the person or their Spirit Guide(s) are always willing to proceed with the transformational healing.

If the human (personality) self is the aspect that the shadow aspect indicates it needs to integrate in specific ways, often homework assignments will need to be carried out after the QTH session. The client may have some resistance following the guidance and completing his/her assignments. If there is resistance, the therapist and client then need to focus on clearing that block, in order to transform that underlying issue preventing the client from following through with and integrating the guidance received in daily life to achieve resolution of the problem. After the person completes the homework assignments (and with subsequent QTH sessions), the shadow aspect can then be integrated, transformed and/or released.

Often, multiple unhealed issues will come up in a single QTH session. When this occurs, the therapist needs to ask the client's I/H Self or guide what is the most important problem or issue to receive guidance and healing on that particular day. If time allows, more than one problem/issue can be integrated or healed in a single, extended QTH session.

Any unhealed issues that are revealed, but not completely integrated and healed at the time the session is ended, should be noted by the therapist for future reference in subsequent QTH sessions. In later follow-up sessions, once a connection with the client's I/H Self or Guide has been established, the therapist can simply ask:

> Is the current level of integration and transformational healing of (name of problem/issue) completed? (or) Is there more guidance or healing that needs to be done to complete healing of (name of problem/issue)? If the answer is "yes," then ask…
>
> Is this the most important problem/issue for _____ (name of client) to focus on healing today? If the answer is "no," then follow the standard script to discover what the most important problem/issue is to work on in the next QTH session.

10. Integration of the Healer/Helping Part with the Problem Part to Create the Transformation

This is the step where the transmutational and transformational healing occurs based on the principle: "Matter can neither be created nor destroyed, but can change form." Hence, trans (trance) – formation literally refers to the changing of form (color, size, shape).

The client is asked to allow the Helper/Healing part to interact/merge with the unhealed Shadow aspect. This is a passive process and the client simply observes the interaction/integration, and subsequent transformation. When the transformation is complete, the client is asked about the inner sensory modalities of the transformation, i.e. "What does the previously unhealed shadow aspect now look, sound, and/or feel like?" Additionally, it is helpful to ask if the particular problem part is completely healed today. If not, ask what is needed to completely heal this shadow aspect.

11. Integrating the Transformation on Physical, Emotional, Mental, and Spiritual Levels

Physical Integration is accomplished by using focused breathing and visualizing the healing energy moving throughout the entire body, to absorb all possible residual energy that may be in other parts of the body.

Emotional Integration is accomplished by asking the client if there is a new, more positive "feeling," or emotional state associated with the new, more whole and healed self.

Mental Integration is accomplished when the transformed self-aspect is asked if it has new, more positive, healthier ways of thinking, or messages or assignments for the person. Integrating new behavior patterns after the session further deepens and integrates the change(s) in the person.

Spiritual Integration is accomplished when several questions are used to deepen the transformation on a spiritual level. For example, "Will your new, healed self abide by the Spiritual Laws of Love and Free Will? Or, "Can you allow the new, healed aspect to fully integrate and reveal itself to your I/H Self?" Or, "Will the new, transformed you agree to balance the Three-Fold Flame of Divine Love, Wisdom, and Power?"

Quantum Transformational Tips

The following is a summary of some key concepts and "transformational tips" for the therapist to remember when using the QTH process:

1. Before you begin each session using QTH, it is recommended for the therapist to clear his body, mind, and spirit using the *Spiritual Alignment, Christ Integration, Transmutation and Protection Meditation* from chapter two, or his own preferred method of meditation or relaxation.

2. Focus your thoughts on "holding the field" to optimize the outcome and have the best possible transformational healing session that day. If the transformational therapist has fear, resistance, judgment or is distracted, you will reduce the possibilities of having a successful QTH session. Abide by the Cosmic Laws of

Love and Free Will by having positive, loving feelings, having an open-minded attitude, releasing expectations and detaching from the outcome you may want. Allow free will, and let go of the need to benevolently control outcomes.

3. Treat the I/H Self or Guide and unhealed Shadow parts the same as you would people. Project a feeling of love and acceptance to help them open up, communicate and reveal their truth. If necessary send or visualize pink light (love) to the helper or unhealed part to facilitate communication.

4. Remember, from God/dess consciousness (Unitary consciousness of 5th density or higher frequency) we are all connected in a single unified field. Realize that by simultaneously focusing on the client and seeing our common humanity, you are helping yourself to simultaneously heal, since we all have experienced variations of the same unresolved human issues and experiences, whether it is fear, anger, rejection, victims and perpetrators of abuse, etc. through our lifetimes of incarnations. There is no healer or healed...only healing! See everyone as your potential mirror and your teacher and healer to find how you can learn and evolve more fully and quickly by finding the common ground and the hidden lessons and blessings in each experience, each day, from moment to moment.

5. There are no victims in the universe! Everything is by agreement, but we often make agreements in our subconscious (sleep, etc.) or superconscious (prayer, meditation, etc.) states and QTH will uncover these agreements so they can be changed.

6. If multiple spirit helpers/guides show up, ask which one(s) can help or answer different questions during the QTH process. Some may come in to just deliver messages or give information to the person (teaching function) while another may be the main guide to actually assist in the integration and transformation of the unhealed shadow aspect (healing function).

7. When multiple unhealed/shadow/problem aspects come up during a single QTH session, always ask, "What is the most important problem or issue to heal today?" to stay on track. Multiple unhealed aspects will come into the light of conscious awareness (the first step of healing) and can be healed in subsequent QTH sessions, as appropriate. If multiple unhealed aspects are located during the QTH session, after step ten (Transformation) ask the person to look in their body where the other unhealed aspects were located to see if those parts have been partially or wholly transformed (which often occurs, due to the interconnectedness of All That Is).

8. Direct and extended spiritual transformational healing sometimes occurs spontaneously in QTH sessions, as evidenced by colored light, most powerfully

violet or green, being seen by the therapist or client at any time during the QTH process, which is discussed in more detail in chapter eleven.

9. If the person merges with his I/H Self or Guides during the process, ask the person to see his I/H Self or Guide outside and in front of himself, as a separate entity, to insure clear spiritual guidance during the QTH process. The I/HS or Guide can be later re-integrated and merge with the client at the end of the session to bring forth greater integration of the human self with the Inner/Higher Self or Guide.

10. When you are taking detailed notes during the QTH process, you may want to label and circle the unhealed problem parts as "D_1, D_2" etc. – if more than one unhealed part, for Dark, Disintegrated part; and "H_1, H_2" for the Healing, Integration aspect, to help you keep track of the different parts that arise.

11. If the person has many homework assignments to complete (to totally integrate the unhealed/shadow aspect), or if the unhealed/shadow aspect has played a great, significant role in that person's life (often protecting them from misuse of power from lack of balanced love and wisdom) he/she probably will not have a total re-integration of the Light and Dark parts and complete healing that day. The assignments need to be completed in order for the unhealed, shadow aspect to be fully transformed and released, and to be able to trust that the person is committed to living by the Universal Laws of Love and Free Will and wise use of power, so that the person will not misuse power as they actualize more of their full, spiritual potential.

12. Quantum Transformational Healing typically results in positive, noticeable changes in thoughts, feelings and behavior in a single session, if the transformational healing session for that day is complete (e.g. no homework assignments). However, in a typical pattern of psychological and spiritual evolution, multiple dis-integrated emotional, mental and behavioral patterns would need to be accepted, integrated, transformed and healed from this and other lifetimes. Many individuals dedicated to years of psychological self improvement and healing, who have sought assistance from healers and mental health professionals for significant periods of time, find much to their dismay, the same or similar unhealed issues re-surfacing in their life, often years later. The process of healing, in which successive "layers of the onion" of the same issue are healed and peeled off, will often occur over a period of weeks, months or years, before significant personality transformation occurs, and the person is increasingly able to access more of her true, full potential, or more evolved Spiritual self.

QTH Frequencies and Patterns of Occurrence of Specific Shadow Aspects

Unhealed Inner Child and Adult Issues

Since I would estimate that approximately eighty to ninety percent of adults from American families of past generations were raised in dysfunctional families, a great many people will have some patterns of dysfunctional (unhealthy) family dynamics, or unhealed aspects of physical, emotional, or mental neglect or abuse, or sexual abuse from childhood.

Similarly, most people will have experienced some events in their adulthood leading to unresolved feelings of hurt, anger, shame, blame, resentment, abandonment, loss, betrayal, etc. from feeling victimized (passively subjected to misuse of power) or guilt (from actively misusing their power) in an abuser or perpetrator role. Additionally, physical dis-ease represents the densification of these unresolved mental-emotional patterns, from childhood or adulthood, and QTH uncovers both the source and the healing solution. As one progresses spiritually, deeper and subtler layers of personal, genetic, ancestral, racial and cellular memory, (including recollections from other lifetimes), will be brought to the forefront of attention of the evolving soul's conscious awareness to facilitate healing, which is the topic of the next sub-category of the QTH healing.

Past/Parallel/Future Lives

Discovering memories of past lives (or less often, future lives), is a natural progression of uncovering even deeper layers of repressed, unconscious material from the psyche. Many mental health practitioners using guided imagery or hypnosis have had unexpected experiences with clients, which, for lack of any explanation of that person's experience in this lifetime, appear to be a re-living of an episode from a previous incarnation.

For example, when non-directive or open-ended suggestions are given to the client, such as "I'd like you to go to the source of <u>name of the problem</u> or, "Now, connect deeply with your unconscious mind to find the root cause of the <u>name of problem</u>," experiences of other past or future lifetimes often emerge. Past/future lives is the 3rd or 4th density term; they are called "parallel" lives from unitary 5th density (or higher levels of consciousness). The emergence of past life content can and does occur even when the client and/or therapist do not have an existing belief in past lives or reincarnation.

The re-experience of dramatic sequences of events with accompanying intense negative or positive physical sensations, emotions, and memories is often a cathartic or strong abreactive expression of karmic pattern revelation (Grof and Grof,1989). In other words, past life memories usually emerge with unresolved negative or karmic content, vs. lifetimes in which there are no significant events or lessons, or karmic sins of omission (not doing) or commission (doing).

Prior to actually seeing a past life for the first time, the person may have dreams about what they believe are past/parallel/future lives, and/or waking experiences of flashes of remembrance. The emergence of both sleeping and waking memories often indicate readiness to embark on exploring past lives in a more in-depth fashion.

The same psychological defense mechanisms of repression (unconscious blocking), suppression (conscious blocking), and denial, which represent decreasing levels of fear, operate to prevent a person from starting to remember and heal past lives. Emergence of subconscious memories of past lives is a natural evolutionary process of re-membering, e.g. reconnecting and consciously integrating all the members (parts or memories) of the life stream.

Spirit Release

Another category of the shadow aspects of the unhealed self is that of spirit attachment of either discarnate (disembodied) astral spirits of deceased humans, or dark "demonic" spirits who have been drawn to or attach to a particular person based on the Law of Similarities or "like attracts like."

Many spiritual healers and practitioners are able to discern and release unwanted spirit energies/entities, which often amplify strong "negative" emotional patterns such as anger or rage outbursts, depression, anxiety, psychosomatic conditions etc., as well as being the driving energies behind most compulsive or addictive behaviors.

Prior to a successful spirit release, the person may have homework (integration) assignments, which representing healing and releasing the underlying "negative" emotions which matched those of the attached spirit and allowed the spirit entity to merge and/or attach to the person in the first place. For example, if a person is being plagued by an attached or possessing spirit that is telling him/her to take one's own life, that person usually needs to clear or heal a significant portion of their depression and suicidal thoughts, general unhappiness with life, and perhaps guilt, low self-esteem or other issues which are underlying, and "resonate" or "vibrate" with the thought and emotional energy of the attached spirit. This resonance of "like type" energies is what allowed the attachment to occur when the person was in a weakened state. The topic of Spirit Release will be addressed in detail in chapter nine.

Spiritual Blocks and Implants

In the process of uncovering various types of "shadow" aspects, another unique sub-category spontaneously emerged, which constitutes a specific type of spiritual block, known as an implant. These implants are spiritual blocking devices which exist in the spiritual (etheric) body vs. actual physical implants (such as microchips). Etheric implants are typically identified as specifically metallic objects in or around the physical body, whereas other unhealed aspects are non-metallic. Since implants are <u>not</u> part of the soul (spirit) of the individual, they are transformed and released (vs. integrated) during the QTH process. Chapter 10 describes in detail the history and origin of etheric implants, as well as transcripts which illustrate the transformation and release.

Case Examples of General QTH Sessions

Next, I will present three samples of transcripts that move from simple to more complex and cover an introductory sampling of problems and issues that can be spontaneously elicited via the QTH process. The split page format of these and all QTH transcripts in the book are organized with the actual transcript on the left of the page, and my teaching commentary and analysis to the right. This format was chosen to deliberately facilitate and enhance "left-brain – right-brain" integration to enable the reader to simultaneously grasp the steps of QTH and flow of the client's process, as well as learn how to interpret and make decisions from the therapist's viewpoint about how to proceed. In the transcripts "T" refers to the therapist and "C" refers to the client.

For the most part, the initial preparatory and ending guided imagery steps have been abbreviated to avoid unnecessary and cumbersome repetition. However, in this first general QTH session, I have provided more in-depth commentary on the right hand side of the page to give a fuller introduction to an actual session and the applicable steps, process and principles of QTH.

This first example was the initial session of QTH with David, a very spiritual businessman who was already familiar with meditation and inner guided imagery processes. He also knew a great deal about many of his significant past lives. In this session, he discovers how his past misuse of power in this life is blocking him and effecting multiple areas of his life, as well as leading to recurrent health problems. There is a partial transformational clearing of a layer of the anger, self-recrimination and guilt, and he receives additional homework assignments to facilitate further healing of this core issue, which was also rooted in other lifetimes of misuse of power.

Session 5-1

T: Deep Abdominal Breathing Open Heart, Open Inner Vision and Hearing, Locate IPOP.

C: I'm by a waterfall..Sacred Falls...with a friend. There's a pool nearby...and he's going to take a swim.

T: Now, connect with your I/HS or Guides.

C: I'm feeling sadness, and resistance to being helped.

Client expresses resistance, which suggests he needs to deepen the connection to his IPOP.

T: Re-anchor yourself in your IPOP. Imagine being at Sacred Falls, looking out through your eyes, seeing the waterfall and pool... hearing the sounds of nature...the sound of the waterfall and the tropical rain forest and sensing the smells and scents...the earth, plants and flowers. Feel the peace and tranquility of being there...now using all of your inner sense abilities to see, hear, feel, and smell...the sensory experience of being fully present right now in that beautiful sacred place...

Here, I re-focus the client on his inner-sensory experience in order to release his resistance.

T: Are you fully back in your IPOP now?

I observe client's body language for a relaxation response, and it appears he is more relaxed.

C: Yes, I'm sitting by the pool at the base of the waterfall enjoying the smell of the ginger that's in bloom.

Make sure client gives description of inner sensory experiences in enough detail to confirm deep connection to IPOP.

T: Now, make a heartfelt call for your I/H Self, or one of your Spiritual Guides, to come and be with you in your IPOP.

C: It's my HS aspect – he looks like King Arthur.

T: Ask your HS, what is the most important or beneficial problem or issue to heal today?

C: The issue of my power – about denying it and not using it.

T: Where is the issue of not using or denying your power, and the sadness and resistance anchored in your physical body?

C: In my throat – it looks cavernous…red and angry. I feel rage…frustrated and total anger turned inward…It's the energies from chakras one through four, all moved up into my throat – issues of sexuality, money, psychic power, plus energy…my misuse of all of them turned into self-recrimination and guilt.

T: What is the purpose or function of the red angry energy in your throat?

C: To get me to recognize how powerful I am in my speaking. But it's causing me to have problems with my health and well being…the anger becomes a sore throat or cold.

T: What does the red angry energy want at its highest levels of intention and purpose?

C: It wants to mimic the shark…needs to cut into the issues…cut itself loose from the guilt and negative energies. It's like a conglomerate holodyne…seeing myself as a victim, living in a role of powerlessness because of the guilt over past misuse of my power. I'm feeling physically and emotionally beaten down and I'm blocking myself with self-doubt, not trusting myself, or the accuracy of my decisions about others.

Client was familiar with Holodynamics(1990), a similar therapy developed by Vern Woolf, and used the term holodyne to describe a core (unresolved) complex.

T: Who can help you to clear the energy in your throat, the anger and guilt…all the negative feelings that are blocking you from your power?

C: Jesus is here now. He's in white robes. I'm kneeling before him with my head bowed. He's blessing me and absolving me of guilt. It feels like I'm going through purification with fire. (client pauses and reflects) I've been going through these before…there's been seven baptisms by fire.

T: What does this fire look like?

C: It's white light.

T: Allow yourself to absorb the white light in your throat and breathe it through your whole body to cleanse and purify and transmute all the self-anger and guilt over misuse of power in all of your cells. (pause)

Now check to see if the red energy in your throat has been completely absorbed and purified by the white fire.

C: No, there's still some red…

T: Then ask Jesus what else will be needed to completely clear these energies in the throat.

C: He says that I need to:

1. get an amulet…a caduceus symbol with a sword and a snake, and also
2. a heart locket…something ornate and regal – an apple red ruby color. I'm seeing it pulsating and vibrating …the ruby red is like the color symbolizing the Sacred Heart of Jesus.
3. And I'm to focus on bringing the white light into the throat on a regular daily basis…to cool the red down.

T: Are there any other assignments to help transform and heal the misuse of power anchored in your throat?

C: Yes, I'm being told to complete more healing when I was in the King Arthur lifetime, to integrate the feminine energy of Gwenevere…to get some music…and pictures of that time…and read about her.

T: Are there any blocks or resistance to completing any of the assignments you've been given so far?

C: No, I feel I will follow through with them. Now I'm feeling mucus in my throat, but I'm bringing in more white light to get rid of it.

T: Great! Ask Jesus if there's anything else to complete our session today.

After absorbing healing energy in the client's main focal point (the throat) in the body, I continue to suggest complete physical clearing of the entire body.

From prior experience and knowledge of this client, who has had many lifetimes in a powerful position (which almost inevitably results in misuse of power), it would be anticipated that this issue would not be cleared in a single session of QTH.

Here, the client gets several "homework" assignments to facilitate complete clearing/ healing of this issue.

Integration of feminine energies is often a key to balancing male/female energies of misuse of (male) power with the feminine prototypical polar opposite of love.

C: I've been having a sore throat lately. My craving for sugar is feeding the sore throat. Instead of more sugary foods, I'm to eat apples...and reminded to again transmute the angry red to ruby red...of the Christ heart.

T: Any other final messages or assignments from Jesus?

C: He says that my hopes and wants and wishes will be realized before Christmas.

T: That's great. Now thank Jesus for his guidance and healing today and open your eyes when you are ready, and come back into the present.

Due to the fact that he was given several homework assignments, and additional knowledge of David's issues with multiple powerful past lives (in which he misused power), additional future sessions would be recommended after he follows through and completes his assignments. This would help him to heal the multiplicity of layers of guilt and self-recrimination.

Session 5-2

Olivia, who was a professional dancer and actress, had only one prior QTH session. She was an experienced meditator who was consciously spiritually connected with her Higher Self. The following two more complex sessions were done one week apart, and related to clearing blocks to her power and creativity (in her stomach and throat respectively), both related to being persecuted and killed as a witch in another life. Since approximately seven million women, as well as many men, were tortured, persecuted, and killed for being witches and healers during the Inquisition, many people have similar past life cellular memories and are similarly blocked in expressing more of their spiritual and/or creative power due to past life fears of being persecuted or killed.

In this first session, the generalized issue of betrayal that Olivia held primarily in the stomach – with specific feelings of fear, disappointment, judgment and denial – was transformed into the archetypal symbol of butterflies, representing transformation and freedom after emerging from the cocoon or chrysalis.

In the second session, which was done one week later, the source (past life) of the unhealed energies of betrayal is further revealed as an additional block in the throat. This deepened the integration and healing from the first session by clearing the block to her creative power in the throat chakra.

These two sessions reveal a typical natural progression in which a core traumatic event (being persecuted and killed in a lifetime in which higher levels of spiritual and creative powers were actualized) can create multiple blocks throughout the body, which all need to be cleared and healed in order to manifest changes in the inner and outer (thoughts, feelings and behaviors) of the person.

T: Deep Abdominal Breathing – Open Heart and Inner Vision – Locate IPOP.

C: I'm on a peninsula…it's foresty…with animals. It's clean and dry.

T: Now, connect with your I/HS/Guide.

C: It's my Higher Self. She's an angel…robed in light.

T: Ask your HS, "What is the most important problem or issue to heal today?"

C: She says it's about betrayal.

T: Ask your HS, "Where in or around your body is the feeling of betrayal anchored?"

C: It's in my stomach (D_1)… a complex of different feelings. It looks like …isolated pockets of marbles or rocks – like cat's eyes, grays and reds with a shell around them.

Similar to hard, encrusted, solidified matter representing densified mineral deposits, which can manifest in the physical body as stones in the kidney or gall bladder.

There's more on the right side…more congested with substance on the right. The left side looks like it has a hole blown through it. It's holding fear, disappointment, judgment and denial.

Typically the stomach (solar plexus chakra), which is the seat of lower intellect and will, is a center point for mental judgments (disappointment and denial) and fear (as well as other negative emotions).

T: What does the energy in the stomach want?

C: It wants to relax…to be meshed, calm and facile. To have liquidity and strength…and to have a reinstatement of my center. But I'm afraid there's not enough room.

> This is an expression of the highest intention and purpose of the unhealed energy, based on the positive qualities it desires.
> This last sentence is the client's ego (human fear) talking.

T: Who can help the stomach get what it really wants…to be relaxed and calm and have liquidity and strength?

C: My HS can help.

T: Is the stomach willing to receive help from your HS?

C: Yes.

T: Then ask your HS to go anywhere in the universe to find the healing solution to give the stomach what it wants.

C: She's bringing back a big lit ball of love… it's a yellow and white ball with lines.

T: Now, allow the big yellow and white ball to merge with the unhealed energies in the stomach, and completely absorb and transform them.

C: It's merging now. I have a pregnant feeling…The rocks and marbles are in a liquid base…they're starting to dissipate… and the shell is dissolving. (long pause… therapist waits about thirty seconds to allow for completion of the transformation)

> Beautiful metaphor for transformation, likened to pregnancy, i.e. giving birth to her new, more healed self.

T: Keep focusing on breathing deeply to clear out all the unhealed energy in the stomach… and then breathe the yellow and white light through your entire body.

> Coaching to enhance breathing and focus intention to clear entire body.

C: The shell has dissolved now…and the cat eye has a message…it's transforming to butterflies flying around trying to find a formation. A butterfly just flew out of my mouth (she says excitedly). My HS likes this game. Now I can see the light moving into my ankle and hip, and my right ear and shoulder.

> Direct reference to re-organization and transformation in a physical, visible manner. Notice the "lightness" and energy shift in client's excitement.

C: (cont.) The message from my HS is, "Be more aware of my angel presence as a bridge integrating the spiritual and the material."

Spontaneous expression of Mental Integration.

T: How does this transformation feel?

C: I feel...actually hypoglycemic...and I'm quivering.

Kinesthetic Integration.

T: That's okay. Sometimes after people go through a deep release and transformational healing, they might feel hungry or thirsty. Just remember to get something to eat after the session...drink lots of water...and rest... because you've gone through a major clearing.

Here, I give her reassurance and recommendations. Her experience is similar to healers who may experience relative hypoglycemic episodes after running a strong influx of healing energy through their physical body, which uses up available blood sugar (energy) that needs to be replenished.

C: My HS says my dance...is a creative synthesis bringing the spiritual into physical expression. My throat is going to be effected to have more physical and verbal expressivity.

Further messages from HS describing future effects of integration.

Here is the second session with Olivia 1 week later:

Session 5-3

T: Deep Abdominal Breathing, Open Heart and Inner Vision, Locate IPOP.

C: I'm seeing a male...climbing up the castle steps. My right side feels achy, my head is hurting and I'm having sensations like muscle releases...in my solar plexus. It's the Inquisition...rocks are being thrown at me...

Client is spontaneously accessing a past life, and having cellular physical memory release in her body.

T: I'd like you to just breathe out any discomfort in your body and let the pictures you were getting fade out. Allow your body to be relaxed and comfortable and let your mind take you to find an IPOP.

I guide her back to her IPOP to anchor in relaxation and peace and then connect with I/HS/Guide to receive clear guidance. Otherwise, client may get stuck in fear or other strong negative emotions and judgment of self or others, which will block or impede progression through difficult scenes of that particular lifetime.

C: It's the same as before...a peninsula... that's foresty...with different animals.

T: Call forth your own Spiritual aspect, your Higher Self, Angelic Self or a guide to join you in your IPOP.

C: I feel holes in me…I'm on a raised bed, old style, Aegean with a gold banister…there's light beings around me.

Client again apparently sees flashes of past life pictures.

I see my H/S…she's an angel robed in light. She says that at the University of Hawaii, the actors and actresses are in the same play or re-enactment. There's a liaison between good and evil. I was persecuted as a witch…my motivational skills were very threatening. My energetic connection with so many people threatened some of their past life hooks. They're threatened by me now….just as they were before.

Client is a dancer/actress and giving a metaphor relevant to her particular profession.

The re-creation of good and evil liaisons she is alluding to refers to multiple "players" from her witch lifetime who are now reincarnated and working together as faculty or staff at the University.
Here, she is referring to problems with other faculty/staff she works with at the University being threatened by her.

T: Ask your angelic H/S what is the most important problem or issue that's blocking you?

C: It's that I feel it's not safe to be powerful. I have to take precautions…so I won't get attacked on this plane. But I need to believe in myself – keep my physical body up to speed with my spiritual body – to be in the largeness of myself. Then I can physically manifest my power…rather than shrivel.

T: So what specifically is the main problem or issue?

Ask for clarification if problem/issue is not clearly and specifically stated.

C: My whole self-image…there's a general block of my creativity. I keep re-creating the old issues – stomach problems, my weight, old injuries, financial problems, and no man in my life.

T: Where in your body is the creative block, which is affecting your whole life and self-image?

C: It's in my neck…it looks like a lid… dark blue-grey steel that sits horizontally… separating my head from my heart. (D_1)

The neck (throat chakra) is the typical center for creative self-expression.

T: What's the lid's function?

C: To protect me from myself...my free-spiritedness...keeping it in check...it's too powerful. The fullness of the connection would freak me out.

T: What does the lid want at it's highest level of intention and purpose?

C: It wants to relax...to trust I'm willing to be my bigness and not get hurt. If I let go, I'd get hit by a truck. It would jump out with a creative inspiration or idea...and I may have been assaulted. I've pulled it up and down... the energy in my throat...to create resilient boundaries...like Jell-O...to let them in and out. Sometimes I get ahead of myself. I have to be more aware of the mercurial barometer of the flow of energy...to expand or contract... the friendly electromagnetic field.

Being hit by a truck is probably a metaphor for the power that would be released if her heart and head were connected as well as being attacked (assaulted) by others threatened by her power.

T: Is the lid in your neck willing to receive help?

C: Yes it is.

T: Can your angelic HS or someone else help the lid in your throat get what it wants...for you to use your power and creative energy wisely...letting it out in ways so you won't get hurt?

C: Yes, she will.

T: Then allow your HS to go anywhere in the universe to give the lid what it really wants. What would that look like or be like?

C: I'm seeing a diamond octahedron... (H_1) about three inches high...with clear crystal refractions of light in my throat now. It's opening my vocal cords...like elevator doors...it's a protective shield and for alignment. I'm feeling the energy shift...in my throat and down to my heart. Now I sense the lump in my throat has moved up.

T: Take a deep breath and breathe the energy from the diamond octahedron all the way down to your heart...then up again through your throat

Here I am facilitating physical integration throughout the body.

T: (cont.) and up into your head. Keep breathing it up and down running the clear white light energy from your heart to your head…and back down again through your entire body (pause and observe client).

C: Now my breathing is breaking up the steel grey lid…I can see it's disappearing (say's excitedly). My jaw feels freer…and my voice has dropped.

Physical Integration

Kinesthetic Integration

T: Are there any messages from your HS?

C: To use my creative power wisely…be more conscious of opening to the flow.

Mental Integration

T: Will you now abide by the Two Cosmic Laws of Love and Free Will?

Spiritual Integration

C: Yes.

Session 5-4

This third example is a lengthier session with Sarah, a very advanced spiritual woman who was familiar and experienced with the QTH process. It illustrates greater complexity with a multiplicity of past life issues, energies and entities being brought to the light of conscious awareness for transformational healing. Some wonderful "nuggets" of spiritual truth and wisdom also are spontaneously expressed by Sarah in this session.

T: Deep Abdominal Breathing, Open Heart and Open Inner Vision, Locate IPOP.

C: I'm on top of a mountain, very high up… with sparse vegetation and a great vista. The sky is covered with clouds.

T: Now, call from your heart for your I/H Self or Guides to come and join you in your IPOP for the purpose of receiving clear, detached, objective guidance for the rest of today's inner healing process.

C: I'm seeing violet light…it's very beautiful. I think it's St. Germaine (SG).

T: Ask SG to make himself visible in a form that you can recognize, to be sure it's him.

C: I know it's him…because he's come to me many times before…we have a telepathic communication.

Here, since I have known this person and her connection with her guides, I do not question her certainty.

T: Okay, then ask SG "What is the most important problem or issue to heal today?"

C: He says it's my urinary system.

T: What specific issue is related to your urinary system?

C: There's fear…and sadness. Something very black…like a circle.

T: Can you ask SG where in your urinary system it's located and more about the size and shape?

C: It's above my pubis…in the lower abdominal area and bladder. The black circle shape is turning into tentacles all over the place…and I see it moving.

The fact that this energy is moving around is both typical and suggestive of an attached, separate entity or spirit.

T: Can you ask the black circle with tentacles what it wants?

C: It wants my life force energy from my sexual organs.

This is its lowest intention and purpose.

T: What does it want at it's highest level of intention and purpose?

C: To live and grow…and move.

T: How long has this part been with you? Did it originate before, during, or after your birth?

C: It's been with me several lifetimes.

T: Is it part of your soul or a separate energy/entity?

The question, "Did it originate before, during, or after your birth?" is an "elegant" way of eliciting past lives, especially for people who may not really believe in the possibility of reincarnation.
Here I query if it is separate from her soul/spirit.

C: It's separate from my soul…it's actually a parasite.

T: When did it originate?

C: It originated from negative thought forms…it's in my DNA…ancestral, negative, astral thought forms residing in the sexual and urinary tract organs of my body.

This coincides with esoteric wisdom about attached spirits and other parasitic entities being originally created from thought forms.

T: What is the name this part would like to be addressed as?

C: It says you can call it the "Black Thing." It's responsible for creating the recurrent urinary tract infections I've been having lately.

T: Can you ask SG for confirmation as to whether this part needs to be integrated (as part of your soul) or released (as an energy formation separate from your soul)?

Checking for confirmation from clear guidance (SG) on whether this is a (suspected) separate, embedded, or attached entity/spirit or a part of her own soul/spirit.

C: He says it's not part of my soul…and it's parasitically attached to me.

T: Would it be willing to be released?

At a higher level of evolution, all life forms including parasites will become self sustaining and independent, not parasitic; the simplest examples being the human progression from the total dependency of the infant on it's parents for sustaining it's life to full independent functioning as an adult. A case in point of ontogeny (the developmental evolution of the individual) recapitulating phylogeny (the evolution of the species or group).

C: Now, Sanat Kumara and Lady Master Venus have come in. Sometimes with me they coalesce into one Divine form.

Here, additional spirit guides spontaneously appear as the healing or helper aspects. Sanat Kumara and Lady Master Venus are Cosmic level spiritual masters.

T: Is that what's happening now?

C: Yes, and they're saying that it needs a teaching…to learn love…and not be parasitic…so it can find it's own higher source of energy…(pause) I feel tears with that. I can feel it. It's a ball…there's a whole sphere

C: (cont.) coming out of my abdomen into my aura. It has a center to it. It's indicating it's willing to receive a teaching from the masters.

T: Are the combined energies of the two masters willing to begin the teaching now?

C: They've already started…there's a triangular prism of rainbow colors moving in to the center of the black thing. It's almost like it's entering into the core. Now the colors are becoming more pink and purple…and white.

T: Just open yourself to fully allow the transformation to occur.

C: I want to ask …what part I play in the communication.

T: Ok, then go ahead and ask your guides.

C: They want me to be a part of the teaching. They're doing an energy shift as a preparation for the teaching. The black thing is receiving it (the energy).

T: Then focus now on allowing the maximal transmutation of energy to be received by the black thing so it can be more receptive to the teaching. (I pause for about thirty seconds to allow for the energy shift).

This is standard procedure of the Ascended Masters and Spiritual Hierarchy to raise the vibrational frequency for both direct clearing and healing as well as to increase receptivity to Higher levels of Truth (teachings).

T: Ask the black thing if it's ready to receive the teaching now?

C: It says it's ready. The teaching is to begin. I'm to be a mediator…for me to experience it (laughs gently) as a necessary prerequisite for my growth as well. The black thing says, "As a consequence of my actions as I live and thrive I cause disease to another."…(client) I want to tell it that I've been having painful bladder and urinary tract infections and there might be some disease process starting… there's been fungal and intestinal infections and problems with elimination in my colon, causing me to lose energy and taking energy away from fulfilling my Divine Purpose and expression of gifts. I'd like to have my health

Illustrates the client's co-participation as a spiritual teacher and healer in her own healing process.

Client talks directly to the black thing to educate it about the affects it's been having on her body and spirit.

C: (cont.) and wellbeing back. I can't have that if you stay attached to me. I lovingly ask you to find your own source of energy. It will be so much more powerful and clear...a much purer source of energy. I do believe you'll be happy with the transition...

A beautiful, loving expression of the truth that all life forms (including humans) are wise to connect directly with their own life energy, as well as Source, to derive greater power and clarity.

T: Now, ask your guides for direction on how to continue to proceed with the teaching and healing process.

C: They say I should forgive the black thing for parasitically using this energy in my body (client now speaks softly to the black thing). I forgive you for using my body parasitically for your energy source. With the guidance of SG, Lady Master Venus and Divine energy source, you can make your own connection to Source (client is silent for a long period).

T: Ask the black thing for it to respond.

C: I'm getting an apology. It didn't realize it was causing so much trouble. It knew it but it didn't care. Now it's starting to care. It's willing to find it's own Divine energy source and connect with it. The Masters are connecting it now (pause). My Divine consciousness is simultaneously working with the black thing, so I'm clear and my mind can understand what's happening.

Many times when the shadow aspect realizes how much suffering/problems etc. it has caused, compassion arises from the understanding and this greatly enhances and expedites the healing process and release.

C: It's receiving the Sunas, a Divine source of golden white light energy...radiating and merging with it. The sun's shining the light down and the black thing is becoming a light core...now the tentacles are becoming silver and yellow.

The transformational integration and healing aspect is the sun.

T: Now, focus on allowing the fullest possible transformation and re-absorption of the black thing into the golden white light of the sun.

C: I just need the Masters to help remove the negative thoughts in my DNA that are still there. This was the matrix that allowed the black thing to come in the first place. As it's clearing and being energized by the golden white sun, it's also shining throughout my body.

Client receives revelation of negative thought forms in DNA as attracting the parasite in the first place (according to the Law of "Like Attracts Like" or the Law of Similars).

T: Yes! Allow it to absorb all the residual energy and effects throughout your entire body.

C: (Client spontaneously affirms) My whole body is a clear vessel of silver radiating through the DNA of each cell of my body. I consciously affirm and choose to release the black thing so it can leave (short pause). It's moving on its own. It's going to be a free-floating energy form in the universe with it's own consciousness.

T: Has it's consciousness changed?

C: Yes, it's more aware of other beings, and how to be in a right relationship. Now, I'm getting guidance that there's energy work that needs to be done here (points to abdomen) to balance it. I need to release and let go of the same thing. (Client pauses and focuses). I feel complete with that. I'm being guided to bring the sun into my solar plexus and second chakra. I'm bringing in the sun's Divine energy…it's coming in to attach where the release took place…(Pause)…Now it's like a galaxy…filled with stars…going from below my navel into my pelvic area and up to my solar plexus. It's swirling silver energy stars against a black sky. I see many stars and solar systems all moving…in black space.

Here, the client has a realization of her human self needing to integrate a deeper respect and right relationship (freer and more separate) with other beings.

This inner guidance from the client reiterates another important principle of healing to always fill an area where something has been removed (usually with one or more colored light energies). The principle is that "nature abhors a void," ergo the void will randomly and haphazardly be filled with whatever energies are passing through nearby.

T: What effects or positive change will this transformational healing have on your physical body?

C: My health will be improved although it may not be sudden and complete.

T: Establish a clear connection with your three combined guides and ask them what else needs to be done to complete the healing of the fear.

C: They're having me check my urinary system…There are negative thought forms embedded there…they say any current thoughts I carry on my person…in my own consciousness…have not been cleared. I need

C: (cont.) to be more loving and accepting without judgment of different expressions of masculine and feminine energies.

T: Who can release these negative thought forms?

C: I can do it on my own…they're telling me I still have some unconscious fears…and to do dream work…Set intentions and write down my dreams.

This recommendation for "homework" assignments suggests a more complete healing is only possible in the future upon completion of these assignments.

T: Are you willing to set intentions for clearing these negative judgments in your dream state and record your dreams?

C: Yes…one dream just came to mind…in a dream…a man came from behind a telephone pole…he was hooded…I was re-visiting and clearing it. I'm setting an intention now to write down my dreams.

T: What effects will this healing have on you emotionally?

Facilitating emotional integration.

C: Now I'm receiving energy in my throat… to bring through the acceptance and expression on a conscious level. I rejoice in it…recognizing it as a great universal energy. I'll have more lightness and purified energy.

Here, client is receiving a spontaneous healing energy transmission to clear her throat chakra.

T: Can you acknowledge and consciously accept this transformation? Are there any mental blocks to maintaining this change?

Eliciting mental integration.

C: There's some mental doubt…It would be good to repeat the transformation that occurred today…But what happened is as true as any other events in my life…There's a certain skepticism about the power and depth of the healing…It's real, not just my fantasy…But I will let go of it.

Interestingly (and unexpectedly) as client descends in vibration and consciousness from her Divine to her Human Self, she questions the validity and depth of the healing today.

T: What effects will today's session have on your spiritual self development?

C: I'm carrying a galaxy around in me! (Laughs) The galaxy and I are one…It's actually universal.

Here, she spontaneously goes back into multi-dimensional (galactic and universal) awareness!

T: Great! Ask your guides if there is anything else to complete our session today? Do you have any blocks on subconscious, conscious, or superconscious levels?

Checking for blocks on the three levels of consciousness integration.

C: No, It's complete. I just verbally deeply thanked my guides to move into my own Divinity and release the parasites.

In the next several chapters, we will explore in more detail the various subcategories of QTH, with examples of sessions including: Shamanic Journeying, Inner Child Healing, Past/Parallel/Future Life Healing, Spirit Release, Removing Spiritual Implants, Spontaneous Spiritual Healing, and Complex and Multi-Dimensional Sessions using QTH.

CHAPTER 6
Shamanic Journeying

Ancient tribal shamanic practices of medicine men and women are a common heritage in almost all native cultures worldwide and have existed for at least thirty thousand years (Eliade, 2004). The term "shaman" originated from the Siberian Tungus Tribe. Shamanic journeying is a contemporary practice of accessing intuitive or spiritual realms for the purpose of guidance or healing. It is the way all native cultures expressed their spiritual connection to nature and the unseen spirit realm. Shamans would typically journey to receive guidance and healing on behalf of a person who was ill. Modern shamanic journeying is a complimentary practice for almost any spiritual belief system, to be used as a vehicle for personal guidance, transformation and healing.

The process of shamanic journeying involves entering a state of non-ordinary reality by eliciting a relaxed (alpha-theta) state via rhythmic drumming, or using other instruments such as rattles, sticks, didgeridoo, or Tibetan bowls. One then contacts his/her spirit helpers or guides, most often in the form of power animals (as in the Hawaiian "Aumakua" or animal guardian spirits). However, within the context of shamanic journeying, guides may also occasionally come from the plant or mineral kingdoms.

Michael Harner, author of *The Way of the Shaman* (1980), labeled the core elements of the shamanic state of consciousness from native shamanic cultures around the world as: induction through drumming, entry into non-ordinary reality, travel through an opening in the earth, and working with power animals and travel with spirit helpers in explorations of inner worlds. It was in this way that shamans and medicine men and women in all native cultures would communicate with specific plants or minerals to facilitate them revealing their unique healing properties and preparations for remedies. Sandra Ingerman in *Soul Retrieval* (1991) describes shamanic journeying as a valuable guided imagery process for recovering and healing the "split-off," or dissociated parts of the self, or soul. Such splitting occurs during significant negative or traumatic events including physical or sexual abuse, loss or death of a loved one, etc.

In shamanic journeying, one begins by inner journeying to a lower (subterranean), middle (astral), or higher (spiritual) world. When journeying to the lower world, a guided imagery process is used to suggest traveling into an opening in the earth, such as through a cave, pond, lake, or hollowed out tree stump; and then travel through a tunnel, looking for a light at the end of the tunnel, which opens into a new landscape. When one emerges into the new inner landscape, the person looks around to meet an animal guide that is waiting to talk with him and give answers to particular questions about life issues or problems. A journey to the middle world is though the earth's biosphere, while the upper world is the higher etheric planes, with lighting that can range from soft to very bright, or the absence of light, or being in the darkness of "the void."

With shamanic journeying, connecting with one's power animals or other spirit guides to seek clarity and the wisdom of their guidance is the vehicle for discovering and implementing the solution to healing. Similarly, in QTH, one goes to an inner landscape, or Inner Place of Peace, to detach from outer reality and connect to a more objective, clearer source of guidance, either one's own Inner/Higher Self, or a spirit guide, which may be animal, human, angelic, or another higher spiritual teacher/healer.

In the next section, I will present some shamanic journeying examples of QTH.

Shamanic Journeying Session 6-1

Jeanie was going through a difficult break-up with her boyfriend, with whom she felt she had shared an unprecedented level of spiritual and intellectual intimacy, but who had been emotionally and mentally abusive. In the following session, she received insight on how he had assisted her in being more verbally expressive, helping her to speak her own truth (albeit in order to verbally defend herself). This helped Jeanie to understand one of the positive functions or higher purposes of their relationship, in order to realize she had learned what she needed and could detach and let go of the feeling of missing the spiritual and intellectual companionship they had shared. Additionally, Jeanie received valuable guidance on how to fill the void in the relationship - with a positive focus on how to re-balance her life and create the future she desired.

Deep Abdominal Breathing, Open Inner Seeing & Hearing & Spiritual Alignment meditation.

C: I'm inside of a quartz crystal. It's clear and serene inside.

T: As you relax in your IPOP…

C: My guide is a white owl…(pause)…now he flew off…(pause) I'm seeing a wild pig now…it's becoming winged.

Here, since she knows the QTH process, she connects quickly with her guides. The appearance of wings suggests a more angelic being in the form of a pig; since wings are typically associated with angels.

T: Is the winged pig your guide?

C: Yes.

T: Ask the winged pig...what problem or issue is most important to receive guidance and/or healing about today?

C: The pig says I should focus on knowing God...letting go of my ego...and pride... about being right. He says I need to focus more on honesty and truth...on speaking what I feel without fear of rejection. I used to be withdrawn and quiet...and would not speak much...before I was in the relationship with Peter (her past boyfriend). He challenged me to express myself more because he was so intellectual and self-righteous. I used to seek to please...as a child, I had a "pleaser program"...always the helper in school but with my parents at home I was rebellious. I tried to please the teachers to be accepted... and to appease my parents.

T: Where is the energy of wanting to please others, and not speak your own truth being held in your body? Just ask the winged pig to help you scan your body to find where the focal point(s) of this energy are in your body.

C: I see a lump...it's in my intestines and abdomen and by the navel. It's black...the size of a golf ball.

T: What does the black lump in your abdomen want at its highest level of intention and purpose?

C: It wants me to slow down...to find some focus. Teaching me lessons in mindfulness. To understand how my thoughts lead to my actions. I'm supposed to set priorities to prepare to fulfill my dream of sailing around the world. I'm to focus on a comprehensive preparation...(pause)...everything else is extraneous.

This client practices "Zen Buddhist" mindfulness meditation.

T: Are there any parts of you that are not in alignment with getting your priorities in order and comprehensively preparing to go on your world journey?

Querying for subconscious blocks to following through with guidance.

C: Yes...I'm doubting that I will have all the people and resources that I will need to make it happen.

T: Ask your guide, the winged pig, for more specific guidance on this.

C: The pig says there will be people to support and sustain me...there is only light ahead... an incredible bright light...I'm seeing it now.

Here is a spontaneous appearance of the transformational, or healing solution.

T: Is the white light here to clear the black lump in your abdomen?

C: Yes.

T: Then be one with, and breathe in the bright white light into the abdomen to help you become clearer to accept and strengthen you for your journey. Breathe the white light into the black lump, and allow the highest level transformation to occur now...(long pause)... What does the black lump look like now?

Facilitating the integration and transformation.

C: It's much lighter and smaller, but it's not all gone.

T: Will the black lump be able to be completely transformed and healed today, or are there some things that will need to be integrated before that can be accomplished?

C: No, not today.

T: Then, ask if there is any other guidance or homework assignments to continue to transform the black lump.

C: My homework is to "sit more." I'm not meditating very much. At night, I distract myself from feeling alone by socializing and talking on the phone, doing reading, and taking classes. I'm being told to decrease my socializing and talking on the phone...

"Sit more" refers to her practice of mindfulness meditation.

C: (cont.) because it's just a space filler, to avoid being alone and feeling lonely. I don't have to feel lonely just because I'm alone. I can use the time productively to meditate and receive guidance for my future direction and set priorities for my trip.

T: If you follow through with sitting more and focusing on receiving guidance about how to manifest your dream, will the black lump disappear?

C: The black lump will hang out for a while…I need to stay really focused…because I will be challenged with different obstacles that I need to overcome.

T: Is there any other guidance before we complete the session for today?

Pacing the client to complete the session due to a limiting time factor.

C: No.

Shamanic Journeying Session 6-2

This is a second Shamanic journeying session with Jeanie in which the owl, which appeared in her first session, reappears briefly to give her some guidance and healing on a distinctly different problem.

Deep Abdominal Breathing, Open Inner Vision and Hearing, Spiritual Alignment

C: I'm laying on a cloud…the sky above is blue…there's a gentle breeze blowing.

C: I see an owl…it's name is "Hoot" and I'm seeing a bundle of logs (D_1) like you'd see on a truck…It's like the logs are…in my body… there's a log jam in my body.

T: Ask Hoot if the logs represent the unhealed issue that is the most important issue to work on today.

C: Yes.

T: Where are the logs in your body?

C: They're in my abdominal cavity (client puts her hand below navel)...here. Now I see a knife there...like it's cutting me. Part of it is going straight in...into my vagina. It's like there's two knives (D$_2$), one knife moves, one is centered above my pubic bone...and it goes straight in.

T: Can you ask Hoot to show you where the knives came from?

C: It seems like it's from surgery...I've had four abortions and my tubes tied. The knife is symbolic...I guess. It represents the energy of cutting...it seems real cold...no life...no being...it's just dead.

It appears like these feelings/perceptions represent both the knife...as well as related cellular memories in the reproductive organs of ending life (abortions) and the possibility of new life (having tubes tied).

T: What do the knives in your abdominal region want?

C: They want to come out...to be warm...and be useful.

C: Now I'm seeing fire. It needed to be thrown in the fire...now the knives are warm. Something else has to be cut out though. Something else needs to be removed...it's the logs (D$_1$).

The fire is symbolic of transformation – not only warmth (heat), but purification of the cold energies of death.

T: Are the logs ready to be removed?

C: Yes...but I have to just let them go. It will happen with or without me. They're floating in water...I'll let them flow. Now I'm letting the water wash through me. There's a hole where the water washes out...it's my vagina where the knives had cut...into the area where the two knives came out.

Here, her "Self" is the "healer"...choosing to let go.

Symbolic "dream-like" imagery of cleansing and release via the healing element of water.

T: Did all of the logs flow out of you now?

C: Yes! And the owl is flying around...it's happy, and saying "hoot, hoot."

C: Now I see a worm...it's playing and crawling in and out of the hole. It has a big smile...and glistening white teeth. It feels comfortable being there...especially in the front.

An almost childlike quality of simplicity in the response of the animals – both owl and worm. Rather than being grotesque, the worm here (which is present only in fertile soil) most likely represents the renewal of health and fertility in her abdominal/vaginal area.

T: Now, I'd like you to check if the transformational healing process involving the knives and logs is complete?

C: Hoot is saying I need to replace them with something. The hole where the logs were is filled with flowers...yellow daisies...and sunshine and warmth. And the knives are all shiny on the wall in my kitchen. They can be useful and decorative, they're very shiny stainless steel...and beautiful. They're happier.

The principle of needing to fill the "void", as in "nature abhors a void" is illustrated here.

T: Are there any other recommendations from your guide the owl to integrate your new healed self on physical, emotional, mental or spiritual levels?

C: The owl says I need to love myself... because I'm doing so many good things. And don't worry about making others wrong or bad.

Positive suggestions of releasing her critical tendencies toward self and others.

Shamanic Journeying Session 6-3

Karen came in with a medical diagnosis of a fibroid tumor in her uterus that she had known about for nearly a year, which she had been using some natural health supplements to treat, with little results. She was having "horrible pains" in her right side lower back...and had not had her period for five months. The past weekend prior to our QTH session she had reported heavy bleeding and lots of clots. Karen had previously been given inner guidance to cut out dairy, red meat, fried foods and caffeine, and had done so with no significant changes in her condition. She was somewhat anxious and fearful about the possibility of needing a hysterectomy if her condition did not improve.

Deep Abdominal Breathing, Spiritual Alignment, Open Inner Seeing and Hearing

C: I'm up in the mountains...seeing grey mountaintops around me. There's a little snow on the mountain. The sky is a light lavender blue...it's still and cool.

T: Open your heart to call for your own I/H Self, or one of your guides.

C: I'm seeing a female butterfly...she's flying in front of me.

T: Ask the butterfly if receiving guidance or healing related to your fibroid is the most important and/or beneficial problem to work on today?

Here, I directly query about the main concern she desires to focus on today.

C: Yes...the butterfly says that the fibroid is a thickening of the uterine wall...but it's not a tumor.

T: I'd like you to connect now with the fibroid tissue in your uterus.

C: The fibroid says, "We're going through a transition as we're getting older...it's from a lot of pregnancies...It says to be patient...and it will reduce it's thickness on it's own.

T: Ask the butterfly or your fibroid if it has any suggestions on how you can accelerate the process of the uterine tissue reducing its thickness and becoming normal and healthy.

C: The butterfly says I need to take better care of my health...to eat less refined sugar and white flour, decrease cookies and pastries... and increase fruits. She says I should also increase my home cooking. There's a cookbook on Healing Foods I have that I could use.

T: Great. Are there any subconscious or conscious blocks to following through with your guidance to improve your diet by decreasing sweets and nurturing yourself with more home cooking?

C: No...I'm ready to do it. I'm scared it might get worse. My ex-husband said, "I'll see you in your grave." That really scared me.

T: Ok. Are there any other suggestions or homework assignments before we complete today's session?

C: The butterfly says I'm out of balance. I'm focusing on my spiritual and emotional (social) aspects...but I also need to take better care of my physical health. She also says, "Take your time...get off the treadmill." (client reflects)...probably because I've been putting in really long hours, and it's creating a lot of stress and time pressure.

T: Ok, thank your guide the butterfly for her guidance and your uterine fibroid for it's assistance in giving you the "wake-up call" to take better care of your physical and emotional health.

As you can see from these three shamanic inner journeying sessions (compared to the previous much more complex sessions in chapter five) these are sessions in which animal guides express their truth in a quite straight-forward and uncomplicated manner. Animal guides typically give clear, to-the-point guidance and direction, and can even facilitate healing, as in Jeanie's second session.

CHAPTER 7
Inner Child Healing

Since a large percentage of children in the U.S. and abroad grew up in dysfunctional families, the need for healing of unresolved childhood issues in adults is widespread. In *Homecoming* by John Bradshaw (1992), which I consider the foremost book on self-assessment and self-therapy for Inner Child Healing, Bradshaw describes the myriad of ways the Inner Child Self can be wounded by a wide variety of dysfunctional family dynamics, including physical, emotional or mental neglect; and physical, sexual, emotional, or mental abuse.

I often use the five developmental questionnaires in *Homecoming* - Infant, Toddler, Preschool, School-Age, and Adolescent – to assess the extent and severity of specific adult behavioral symptoms that are a direct reflection of family of origin dysfunction, neglect or abuse that were present during the respective developmental age ranges. These questionnaires provide valuable clues as to the unhealed issues the client is experiencing, and I use this information to develop an individual script for doing an Inner Child Healing recording that can be played preferably daily for three or more weeks, since it is often stated that it takes at least twenty-one days to change a habit, or create permanent personality and behavior change. In addition, Bradshaw's self-therapy exercises (at the end of each of the five developmental age chapters) are powerful tools to create healing, maturation and transformation of the Inner Child Self and the personality.

John Bradshaw stresses the importance of "original pain work" in order to heal the wounded inner child's sense of being flawed and defective, which is rooted in feelings of "toxic shame" about parental neglect or abuse. When a child is neglected or abused, the genuine, authentic, spontaneous and naturally curious child becomes injured and buried beneath layers of repressed negative feelings of hurt, anger, fear, confusion and low self-esteem.

Furthermore, consolidated or crystallized personality patterns can develop in persons who grew up in dysfunctional co-dependent family systems. In *Co-Dependence, Healing the Human Condition* by Charles Whitfield(1991), he describes four frequently seen personality complexes and their characteristics:

Rescuers and Fixers – who neglect their own needs while focusing excessively on rescuing, fixing or helping others;

People Pleasers – who acquiesce and comply with other's wants and needs to gain approval and acceptance;

Overachievers – who compensate for feelings of inadequacy, inferiority or emptiness by needing to feel adequate or superior to others via overachievement; and;

Perfectionists – who are driven by fear of making mistakes, avoidance of failure or being found imperfect.

In order to heal the wounded Inner Child Self and correct dysfunctional relationship patterns that develop from unhealthy family dynamics in childhood, one begins by accepting, expressing, releasing, and transforming the feelings and associated unwanted thought and behavior patterns. However, first one must acknowledge the ego's resistance or defense mechanisms to knowing and accepting one's unhealed issues. The classic Freudian ego defense mechanisms that numb or distract us from our original pain and block awareness of subsequent relationship dysfunctions, in approximate order of increasing dissociation or dis-integration are: 1) minimizing (it wasn't that bad); 2) denial (it didn't happen); 3) suppression (conscious forgetting); 4) repression (unconscious forgetting due to severe pain or trauma); 5) conversion (symptom substitution); and finally, 6) projection (it's happened/happening to you, not me). As one progresses through healing his/her childhood, the ego or personality self becomes more whole and reintegrates its lost or dissociated feelings and experiences. Henceforth, the ego's defense mechanisms subsequently greatly diminish or disappear, as they are no longer needed to protect the ego from knowing the truth.

The QTH process can be utilized for healing the wounded Inner Child Self (and can create a more integrated human adult personality self), by bringing the unconscious, unhealed core issues and dysfunctional patterns into conscious awareness, as one is being guided through the transformational healing process by the superconscious or Spiritual Inner/Higher Self or Guides. If a person has unhealed Inner Child issues with parents and/or outer authority figures, it can often lead to projections, distortions and/ or blocks to listening and following guidance from one's I/H Self or Guides (as Inner, Spiritual "authority figures"). For example, lack of trust, anger, or fears of abandonment stemming from a critical, judgmental parent, if unresolved in adulthood, can lead to resistance, conflicts and rebelliousness towards outer authority figures in adulthood. In essence, this same resistance to following the Inner guidance from one's I/H Self or Guides will be a direct "mirror" or reflection of the same resistance and distrust toward outer authority figures.

That is one reason why healing core childhood issues is so foundational and important for spiritual self-development – so we can receive, trust and follow through with the guidance received from our own Inner Parent (using Bradshaw's model) as well as our own I/H Self or Guides.

The following is a checklist of some of the most common adult issues or problems integrated and adapted from Bradshaw's book *Homecoming* (1992). These adult behavioral symptoms reflect unhealed dysfunctional family dynamics during childhood. To assess the number of dysfunctional thoughts, feelings and behavior patterns currently affecting you, please put a check in front of each item if it applies some or most of the time. Do not spend time analyzing or thinking about your response, just place a check if your initial response is a "yes" to the item.

Inner Child Healing Questionnaire

1. _____ history of oral or ingestive addiction (overeating, overdrinking or over-drugging)
2. _____ over-reliance on others to take care of certain needs
3. _____ trouble identifying your own feelings and needs
4. _____ difficulty expressing your own feelings and needs
5. _____ not trusting your ability to make your own decisions
6. _____ excessive reliance on others' opinions/feelings to make your decisions
7. _____ feeling disconnected from your emotions
8. _____ neglecting your physical needs (good nutrition, rest, exercise, etc.)
9. _____ fears of abandonment/rejection
10. _____ feeling like you don't fit in or belong
11. _____ being so helpful in your relationships with significant others to create dependencies so they will not leave you
12. _____ excessive need to be valued and esteemed by others
13. _____ excessive need to be touched and held
14. _____ being socially withdrawn OR overly social
15. _____ difficulty trusting others OR being overly or inappropriately trusting and gullible
16. _____ fear of exploring or trying new experiences when you are in a new place
17. _____ obsessive/ruminative tendencies to dwell on anxiety-producing thoughts (ex: excessive worry and preoccupation with cleanliness, fear of germs, etc.)
18. _____ compulsive tendencies (ex: excessive need to be neat and clean OR sloppy and dirty), with the need to perform repetitive behaviors to reduce discomfort or anxiety
19. _____ inappropriate or rigid boundaries with others (almost always saying "yes" or "no" to requests or invitations)

20. _____ tendency to go along with other's wishes to one's own detriment
21. _____ excessive criticism of others or tendencies toward negative gossip
22. _____ avoidance of conflict or difficulty negotiating and compromising in relationships
23. _____ trying to control your own OR others feelings
24. _____ feeling responsible for others feelings
25. _____ not asking for clarification of unclear communication
26. _____ acting on unchecked assumptions or confusing information
27. _____ excessive negative self-talk or self-criticism
28. _____ feeling typically inferior OR superior to others
29. _____ feeling uncomfortable in social situations
30. _____ lack of ability to develop and maintain close, enduring friendships
31. _____ being overly strict or overly lenient as a parent
32. _____ excessive competitiveness
33. _____ frequent conflicts with significant others (family, friends, and co-workers)
34. _____ procrastination or trouble finishing things
35. _____ excessive fear of making mistakes
36. _____ difficulty accepting constructive criticism / overly defensive when mistakes are pointed out
37. _____ lying to cover up personal weaknesses or behavior you feel is unacceptable
38. _____ frequent conflict with authority figures
39. _____ difficulty accepting rules and regulations OR rigid adherence to rules
40. _____ falling into the role of overly compliant or rebellious child when visiting parents
41. _____ confusion about one's identity in love or work (sexual, career, etc.)
42. _____ socially overly conformist or non-conformist
43. _____ a dreamer who fails to take action to achieve important personal, relationship, or career goals
44. _____ lack of identifying and adhering to one's own values and belief systems
45. _____ close friendships with only people of one sex
46. _____ difficulties maintaining sexual relationships with the opposite sex (or same sex if homosexual)
47. _____ excessive obsession or pre-occupation with sex (real or imagined), masturbation or pornography

Now, count the number of check marks. If you have five or more items checked, you would benefit from doing some Inner Child Healing work, either using Bradshaw's techniques in Homecoming, or using the QTH process to do Inner Child Healing.

The standard QTH script can be utilized to do Inner Child Healing, since a specific age Inner Child Self will emerge as the most important aspect of the shadow, unhealed self which has a problem or issue for the healing focus that day.

The following addition to the basic QTH protocol involves a few modifications based on the principle of "triangulation" of the three-part model of consciousness integration. Below is a depiction of the QTH "triangulation" model for integration and healing of the Inner Child with the Superconscious (Parental aspect, I/H Self or Guides)which sends love, healing and guidance to and through the Adult Self, and then to the IC Self.

Superconscious
Healed Biological Parent (or surrogates), Inner Parent Self, I/H Self or Guides

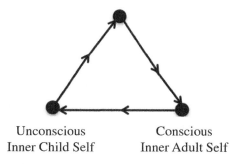

Unconscious   Conscious
Inner Child Self   Inner Adult Self

Figure 7-1
Inner Child Healing Triangulation Model

In the QTH Inner Child Healing triangulation model, there can be several choices for the superconscious or Parental Self aspect(s). All of the four options below can be the source of loving, healing energy, and also provide guidance and direction for the transformational healing of the IC self.

1. The more whole and healed biological parent of the client can serve the role of the helper, or healing part. This can work only if the client can actually imagine the biological parent as sufficiently transformed so as to be able to send loving, healing energy to the IC self.

2. Another adult person who was a real loving, significant, positive role model in the client's life when she was a child, can also be the Parental Self (surrogate). Examples of substitute "real life" parental figures would be the biological grandparent, aunt or uncle, or the parent of a close friend.

3. The client's own Inner Parent or Adult Self aspect can be the superconscious, healing aspect, or

4. The I/H Spiritual Self or Guides, as per the standard QTH protocol.

Here are some additional tips for using the QTH method of Inner Child Healing. Since the IC self often needs to have a greater feeling of safety and security, I usually use the term Inner Place of Safety (IPOS) instead of the Inner Place of Peace (IPOP) at the beginning of the QTH session.

If the Inner Child (IC) self has never been previously communicated with prior to the first healing session, it may typically need additional loving energy (which the client can visualize and project as pink light) to feel willing to come forward and express itself.

During the course of multiple sessions of IC healing, different ages of the IC Self will naturally emerge for healing. To elicit the IC self, say "I'd like you to call forth whatever age child needs healing the most today...to make its presence visible to you now." I often give the clients the choice to have the IC self appear either 1) inside of their body, such as in their heart center, or 2) in front of their body, whichever is most comfortable or preferred that day.

In a typical series of QTH IC healing sessions, there is a natural age progression often from the younger to older age inner child(ren). Sometimes, however, there is a progression from the least to the most severely psychologically damaging experiences (which may follow an unpredictable or variable age sequence).

Next, I will present three QTH IC Healing transcripts to elucidate the process and variations in this application of QTH.

Inner Child Healing Session 7-1

This first example is of a basic IC healing session using the standard QTH format. This was James' first experience with QTH. Interestingly, he spontaneously associates to a pre-birth memory when he was in his mother's womb. He then went on to heal a layer of unresolved issues around feeling unloved and psychologically scapegoated and abused by multiple family members.

Deep Abdominal Breathing, Open Inner Seeing and Hearing, Spiritual Alignment and Locating IPOP.

C: I'm in Puerto Rico...on a grassy hill...the grass is clean and bright and thick...it's like everything is new.

T: Just immerse yourself in seeing the colors and shapes...and hearing the sounds...in your beautiful Inner Place of Peace on that grassy hill in Puerto Rico...smelling the scents in

Deepening the inner sensory experience of his IPOP.

T: (cont.) the air...and feeling as if you are there right now...(pause)...Next, I'd like you to open your mind, heart and spirit to connecting with your I/H Self or guides... relaxing and softening your inner vision and just allowing your own spiritual self or guides to appear in a form you can recognize.

C: My Higher Self is here...King James. And there are many Ascended Masters.... including St. Germain.

T: Ask King James and your Ascended master guides, which one of them is your main spiritual guide for today?

C: It's Uriel...she looks like she's in a human form...blonde, blue-eyed and radiant...She needs beautiful clear energy from me to be there. She's smiling and laughing...Uriel is giving me an assignment...to be clear and focused...and drop all my attachments...and release my blocks or resistances.

Uriel is one of the seven major Archangels.

T: Ask Uriel what is the most important problem or issue to focus on receiving guidance and healing on today?

C: She says I'm not receiving love... (pause)...love is all around me...the love of the Universe and the Masters.

T: What is blocking you from receiving the love of the universe and Masters?

C: It's fear...fear of being alone.

T: If the energy of fear was anchored in a certain place in your body, where would it be? Just scan your body now from head to toe, asking for clear inner vision from your guide Uriel.

C: It's a grey metal plate in my heart. Now it's going horizontal and changing shape...I'm seeing it as a knife or sword.

The plate (like armor) for protection may be distinct from the knife or sword...or it may symbolically represent the client's energetic transformation when he was a child from feeling the need for self-protection (armor)... to experiencing anger or aggression (knife or sword).

T: What does the knife or sword represent?

C: It's anger and fear...it's so sad...I tried so hard to love...but I withdrew back into myself.

T: How long has this knife or sword been in your heart area?

C: When I was a child around six to eight... He's so sad...so hurt...trying to be accepted and loved...he doesn't understand why he's punished so much. People in his family are so serious...they can't have fun. He's hiding... and angry. My sister...Dad and Mom...no one is really happy.

Client spontaneously regresses to a dissociated (use of the word "he") inner child self between the ages of six and eight.

T: What does he want at his highest level of intention and purpose?

C: He wants to be outside...to explore and learn...not be so serious. And mostly he wants to be loved and accepted. He's been programmed that he's a special little angel... but also a devil...by my sister.

T: Was there any love you got from your parents or sister when you were a little boy?

Questioning about whether there is any positive, loving energy he got as a child, to balance out the picture.

C: My mother...she wants to love me...but my father...he'll be angry...Why didn't I get that love? I can see my mother holding me... hugging me...why didn't she love me more... was it karma? I have so much anger at my father.

Client freely associates back and forth between the energies related to mother and father.

T: Ask Uriel why your mother didn't love you more?

C: My mother was addicted to codeine and prescription drugs. Now I'm watching something that happened between my mother...my dad...and me. She thought I aligned with my dad...and she stopped loving me...(pause)...I think my dad...he abused and beat my mom up. He pushed her down the stairs when she was carrying me...she's crying...and he's angry with her. He used to make my mother have sex with him...I felt not loved...he didn't love and respect my

Here, he has a spontaneous flashback of memories from when he was in his mother's womb.

C: (cont.) mother or me even when I wasn't born! I hate sex...I picked up my father's hatred and went to a very dark place....(client drifts off)....

T: Where are you now?

C: I don't know...somewhere else...it's dark here.

Here, I had a sense the client got lost in some inner place that was dark and confusing.
So I directed him to center himself in his IPOP, and then reconnect with his guide Uriel.

T: Then, I'd like you to go back and anchor yourself in your Inner Place of Peace...on the grassy hill in Puerto Rico where everything is clean and bright.

C: Ok...I'm there now.

T: Now call forth Uriel...your angelic guide... to reconnect with her.

C: I can see her...she's smiling at me again. I want to see where I bought that I'm dark... I'm seeing the words...and programs...of my parents...other people...and Christianity... instilling that I'm bad and evil...and so much fear of dying and damnation. I'm seeing both my sisters had me so scared...they used a Quija board...and spirits came in...They had me so scared...My sisters hated me...They thought I was just like my father...James Jr... the incarnate little devil...but that's not true!

Client begins another free flowing stream of associations.

Typically, the Quija board will attract lower level astral and/or demonic spirits and is NOT recommended to facilitate contact with the spirit world!

I just want to quit being tortured...and taking on so much anger and hatred toward women... They used me and hurt me (said with an air of sadness and resignation).

T: Where in your body is the anger and hatred?

C: In my heart...like where the knife and sword was...it's like a grey cloud and flashes of metal...in there...

T: Ask Uriel to assist you...and ask the grey cloud and blades what they want at their highest level of intention and purpose.

C: They want to not be angry...I don't want to be angry at them...and feel bad about myself.

T: Ask the grey cloud and blades, who can help them to get what they want?

C: Uriel can...She's bringing in some white and greenish tinged light. The white light is clearing and washing away the grey...now it's cleared my heart! It's clean and sparkling with pure white light!

T: Great! How will this change manifest on the emotional, mental and spiritual levels?

Checking for the signposts of clearing on the emotional, mental and spiritual levels.

C: I'm not angry at my mother and sisters anymore! We're all dancing around in a circle and holding hands...I'm not angry at them and I love them. It's like I don't have to do things to prove myself anymore. I can love myself...and not be afraid to look in the mirror.

A wonderful symbolic representation of the transformational healing!

T: Are there any other messages or assignments from Uriel?

C: Just to love myself...accept that I'm good...and let go of all the negative feelings about myself and my family.

T: Will you commit to loving yourself and releasing all the negative feelings about your family from your childhood?

C: Yes...I'm doing it now.

T: Then as we close...thank yourself and Uriel for assisting in your healing session today.

Inner Child Healing Session 7-2

Rebecca was seen for approximately one year prior to this session, and had been plagued with depression and post-traumatic stress disorder related to severe childhood mental and physical abuse by her stepmother, and severe emotional and sexual abuse by her father. Rebecca's father remarried when she was twelve years old, and her stepmother made her cook, clean and care for her younger siblings, and so she became a "parentified child." Her stepmother would beat her when she did not clean the house well enough.

In her life currently, she was feeling lonely and not needed due to a recent break-up with her boyfriend. Since her last child had moved out and she was living alone with no boyfriend and an "empty nest" for the first time in many years, she was quite depressed. In this session, Rebecca gets a deep understanding of what drives her obsessive/compulsive need to clean her house whenever she feels lonely and not needed, or angry.

This session also illustrates the QTH adaptation of Inner Child healing using the "triangulation technique" previously described, in which the (1) Superconscious - Parental aspect, I/H Self or Spirit Guide(s) sends love and strength to and through the (2) Conscious Adult Self and then to (3) the unhealed Inner Child Self, for healing.

T: Deep Abdominal Breathing, Open Inner Seeing and Hearing, Spiritual Alignment.

T: Now, I'd like you to find a nice, safe place for your wounded inner child to be able to express herself. Just let yourself find the Inner Place of Safety that looks...or sounds...or feels the best today...a place for your inner child self to feel safe.

C: I'm in my bedroom...I'm two yrs. old. She's crying...she wants her mommy. (Client bursts out in intense crying) I want my mommy...(wails) I want my mommy...

Client immediately and spontaneously accesses the specific age of the inner child aspect that needs healing the most that day.

T: Where is your mommy?

C: She's gone. (client wails) I'm not gonna have my mommy...(crying)...I want my mommy back. (continued sobbing) I'm scared...

Her parents had separated and later divorced when she was two years old.

T: What does your two-year-old self really want?

C: She wants love...she wants somebody to love her...it's like there's a hole in her heart... it's dark and empty there.

The dark hole in her heart is where the disintegrated unhealed (D_1) energy is located.

T: Who can help her to get the love she needs? Who can fill that empty place in her heart?

C: I don't know.

T: I'd like you to ask her...who can help her to give her the love she needed then...and now...to heal? Go anywhere in the universe to find your own Inner/Higher Self, or a Spiritual Guide...or whoever else she needs who can give her love.

C: I see wings...they're white...with pink and yellow tips...It's an angel.

T: What's the angel's name?

C: It sounds like Ariel...

T: Ask Ariel if she will talk with you?

C: She said yes.

T: Can she send love to your grown-up adult self...and the little two-year-old girl...to strengthen her?

Here is the "triangulation" technique – her spiritual Guide Ariel sends love to her Adult Self...who in turn sends the love to her own Inner Child Self.

C: Yes...(client starts to cry gently)...I'm feeling the warmth...and love...(client has spontaneous insight and exclaims)...She was there when I was a little girl! I wasn't totally alone...after all...

T: Yes, your loving guardian angel Ariel was there...Our angels are there for us in our times of greatest need...quietly loving, comforting and guiding us...through our lifetime... during our most difficult times.

I chose to elaborate here and strengthen the fairly common belief in guardian angels... being with us throughout our lifetime.

C: I feel her wings around me...keeping me warm and safe...it helps me to stop crying because I feel her love...

T: Wonderful! Just let your little two yr. old absorb all the love she could possibly need... right here and now...extending from when you were two yrs. old through your entire lifetime...feeling love...permeate every cell and atom in your body...until your little child self is glowing...and happy and radiant from all that love.

Here, I use language to integrate the healing... throughout her entire body... from the past to the present and into the future.

C: She's smiling...a big smile now...she's hugging Ariel...

T: Is the hole or dark empty place in her heart still there?

Checking for any change in the location or place of unhealed energy.

C: It's not there...I see a soft...golden pinkish light instead.

T: Great! Ask Ariel if there are any other messages, guidance or healing work for us to do today?

Checking for completion or further guidance.

C: Yes...(pause)...I've been feeling lonely... and angry and not needed...since my daughter moved away. It's hard for me to be living alone...if I'm at home...I clean house...it's cathartic...if I clean house...I feel better. My friends say I'm a "clean freak" ...(client starts crying again)...My stepmother use to beat the crap out of me for not cleaning the house good enough. It started when I was around twelve...until I was fifteen.

Here, client begins to "free associate" about her current life, and her obsessive-compulsive need to clean as a way to deal with her uncomfortable feelings.

T: Is Ariel still there? Can you see her?

C: Yes.

T: Ask Ariel to show you where, in or around your body, you are holding the feelings related to your stepmother beating you for not cleaning the house well enough.

C: It's my whole body...she hit me all over... my whole body has been hurting lately... I've had both my hands and feet swell...and various body pains...the past 2 weeks.

The 2nd holodyne or energy complex (D_2) to be healed is throughout her entire body.

T: Ask your body who can help it to release the pain?

C: Ariel is...she's filling my body with the golden-pink light...it's melting away some of the pain...(30 second pause)....

T: Is the pain throughout your body gone now?

C: Most of it is...she was like a "wicked stepmother" who used the "white glove." It was like her motto was "Praise the Lord and punch out the kids." She was big on going to church...but a hypocrite at home.

Here client has a "cathartic" expression of some pent up angry thoughts and feelings about her stepmother.

T: Will all of the pain be able to be cleared today?

C: No.

T: Ask Ariel if there is anything else we can do today, or for you to do in the future...to heal your entire body of the cellular memory of the pain?

C: She says to picture the golden-pink light all throughout my body...at home.

T: How often would Ariel like you to visualize the golden-pink light filling your body?

It is important to ask for more specifics on how often to do the homework assignment.

C: Everyday...for about 10-15 minutes.

T: Will you agree to do that...to love and heal yourself more?

C: Yes.

T: Is there anything else? Any messages from Ariel? Or other assignments to complete the healing session today?

C: No...that's all.

T: Okay, great. Just visualize and integrate the healing of the golden-pink light...in your heart (D_1) and throughout your body (D_2)...feeling the love, the warmth...and the healing...integrating it on all levels...your subconscious, conscious and super-conscious minds...and in your physical, emotional, mental and spiritual bodies...And then open your eyes...when you are complete with that...

Reiterating the two core complexes that were healed today, and asking for the client to integrate the healing on the three levels of her mind, and the four bodies.

C: Okay...I'm done.

Inner Child Healing Session 7-3

This last inner child healing session using QTH was with Katherine, a very spiritually and psychically developed woman who was easily able to access multiple spiritual guides and her own Inner Goddess Self aspect to receive guidance for personal Inner Child, as well as past life and planetary healing.

In the following session, Katherine goes from pre-birth memories while in the womb and picking up her mother's feelings, to remembering sexual abuse incidents for the first time and clearing some of the root of the fear of being in (and staying in) her body, which is a core issue related to a past life. She is then guided to see another past life in which she was the sexual abuser, to help her to heal and forgive herself and all others, whether in victim (this life) or perpetrator (past life) roles. This past life segment is included here, instead of being placed in the next chapter on Past/Parallel/Future lives, in order to illustrate how "tracking" the source of unhealed issues can extend from the past in this lifetime, to a more distant past in another lifetime. Often the person will be in a similar role, (such as another victim lifetime) or in the case of the following example, an individual will be in the opposite role of perpetrator, which illustrates the importance of understanding, accepting, integrating and healing both polarities in order to transcend 3rd density duality and reintegrate all in a unified field (5th density) of transformational healing.

Sexual abuse issues, especially incest dynamics, are generally some of the most difficult to work through, with the multitude of emotions and effects on several key relationship patterns. This session was one of several sessions for Katherine related to healing both victim and perpetrator roles in this and multiple past lives, to release feelings of low self-esteem, shame, guilt, and depression symptoms.

T: I'd like you to visualize a sphere of brilliant, golden white light above your head. Breathe in and see a golden diamond white light illuminating your head and crown... (pause)...Now, allow the sphere to descend into your head filling your head with bright, scintillating, sparking golden white light... (pause)...Now, have the sphere of GW light descend through your body, at your own pace breathing out GW light into your body, progressively from your head, down through your torso and legs until you can feel or see the GW light filling your entire body. Just say "now" when you are complete with that.

Here, I did only the spiritual alignment meditation, since I knew she could readily get in a state of clarity, and was familiar with the QTH process from prior sessions.

C: Now.

T: Next, I'd like you to locate an Inner Place of Peace (IPOP), whatever looks or feels the best for you today.

C: I'm in a void.

T: Okay. Now just connect deeply within the void, feeling the higher vibrational frequency and a deep, pervasive sense of peace and expansiveness. Notice any gradations of color, and any sounds that you may hear as you are at one with the void.

Next I'd like you to connect with your Inner/ Higher Self, Goddess Self, or one of your Spiritual Guides for the purpose of receiving clear inner guidance.

C: I'm seeing Archangel Michael to my right…and also Divine Mother Mary.

T: Great! Ask Archangel Michael and Mother Mary what is the most important problem or issue to heal or clear today?

C: I'm seeing a little girl…(pause)…It's my Inner Child…She's feeling scared…she wants…to help me clear the fear (a "palpable" level of fear could be heard in the clients voice).

T: Okay, just breathe…and relax. Breathe out the fear…and re-connect with your Guides. Let their Divine Love, which is the opposite of fear…fill your adult self…feeling that love flow into your heart…and out to the little girl that is your Inner Child Self. If you like, visualize violet light streaming forth from Archangel Michael and Mother Mary to your Inner Child Self, surrounding her in a field of violet light, which is the transmutational ray of love (pink) with purple. See a bright beautiful violet sphere bathing your little girl to transform and heal her fear…Now, ask your IC Self if she is still feeling fear.

C: Yes…but it's a lot less.

This client had previously accessed a void as her IPOP, which was at a significantly higher vibration or level of consciousness, relative to her normal awake state.

From prior sessions, these were two of her most frequently appearing guides.

Since I could feel and hear a significant level of fear being expressed, I followed with specific relaxation suggestions to release some of it before proceeding with the standard QTH protocol.

This is an illustration of the QTH Inner Child Healing "triangulation" technique using the greater love, wisdom and power of one's I/H Self or Guides, to send healing to the client's adult self, and then to the Inner Child Self.

T: Is she willing to find out what she is afraid of...the source of her fear? Is this fear the most important problem or issue to clear today?

C: Yes...we need to find out where the fear is coming from...and clear it first.

T: All right then...just breathe and relax even more deeply...allowing yourself and your IC Self to go to the source of the fear.

C: It feels...like I'm looking at a womb... there's tissue all around me...it looks watery...pinkish tissue. I'm feeling nervous...apprehensive...it's my mother... her confusion and reluctance...It's me and my mother...both of us feeling fear...uncertainty and apprehension...about me being born. My mother is "numb." (pause) Now I'm being born. I feel blank...I'm out of my body...I popped out of my body. There's a doctor or nurse holding me...(pause)

Client is re-experiencing being in the womb, a good example of the pre-birth awareness and imprinting of the mother's feelings on the fetus.

Here, she remembers dissociating and recalls her spirit leaving her body, which usually occurs with shock, trauma or when the person has strong negative feelings.

T: What's happening now?

C: Now I'm home at my grandma's...there's a man...I'm afraid when his hands come... He has sexualized energy directed at me. It's my grandfather...he's doing it because I can't talk...(pause)

I'm aware of a penis in my mouth...it's him or somebody else...it's my father! I'm around three months old. My grandpa had "off" energy...he was tall and big. There was vaginal and anal penetration...for a short period...it happened a few times between three and six months. My father thought nobody would ever know. I think he was intoxicated too...

Understandable confusion here about whether the sexual abuse perpetrator was either the father or grandfather (or both). This is typical, since a 3-6 month old infant's vision is not yet fully developed and is fuzzy and unclear.

My adult self knew this, but I couldn't believe it. I denied my own feeling. I remember the hands and penis...but the faces...were fuzzy.

Here client makes an "aside" comment about denying prior feelings and knowingness that this had happened.

T: What effect has the sexual abuse had on you?

C: The effect on me was a dissociative pattern...of not being in my body as much. My soul knew before I came in that it would happen...it was set up for me to stay out of my body. It created confusion about love and sex...and...soul bruising. It's created a feeling about penises...part of the time it's something I don't like...if forced on me or I'm pushed into sex...and other times... there's a fixation...I'm never in the middle... (pause)...There's no sex life with my husband now, but when we first dated in the 80's...it was very frequent...It's either a fixation or repulsion...and then it cycles again...I have the same feeling about female genitals... ambivalence.

Client reflects on the origin of the issue of "not being in her body," which she had talked about in previous sessions. This is often called a soul (or spirit) split.

This is a nice illustration from a Freudian perspective of how an unhealed issue can manifest in both poles or extremes, in this case, either fixation (love), or repulsion (hate).

T: Where in your body do you experience the mixed feelings about sex, and both male and female genitals?

C: It's in my solar plexus (D_1)...and 2nd chakra (D_2)...there's self-condemnation...and an intense fear of sexuality. When my mother was pregnant with me she was in fear...she was in a turbulent marriage...and there was no place of comfort and safety to feel okay. I couldn't bond with her...her heart was closed off in fear...from adrenalin. I didn't know if I was okay. I didn't feel love from her...only my angels. But I didn't really know how to love myself.

T: Is the issue of not loving yourself the same as self-condemnation?

C: It's basically the same.

Clarifying which issue...self-condemnation or fear of sexuality...is being discussed.

T: Is that the issue that's anchored in your solar plexus?

Locating which of the two areas – solar plexus (3rd Chakra), or 2nd Chakra, is the locus of self-condemnation.

C: Yes.

T: What is the highest level of intention and purpose (HLIP) for you to have picked up such a fear, and lack of love from your mother in the womb, and self-condemnation?

C: It has led me to serving others...over myself...to get love from others. This is a pattern in my life...it must be karmic. I'm tracking the judgment back to the source...(long pause)...It's a primordial memory of the fall...stepping down into 3-D...it was a "hell-hole." I felt it was wrong...and ugly...a bad choice. I came from an Arcturian temple...a place of beauty and healing...to this place. I lay in a crumpled heap on the ground...in despair. I don't want this. I couldn't accept I had chosen that life. I have to change that... then and now.

Here, client who is very adept at accessing past lives, is able to quickly transition into another lifetime.

I now take responsibility for choosing that life. I affirm that I accept 100%, choosing that life...and this life. (Aside) It was very painful...I had come from a place that was glorious and noble.

Here, she spontaneously affirms and integrates new cognitive (thought) patterns using positive affirmations to let go of the erroneous belief about her soul long ago not choosing to descend to the denser energies of planet Earth, from a much higher plane(t) and vibrational frequency.

T: How does your solar plexus feel right now?

C: My feelings are frozen...full of residual nausea, despair, and dread...I feel sick to my stomach. There's enormous regret, shock, trauma...fear and loss.

T: What percentage of the energy in your solar plexus and 2nd chakra of self-judgment and condemnation has been cleared today?

Gauging our progress in the session today by obtaining a percentage of the two issues cleared.

C: About 20%. It will eventually clear.

T: Take a deep breath...breathe the pink light of love and the violet light of transmutation into your solar plexus. Visualize a beautiful pink and violet orb or sphere in your solar plexus...and call to your soul and Divine I Am Self for healing and acceptance of choosing that particular incarnation.

C: I'm sensing some more of the self-condemnation and guilt energy...coming from another lifetime.

T: Take a deep breath...allow yourself to flow into the memory of another lifetime related to guilt.

C: It's the past life in Egypt. I'm in a room…I see torches around…it looks like a thousand children's corpses…with ages from about five to eight…(pause)…It was me…who killed them. I was a male priest…in a sexual death cult…with a spiritual connotation. The parents gave up the children to the cult… to do what they wanted. The cult used these children to harness energy. They took the child into a high spiritual energy…sometimes sexually…and killed them to release the energy, which was offered up to Anubis… (pause)…It was experimental. In a negative sense, I was manipulated sexually…I went out-of-body…I told myself it was a good. I learned about sexual power…power gathered through negative methods…because of fear and manipulation.

This client had prior experience with conscious memories of this lifetime in Egypt.

T: Was that the lowest level of intention and purpose…learning how to harness sexual power?

C: Yes…it was learning how to connect with spirit…and connecting the spiritual power to the physical world.

In Egyptian mythology, Anubis was the God of Sex/Death and the underworld initiations. Similarly, dark sexual abuse rituals have been described and documented historically in various countries in dark and/or Satanic spiritual cults.

T: What was the Highest level of intention and purpose? (HLIP)

C: Because of their innocence…in the afterlife, it was bringing these pure souls… the children…straight to heaven.

T: What are you feeling right now?

C: Guilt.

T: Anything else?

C: Mostly guilt.

T: Is the guilt the same feeling underlying the self-condemnation in your solar plexus and 2nd chakra?

C: Yes.

T: Now, I'd like you to re-connect with your guides and ask for guidance on how to release and heal the feelings of guilt.

C: Archangel Michael and Mother Mary said, "Don't go into guilt." They're sending healing energy...pink and bluish purple light...to cleanse and release the guilt.

T: Just breathe in the pink and bluish-purple light...continue to breathe it into your solar plexus and 2nd chakra and release the guilt... fill your entire body with the light...(physical integration)...transmuting and healing the guilt...(emotional and integration)... affirming knowledge...(mental integration)... of your soul's agreement to experience playing a "dark" role in Egypt and learning how to master and control the spiritual and sexual energies of life and death. As you remember the highest level of intention and purpose, allow yourself to experience it without judgment, releasing the guilt... breathing it out...Continue to breathe in the pink and bluish purple light, absorbing all the guilt, and transmuting it into Divine Love, understanding and compassion for the roles of both victim and perpetrator...played by all as part of their soul's pre-agreement for that lifetime. (pause)

Using spontaneous languaging to integrate the healing on physical, emotional, mental and spiritual levels.

Here I took the opportunity to integrate universal spiritual understanding of her soul's agreement to experience the dark role, and to release all judgment and guilt.

C: I'm feeling a lot better...much less guilt.

T: Are there any other messages or guidance to complete the session today?

C: Archangel Michael and Mother Mary say to call on both of them morning and evening to work on my energy.

T: Will you agree to call on them twice a day to continue the healing and releasing of guilt?

C: Yes.

T: Okay then, thank your guides and your own human and spiritual Inner Goddess Self for the love, strength and courage to remember and heal the past life issues of

Closing is facilitated by expressing gratitude and reviewing core components of issues that were revealed (and partially cleared) in the session.

T: (cont.) self-condemnation and guilt in your role as a perpetrator of sexual abuse; and healing the dissociative fear when you were a victim early in this life. Take a deep, slow breath...coming back to the present...feeling alert, refreshed and choosing to remember, integrate, and continue the healing begun today.

CHAPTER 8
Past/Parallel/Future Lives

Historical Foundations of Karma and Reincarnation

The concepts of karma and reincarnation are fundamental beliefs in both Hinduism and Buddhism. Karma, which means action or reaction, is often explained as a concept of spiritual evolution based on cause and effect. From the Christian perspective, karma is the roughly equivalent term for sin, with two main categories: 1) Sins of omission (failure to use power with equivalent love and wisdom), and 2) Sins of commission (active misuse of power without balanced love and wisdom).

First, let us review some of the historical references to the belief in reincarnation from pre-Christian, Biblical and early Christian times.

Pre-Christian References to Reincarnation

The ancient Greek philosopher and mathematician Pythagoras taught that the soul is immortal. After the death of the physical body there is a period of psychic cleansing in the spiritual realms. The soul then reincarnates in a body, and this cycle repeats until the soul eventually becomes free from the cycle of reincarnation.

Socrates and Plato were probably the most important and renowned philosophers who espoused the doctrine of reincarnation. In Plato's Meno, and later in the Phaedo, he proposed that the soul is immortal and does not cease to exist when the body dies (Walker, 2003).

Reincarnation: Biblical and Christian References

References to Jesus as a reincarnation of one of the prophets appear multiple times in the Bible. For example, when Jesus came to the region of Caesarea Philippi, he asked his disciples, "Who do people say the Son of Man is?" They replied, "Some say John the Baptist, others say Elijah and still others, Jeremiah or one of the prophets" (Matthew 16: 13-14). The suggestion here seems to be that if a prophet were to appear, he must be the reincarnation of one of the prophets from the past, and so Jesus is asking the disciples who the people think he is a reincarnation of. The idea of the reincarnation of the prophets is apparently taken for granted as a common belief of Jesus and his disciples, and the sole point of the question is to find out who the multitudes believe him to be.

Jesus later confirmed that John the Baptist was the reincarnation of Elijah the prophet. In Mathew 11:11 he states "I assure you, of all who have ever lived, none is greater than John the Baptist," and then goes on to speak further of John the Baptist saying, "And if you are willing to accept what I say...he is Elijah...the one the prophets said would come" (Mathew 11:14). More Biblical evidence that Jesus taught the doctrine of reincarnation can be found in two excellent books: *Why Jesus Taught Reincarnation*, (Puryear, 1990) and *Reincarnation for the Christian* (Howe, 1974).

Reincarnation continued to be a prominent and well-respected belief among the early Gnostic Christian and Jewish theologians and historians in the first five hundred years after Jesus' death. The Jewish historian Flavius Josephus (37-93 A.D.) in the book Jewish Antiquities discusses reincarnation as a commonly accepted belief originally expressed by Jesus to his disciples. He described the immortality of the soul - that those who deport out of this life are again sent into bodies. In the afterlife they go to either heaven or hell (Hades) based on their actions during their lifetime. Other Jewish philosophers such as Philo of Alexandria (20-50 A.D.), Hillel, and Jehoshuah ben Pandira are to this day respected figures in Orthodox Judaism who taught the doctrine of reincarnation (Walker, 2003).

Origen ((c)188-254 A.D.) is considered by many as the early Christian Church's most prominent and influential theologian and was a prolific writer of some 6,000 works. He taught reincarnation based on the logical deduction that if one believes in a righteous, just God, there is no explanation in orthodox Christianity for the inequities and diversity of circumstances into which men are born. Thus, the principle of the law of karma must govern God's actions so that "the position of every created being is the result of his own work and his own motives." In placing responsibility on each person for his own actions, he incited quite a controversy among the orthodox theologians, who denounced his pure doctrine as anathema, to keep the masses enslaved in the blind obedience to church authorities (Prophet, 1994).

The Roman Emperor Justinian wrote a letter to the Patriarch of Constantinople calling Origen a "pernicious heretic," and in 543 A.D. issued an edict refuting Origen, and convened a synod in Constantinople (which was opposed by Pope Vigilius). Then, in 553 A.D. Justinian convened the Second Council of Constantinople, also known as the Fifth Ecumenical Council, in which the doctrine of reincarnation and most of the

Biblical references to it were banned from Church doctrine.

The great tragedy is that Christians to the present day have been misled to believe there is only one lifetime, and that reincarnation was never a part of Christian beliefs. It has been a well kept secret that for five hundred years after Jesus' death the doctrine of reincarnation was well accepted and expressed by prominent pillars of early Christianity such as St. Augustine, Clement of Alessandria and Origen (Walker, 2003).

Banning the doctrine of reincarnation effectively removed the responsibility and control over the state of the individual's destiny as determined by God. Church authorities thereby established more institutionalized control over the Christian masses. The Church forefathers inculcated the Christian masses into believing that their salvation rested in unquestioning blind adherence to the remaining partial truths and doctrinal dogma, and that simply belief and faith in Jesus who died for us and forgives us of our sins, is sufficient. They deliberately omitted teaching the importance of personal responsibility in atoning for one's sins or clearing one's karma and fulfilling one's mission and purpose.

Open-Minded Pragmatism

Since I was raised in a strong Catholic (Christian) tradition, I initially had (like most people) no affinity or interest in the topic of reincarnation or past lives until it was time for my personal awakening to this truth. In late 1982, I had a past-life reading and healing by a spiritual channel of the Ascended Masters. Then, in May of 1983 I underwent a four hour hypnotic regression by a visiting spiritual healer and hypnotist in which I viewed four past lives. Later that year, in October 1983, I was spiritually guided to do my 1st past life regression, and since then have offered past life therapy as one of my tools for healing.   Since the existence of past lives can neither be conclusively proven nor disproven, I invite all those with healthy scientific skepticism to be open to the heuristic and therapeutic value of experiencing and doing "past-life" therapy.

Many mental health professionals such as psychiatrists, psychologists, and social workers using hypnosis, guided imagery or relaxation techniques to facilitate clients' access to their unconscious, have accidentally stumbled upon experiences reported by the client which appear to be best explained as the remembrance of another lifetime. And this often occurs from giving instructions to the client to "Now go to the source origin, or root cause" of a particular symptom or problem. As most past-life therapists have discovered, the often intense emotional abreactions, such as crying, screaming, flinching, shaking, etc. tend to be convincing to both the therapist and client about the validity of the remembrance of past lives. More importantly, however, is the remission of symptoms experienced by the client following past-life regression. Hence, an open-minded attitude about the possibility of past lives, allows for both the client and therapist to utilize any past-life experiences that spontaneously emerge via hypnotic or guided imagery techniques such as QTH to be expressed, transformed and healed. The Association for Past Life Research and Therapies, founded in 1981, and the Spiritual Emergency Network, founded by Stanislav Grof, M.D. in the 1980s, both include referrals to spiritually-oriented therapists, including those who engage in past-life therapy.

From the perspective of Jung's view of the collective (racial) unconscious, these recollections of a sequence of events in another lifetime may be explained as not only personal, but alternately ancestral memory, since Jung and other more contemporary spiritually-oriented transpersonal psychiatrists and psychologists embrace the unitary holographic model of quantum physics, i.e. that all individuals contain the genetic and cellular memory not only of their race and ancestors, but the entire history and memory of the human species on planet Earth, and the cosmos as well. Additionally, since the personal and collective soul memory also encompasses other extraterrestrial embodiments, this extends the level of soul and cellular memory from not only personal and planetary, to galactic, intergalactic and cosmic memory.

Dr. Bruce Goldberg, author of *Past Lives, Future Lives Revealed* (2009), was a dentist who, after receiving training in clinical hypnosis, sought to prove or disprove reincarnation. He became convinced of the validity of reincarnation and the laws of karma from his results of conducting thousands of past life regressions, as well as future life progressions.

Edith Fiore, author of *You Have Been Here Before* (2005) also became involved in doing hypnotic past-life regression. She was raised a Protestant Christian, then became agnostic as an adult, and only later through the accumulation from experience with clients came to accept a belief in reincarnation as a reliable possibility, and convinced that her clients reports of past lives were not made-up fantasies.

An early pioneer in research and documentation of reincarnation was psychiatrist and Professor Ian Stevenson, Ph.D., at the University of Virginia Medical School. He documented over two thousand case histories, including those of very young children, whose detailed memories were described in his book entitled *Twenty Cases Suggestive of Reincarnation* (1980).

In *Reliving Past Lives: The Evidence Under Hypnosis* (2000) by Helen Wambach, Ph.D., a psychologist, the author describes her findings from guiding more than 1,000 people into past lives via group hypnosis. In *Life Before Life* (1984) she reports findings culled from seven hundred and fifty people in group hypnosis, all of whom related to experiences of reincarnating in another lifetime. Interestingly, her results corroborated many of the common spiritual beliefs and theories of reincarnation.

Finally, Dr. Valerie Hunt, an internationally renowned researcher in human energy fields and author of *Infinite Mind* (1996), uses the term "lifehoods" to transcend the linear past or future life time-space construct. Her use of lifehoods corresponds to my use of parallel life (5-D) terminology, where everything exists in the everpresent "now" from the soul's perspective. Dr. Hunt reiterates the importance of uncovering memories from other lifehoods which carry the true psychological source, and emotional residue relating to present-life problems.

Therapists who use past life regression therapy have discovered that a wide array of emotional, mental, and physical symptoms can have their "roots" in one or more past lives. However, problems with depression, generalized anxiety, panic attacks, phobias, headaches, neck and back pain, other body pains, arthritis, and allergies are some of the more common problems that have been found to be causally related to unresolved past life negative events or traumas.

Psychiatrist Shakuntala Modi, M.D. in *Remarkable Healings* (1997), analyzed a patient sample of one hundred clients out of hundreds of cases in which she facilitated treatment using past life regression therapy, as well as spirit release and soul integration. The most common psychological symptoms were depression, generalized anxiety, panic attacks, psychotic features, bipolar disorder, and specific fears or phobias. The most frequent physical symptoms were headaches, neck and back pain, general aches and pains, allergies, weight problems, PMS and gastro-intestinal symptoms. She found that twenty percent of the clients primary symptoms, and seventy percent of secondary symptoms, were related to past lives.

Past/Parallel Life Therapy Using Quantum Transformation Healing

It has been postulated that each soul will experience an estimated one to two hundred or more lifetimes (Stevens and Warwick-Smith, 1988). Many of these lifetimes are very mundane, prosaic, and uneventful, with an absence of significant negative content expressing itself in residual symptoms or problems in the current life, and also lacking any significant advancement in soul evolution.

A logical progression in therapy is to clear and heal all factors , both conscious and unconscious, from the client's current life, that relate to a particular symptom or diagnosis. If symptoms remain after doing sufficient healing of one's current life issues, then the remaining symptoms may logically be causally related to unhealed experiences from other lifetimes, (but may also be caused by disembodied spirit influence or attachment, to be described in detail in chapter nine).

The standard script and format of QTH presented in chapter five allows for the individual expression of problems or issues including those stemming from past/parallel/future lifetimes. When this occurs, the client will typically state the unhealed problem or issue (Ex: anger) and can identify the source as coming from a past life. The therapist can then simply guide the client into the relevant lifetime by saying "Now ask your I/HS or spiritual Guide to guide you to that past life that is the source of the (name of unhealed emotion). In hypnotic terminology, this technique is called an "affect bridge," since the affect or emotion is focused on, and intensified to create the connecting link to the past life.

If the client is unable to directly transport themselves into the past life using the affect bridge embedded within the basic QTH process, the following Past/Parallel/Future life therapy script using the "Ascension Technique," illustrated in the seven step process to follow, can be utilized.

Past/Parallel Life Therapy "Ascension Technique"

1. Deep Abdominal Breathing

   Allow yourself to relax comfortably on the surface on which you are sitting (or lying down). Breathe up deeply from your abdomen, below your navel, expanding your stomach, drawing in your breath up through your solar plexus… into your chest…and up into your shoulders. Hold briefly at the top of your inhalation … then exhale slowly, dropping your shoulders, contracting your muscles and exhaling out all the air in your chest, …then contracting your solar plexus or stomach… and abdomen. Continue to breathe deeply, inhaling up from your abdomen, all the way up to your shoulders, … and then exhaling down, down from your shoulders…all the way down to your abdomen. Continue to do several cycles of this breathing, getting more and more deeply relaxed each time you breath. Let go of any physical tension in your body, and release any unwanted thoughts and feelings by focusing on breathing them out, each time you exhale.

2. Ascension Technique

   Continue to breathe, slowly and deeply, but in a more normal, relaxed fashion. I'd like you now to shift your attention inward to your spirit. Imagine that your spirit, which is in your body, is going to ascend, lifting up and out of your body through the top of your head. Breathe your spirit up, drawing your spirit body up from your feet, up through your body and breathing in up and out through your crown, or top of your head. Your spirit will remain connected to your body by a crystal white (silver) cord, so that you will always stay connected to your body through this cord. Focus intently on breathing your spirit up and out of your body. See your spirit now floating above your body. Let me know when this is happening by saying "now". (Repeat and paraphrase as necessary until person is successful with this). Continue to visualize your spirit floating up higher and higher, looking down at the landscape and houses, and continuing up above the cloud level. In a little while, your spirit will float through a layer of fluffy white clouds. When your spirit is up above the clouds, allow your spirit to rest and pause, and just say "Now" when you are at that point. Optional: You may do a guided imagery process to connect the person with her I/HS or one of her spiritual guides for guidance and support, as per the QTH basic script.

3. Travelling through the Time/Space Tunnel (4th density bridge)
    Imagine now in front of you is a tunnel, and as you look through the tunnel, at the end of the tunnel is a bright, white light. As your spirit moves into the tunnel you will be able to travel through time and space going back (or forward) in time to another place, another lifetime. (If the person has a spirit guide, they will travel through the tunnel together). We ask your own I/HS or spirit to guide you to the lifetime that would be the most important or beneficial lifetime to see and heal today. Alternately, you may ask to be shown: 1) the most important other lifetime with _____ (name of person in this lifetime) to see and heal today: or, 2) the most important past/parallel/future life to understand and clear your karma with _____ (name of person in this lifetime), or 3) the most important lifetime to heal any negative or unwanted physical, emotional, mental or spiritual symptoms, etc. (name specific symptoms). Now, let your spirit move into the tunnel, and feel yourself tumbling and turning, moving through the tunnel …towards the bright light at the end of the tunnel. When you get to the end of the tunnel, you will be in another time/space dimension, immersed and resting peacefully in the bright white light. Then, when you are ready, you will be able to drop down into another lifetime, the lifetime which is the most important lifetime to clear and heal today. I'm going to count from one to five. When I get to five you will be at the end of the tunnel, immersed in the bright, white light. Just pause when you get to the end of the tunnel. One… two…three…four…five. Now, you are at the end of the tunnel surrounded by the brilliant white light.

4. Descending into the Past/Parallel Life

Next, I'd like you to imagine dropping down into another lifetime, another time and place, into the most important lifetime to re-experience and heal today. In a few moments, I'm going to count from one to ten. When I get to ten, your spirit will be in another body, in another time and place, and your feet will be resting on a particular surface. Ready, now…one…two…three…four…five…half way there…six…seven…eight…nine…ten. Now, allow yourself to touch down upon a surface. Look down at your feet, and tell me what you are wearing on your feet (pause to allow response). Now, look at your body, moving from your feet, up your legs, and notice what you are wearing, and if you are male or female. (Ask client for description of clothing and gender).

5. Exploring the Past/Parallel Life

Now, imagine your spirit moving out of your body and being able to look at yourself, and see your face. What do you look like? (Ask for details re: hair, eye color, and features). What is your name? Now go back into your body and gaze out through your own eyes, looking around you. What do you see? Ask for specific details of scenery, other persons, what is happening, etc. How old are you now? Pause until you receive a response to questions or move on if person is unsure. (Ask spirit guide for the answer and help at any points during the process). Where are your parents? If person is an adolescent or adult, ask if they are single or married, and information about these significant relationships, if and when they see or contact these persons. To determine who a person is that they know in this lifetime ask, "Do you recognize _____ from this lifetime? As you look at _____, just perceive his/her (soul) essence, relaxing your focus, and allow who they are in your current lifetime to come to you." Continue to explore what you may intuitively feel is significant and then say "Is there anything else that is important to know before we move on to the next most important event?" When the person indicates that there is nothing else important to remember from that particular scene or event, then say "I'd like you to move forward in time to the next most important event. I'm going to count from one to three. When I get to three, you will be at the next most important event…one…two…three." Ask, "Where are you now?" "What are you doing?" Move through all significant scenes until you have progressed the person through their physical death in that lifetime, if possible. Always remember to have closure at the end of the session by releasing (via processing out feelings and thoughts from the session in a normal alert state after the QTH part of the session is ended), or doing healing work on the emotional issues that are uncovered.

6. Understanding Karma and Clearing/Healing Unhealed or Negative Energies
Say "Now as you review your lifetime, what were the major lessons that you learned?" Allow person to reply. Ask about karmic debt. "Who do you still have karma with from that lifetime?" Ask the person (or their spirit guide) how this karma can be cleared. Ask, "Are there any unhealed energies (negative emotions or thought patterns) from that lifetime?" If so, ask the person where this energy is anchored in their physical body. Here, you can use the full QTH basic script. Or just do an abbreviated version and ask the person to just send love energetically and/or ask the person to visualize sending pink and violet light (love, compassion and forgiveness) to the area of unhealed energy. Have the person ask their unhealed energy if it will talk with them. Ask that part what it needs to be healed. Follow the response(s) of the person, and give that part what it needs to be healed. Or ask the unhealed energy "What colored light can assist you in absorbing and transforming this unhealed energy? (Use violet light for the most powerful transformation and healing effect). Have the name of color light come in and completely absorb and heal all the old, unhealed energy. Check for sensory experience of validation of change in the person. Ask, "Does the part of your body where the unhealed energy was, look or feel different?" Finally, ask the person or their spirit guide "Is there anything else we need to do today to complete this session?" Ask for homework assignments, or anything else the person can do to clear karma from that life, or advance his spiritual evolution.

7. Returning to the Present
Now, I'd like you to shift your focus to come back to your present lifetime. I'm going to count backwards from ten to one. As I count, I'd like you to travel quickly back in time and space, to come back to the present when I get to one. Ready?...one...two...three...four...five...half way there...six...seven...eight... nine...ten. Now, come back fully in your body, remembering and integrating everything you have learned and healed today. When you are ready, open your eyes, stretch your arms and legs, and wake up, alert and refreshed.

Next, I will present three samples of past life therapy sessions using QTH.

Past/Parallel Life Therapy Session 8-1

This is a touching and poignant past life healing session of ill-fated lovers, a theme which was uncovered as a repeat pattern for Gerald in two other lifetimes of strong, but unfulfilled love with his current wife. He had prior experience with QTH past life therapy. The purpose and specific request in this past life regression was to understand the karma and/or "unfinished business" with his current wife, in order to facilitate an understanding of why he was blocked, unwilling, and unable to accept her wishes for a divorce.

T: The client is guided through the Ascension Technique as a substitute for locating his Inner Place of Peace, and is guided into a spiritual place of peace beyond the clouds.

C: I'm in an empty space.

At times, the inner or spiritual IPOP may be in a void, or empty space, with nothing visible in their inner landscape.

T: Now I'd like you to connect with your HS or Guide.

C: It's St. Jude...he's wearing a white robe... and looks like Jesus Christ...but he's not.

T: After client is guided through a time tunnel to the light at the end of the tunnel, his guide St. Jude is requested to guide him to the most important lifetime for healing of the relationship with his current wife.

Spirit helpers will almost always accommodate a specific request to view and heal a given lifetime, unless another problem or lifetime is more important to integrate and heal.

T: I'd like you to descend into the most important lifetime with your current wife, Theresa...(pause)...What are you wearing on your feet?

C: I'm wearing sandals. I can't tell if I'm in ancient Greece or Atlantis. The roads are very flat and level. I'm wearing a white robe. I have curly hair...short and full.

Client quickly accesses the place, time period and his age in that lifetime, although it often may take longer for the person to "reorient" their consciousness to obtain that information.

T: Ask St. Jude where you are and what year is it?

C: I'm in Egypt, around 1290 B.C.

T: How old are you?

C: I'm 25...(pause) and I'm Hebrew...a slave. Now I see Theresa. She's wearing a brown robe...carrying water. She has brownish black hair...and she's Egyptian. I love her very much. I feel this pain in my heart.

T: What is the pain related to?

Accessing the problem/issue on a sensory level.

C: I was a high slave...beautiful, intelligent, and helpful. My job was looking after the affairs of the Pharaoh. I gave it up for the love of this woman...I gave up so much to be with her. Because of her I got demoted. I was strong willed then like I am now. (client has past life trait carryover insight) And...I'm hurting in my heart.

T: What's happening now in the scene you're in?

C: They're whipping me in public. I see her face in my mind...She's indifferent... showing no emotion.

Beginning to access the core unresolved emotional issue in that lifetime.

T: Then what happens?

C: After I'm whipped...and the Egyptians leave, I go over to her...she's looking at me with love (client pauses for a long time).

T: When I count to three, I'd like you to move forward in time to the next significant event. one...two...three. What's happening now?

I utilize a pacing technique to quickly move him forward to the next significant event by counting slowly to three.

C: We're in her cottage. She's about eighteen or twenty. We're making love...and very passionate (pause). There are two guards at the door. They're ordering me to leave and take me out of her cottage. I'm screaming "No, No, No..." (client has look of anguish)

Here, Gerald was not in an intolerably emotionally painful state. If he was, I would use the "dissociation technique" of having his spirit separate from his body to lessen his pain. That way, he would be observing himself (like watching a movie about himself) instead of in his body (fully associated) and feeling the intensity of his pain.

T: Now, ask St. Jude if there is anything else important to remember at this point in time?

C: No.

T: Then go to the next significant event by the time I get to three...one...two...three...

C: I'm older now...and bearded. My hair is thinner, I'm about thirty-two or thirty-five. I've been reassigned to hard labor. I self-destruct by getting beaten.

T: Where is the woman who is Theresa?

C: She's older...she's put on weight. She has two kids now. They're both boys...about five years old and two years old...(pause).

T: Now relax your inner vision. Perceive the essence, not the form, of these two children, to discern if they are anyone you know in your current lifetime.

C: They're both boys...about five years old and two years old...(pause). Gerald sounds shocked, surprised and says "The two year old boy is Ashley! (name of his daughter in this current life). Then he has a realization... "They're my children!"

T: What's happening now?

C: She feels sad...her eyes are so sad... watching me get beaten again. She wishes she could cleanse the wounds and help me. After the beating...she comes out and holds me... and leads me away. She's saying, "It just can't be..." referring to our relationship.

T: Now, go to the next significant event. one... two...three...

C: I look like Charleton Heston...I'm thirty-five...at my son's grave. Both of them (our children) have died of disease. She's standing by my side. (Then client has own realization). I came back from the future to remove a block between us. I want us to have happiness between us instead of sorrow.

T: Is the sorrow the most important core issue to heal from that lifetime?

C: Yes.

Interestingly, and somewhat paradoxically, we can have greater clarity in our inner vision by softening our focus and detaching. The key language pattern which helps access if someone in a past life is in our current life is "Perceive the essence of the _____ (name or role of the person in the past life).

T: What does the sorrow want at its highest level of intention and purpose?

C: It wants to be cleansed and healed.

T: Where do you feel the sorrow?

C: In my heart.

T: What color is the sorrow?

C: It looks grey…like a kind of cloud.

T: Who can help you release the sorrow in your heart?

C: (Excitedly) Now St. Jude and Jesus are hugging all four of us. Jesus loves both of us and wishes us to be together and have more children. Theresa has tears in her eyes – I tell her to smile and be happy…not be so serious.

Here he spontaneously witnesses the healing solution occurring. Jesus spontaneously appears as a 2nd spiritual guide. This often happens when the client is familiar with the QTH process as this client was.

T: What is St. Jude doing?

C: He says, "Have faith…I'm taking your prayers before the Father." (spontaneously and excitedly) "I see a whole flock of white doves, hundreds coming down. They have olive branches in their beaks. They're flying all around us."

Here, the client goes directly into mental integration (the verbal message) and sees another symbol of the spontaneous spiritual healing that just occurred with St. Jude, Jesus, he and his wife – a flock of white doves.

T: Now look in our heart where the grey was. What do you see?

Always check to see if the unhealed energy has been completely absorbed, re-integrated or healed.

C: They grey is gone…I don't feel sad anymore. I have faith maybe we can be together in the future…Theresa has the gift of faith…(client reminisces and drifts off).

The "faith" is evidence of the emotional healing and integration.

In discussing the thwarted love relationship Gerald had in Egypt with his current wife after the past life regression, he gained a deeper understanding of why he had stayed so long in a strained and difficult married relationship with her in this lifetime. In subsequent sessions, Gerald discovered that he had loved her intensely over many lifetimes and finally successfully married her in the current life. He now understood that he had fulfilled his obligation to marry her, since he had fathered children with her in this and another past lifetime, but in prior lives he had been prohibited from marrying her due to political forces. He was able to put to rest his sense of unfulfilled obligation to her, understanding that although he still yearned for them to continue as a couple, a clearer connection with Jesus and St. Jude allowed him to detach more fully and allow her the expression of her own free will. Despite the parallel life healing (with Jesus and St. Jude) that occurred in this session, his wife was not advancing in her spiritual and personal growth. They were growing apart, and so he was able sometime thereafter to go along with her wishes for a divorce.

Past/Parallel Life Therapy Session 8-2

Allison was quite developed in her psychic, healing and spiritual connection abilities and was able to quickly access and view three past lives in the following example. This is a good example of a session with multiple unhealed issues and past lives in extraterrestrial civilizations. The unhealed disintegrated shadow aspects are labeled D_1, D_2, etc.; and the corresponding transformational healing aspects as H_1, H_2, etc.

T: Deep Abdominal Breathing, Spiritual Alignment.

C: I'm seeing an alien (client's face contorts as she focuses on the alien).

Since her face contorted, I sensed that logically it was not a "positive" alien guide, as well as with my intuitive, feeling sense, and was a shadow aspect probably in need of healing. I return to following the QTH steps in sequence of first finding an IPOP, and connect her with her Spiritual Self aspect or guide to get clear, spiritual guidance when a shadow aspect appears prematurely in a QTH session.

T: Just relax and let the image of the alien fade. I'd like you to focus on anchoring yourself in an inner place of peace. Allow yourself to find a place where you feel safe, peaceful and relaxed. Breathe and shift your focus into finding a place that seems the most comfortable for you right now.

C: I'm in a glen...with fairies.

T: Now call from your heart for your FPS, I/ HS, whatever you call your Spiritual Self, or one of your guides, to come and be with you in your IPOP.

C: I see my Higher Self. She has wings. They're huge…and white.

T: Look into your HS's eyes to connect with your own soul. Send love from your heart to your Higher Self aspect and feel it flow back and connect your hearts. Now, ask your Higher Self if the most important issue today is related to the alien.

Used to deepen the connection to her Higher Self.

C: She says yes.

T: Then let the alien come back into your IPOP.

The shadow aspect is re-introduced after being placed on "hold" until she is in her IPOP and her HS is strongly anchored.

C: The alien says he doesn't want to be hurt. He wants a guarantee that he won't be hurt. He says his job is not finished yet.

T: What is his job?

C: To keep me down. He says it's not time for me to go forward. There's lots of wisdom I hold that doesn't belong to me. If I would access it now, I'd be hurt.

Confirmation of restrictive blocking aspect and dark polarity.

T: What does your HS say?

C: My spirit tells me there are no victims… that I can keep the knowledge too.

T: What is the alien's name?

C: He wants to be called Ra.

This being is obviously not Ra, the Egyptian Sun God!! It is attempting to fool the client into thinking it is primarily a powerful being of light.

T: Ask your HS if this is correct?

C: She says it's not. Now I'm being taken aboard an alien craft (with a surprised tone). Now I'm seeing Ashtar and Jesus…and my HS with the alien. The alien is showing me the agreement I signed. He's animal like in look. (Client puts hands over her eyes). The

Since the name of the alien is not important, I allow the client to proceed with her own process. Spontaneous appearance of two other "Light Guides": Ashtar – a Cosmic Commander of an Intergalactic fleet of ships serving earth, (Tuella, 1985) and Jesus. The problem/issue is

C: (cont.) alien is telling me I haven't fulfilled my end of the deal. There was a time capsule...I agreed to keep it secret...for the dark side of this civilization. Now Ashtar is reaching for the agreement...he's ripping it up. The (alien) commander has a wolfish face.

T: What does the alien commander want?

C: He said I was sent to guard the ship. His belief is that the information is not free and available to all in the universe...there was a war...they used my mind as a computer... to guard and hold the information. My agreement was part of a larger agreement or peace treaty. His agreement was not to use it (the information). There's a council of three light bodies forming in front of my eyes. They're all part of one consciousness. They say he has no power over her. Now the alien commander is holding my hand...telling me I hold the wisdom of the universe within me and that wisdom cannot be released. The Council of Three tells me I'm very controlled by my mind...that I need to let love out and access the power. I hold the three keys of love, wisdom and power...all very strong. Wisdom will control the mind, my body has the power, but in my heart, fear holds the power down. The message they're giving me is walk through the illusion of fear...release the mind...and allow the Spirit to be. If I let love in, it will open the way for many, and gifts will come in abundance.

T: Where is the problem of blocking love, wisdom and power anchored in your body?

C: I see a plug...it has many layers...in my root chakra (D_1). It's related to core issues about my weight (client is significantly overweight). But people will come in to help. I feel a tingling there...I felt the same tingle before in my left foot chakra.

T: Ask the plug what it wants at its highest level of intention and purpose?

being revealed in her natural progression.

Here, I seek to uncover what the commander wants at his lowest and/or highest levels of intention and purpose.

Uncovering details about the problems/issues in that lifetime.

What a beautiful spontaneous illustration of the importance of the threefold flame – love, wisdom, and power...and the greatest of these is love!

C: It wants me to be free...only if I will use my power wisely...balanced with love and discernment...and wisdom to not make agreements to assist the dark.

T: Are you willing to have your freedom by balancing your love, wisdom, and power?

C: Yes (tentatively). The Council of Three is telling me the agreement is gone (H_1): It's broken. They say it's part of an exercise to get me on my way up...the debt has been paid. The commander accepts this. Now I hear the words "You're coming home." (Client gets a scared expression on her face).

The tentative "yes" and scared expression on her face indicated she is not totally clear to accept more love, wisdom, and power and the integration/healing is not complete.

C: Now I'm going in to a cave. There's a strong feeling of death here. Children have been burned to death...babies and clothes charred. I was involved in doing this...in an alien lifetime. I had a skeleton-like body and a big head. At the panel...I was operating an incinerator...because of overpopulation. There were two civilizations. We were underneath the surface. Above the surface of the planet was another civilization...more human looking.

Before I can proceed to uncover whatever she is afraid of that is blocking her, in order to complete the integration and healing, another past/parallel life emerges into conscious memory.

We stole children from the other surface civilization and killed them...because they were taking away our resources. I was picked for the job because I could shut down my emotions and leave my body at will.

T: How do you feel about what you did?

C: Very bad...guilty (pained expression on her face). But I was numb then...there's a numbness in my stomach and abdomen (D_2) It looks dark...and a cap over my crown (D_3).

Here, she describes two more places where the emotional/mental blocks are anchored in her body.

T: Ask one of your guides...whoever has the answer...which area, the crown or the abdomen/stomach, is more important to focus on now.

C: She says the stomach/abdomen.

T: Ask the stomach/abdomen what it wants at its highest level of intention and purpose?

C: It wants the children to forgive me. The Council of Three is saying the children have forgiven me. They were not stupid. They knew this would happen to them in that life... that they would be killed to help save another civilization.

Validation that there are "no victims in the universe", and that our soul chooses major life themes and events prior to incarnating.

T: Can you forgive yourself if the children can forgive you...knowing this was part of the plan for everyone in that lifetime...to play out these roles?

C: I guess so...(pause). The children are coming back to life (with surprise and excitement in her voice). When the children died...they were grey...now they're pink and healthy. The children are being taken up by Mother Mary (H_2) (sense of relief in her voice).

Spontaneous transformational imagery of resurrection and healing.

C: I'm seeing that my fetus died in the womb, and I died as the mother. The pregnancy was the result of a rape...(long pause)...Mother Mary and Jesus just came in to heal my little child.

I sense this is yet another third past life that is briefly brought into her conscious awareness to be healed, related to the karmic retribution (death of herself and her child) as a result of the alien lifetime when she killed the children.

T: How does that feel now?

C: Better...not numb and like death in my abdomen and womb. (D_4)

Now we have two past lives related to blocking in the stomach/abdominal area (as an alien and mother). Other unhealed shadow aspects are anchored in the crown (alien lifetime) and the root chakra from the lifetime with the alien commander. So far, there has been only a partial healing of the issues from the three lifetimes.

T: Now, ask your HS and/or guides what else needs to be done in order to completely heal and integrate the three past lives, and the energies in the root, abdomen, stomach, womb, and crown?

C: My HS says to do the Rainbow Bridge.

Therapist would ask how to do The Rainbow Bridge if not familiar with this technique.

T: Okay, then visualize a sphere of white light in your root chakra, bright white light. Breathe and expand the white sphere until it gets stronger and brighter. Then breathe it up from your root to your crown and through your arms and legs...taking all the time

T: (cont.) you need to clear your body with the white light,…aligning yourself with your HS and purifying and clearing out all the old energies, especially focusing on the specific areas you mentioned where the blocks are held in the body. Let me know when you are complete with that by saying "now."

C: Now.

T: Then visualize the seven colors of the rainbow…red through violet, in their respective chakras. See all of the colors bright, clear, and glowing, and let me know when that's complete.

The basic "Rainbow Bridge" is 7 colors from the (root to the crown chakra) of red, orange, yellow, green, blue, indigo, and violet. This client already knew the rainbow bridge meditation sequence so there was no need to go into more detail in the guided imagery process.

C: It's complete.

T: Are all the areas where you had unhealed energy in your body, the plug in your root, the numbness in the stomach/solar plexus and womb, and the cap on your crown – all looking and feeling clear…filled with bright rainbow light colors?

Check for complete healing in all areas (D_1, D_2, D_3, D_4) previously mentioned.

C: Yes, I can feel the energy in all my chakras…the plug is gone…as well as the numbness.

Physical and emotional integration

T: Does your HS or guides have any other messages or assignments for you?

Mental integration

C: If I stay out of the way of my ego, and listen to my heart…only love…other doors will open up. My HS says I also need to take a more assertive role with D's (a friend's) two children…and to not let her pressure me into babysitting. (Client has insight) I can see now it was a karmic debt I was repaying. But there's no right or wrong as far as the babysitting goes. I'm not their savior.

She makes another past → present life connection regarding karma with children.

To recap this rapidly paced session, there was apparently sufficient clearing of D_1 – the plug in the root chakra from the 1st lifetime with the appearance of the alien commander, and Ashtar and Jesus ripping up (and rendering null and void) the past agreement to not reveal the information she held. After the Rainbow Bridge meditation at the end, she saw that the plug was gone (H_1). The other lifetimes and areas of unhealed energy would need to be revisited and checked for the need to do further integration and transformational healing.

Past/Parallel Life Therapy Session 8-3

Diana had a long history of depression and frequent severe migraines, and she was taking prescription medication for both. She had many prior QTH sessions, uncovering and releasing other lifetimes related to guilt (over past perceived misuse of power) and feeling victimized, both of which led to her current feelings of depression. In addition to being quite familiar with the QTH process, and doing past life clearing and healing, she had also studied hypnosis, spiritual psychology and Goddess cultures.

T: Spiritual Alignment, Locate IPOP.

C: I'm in a healing temple…very beautiful… with crystals, gardens…and waterfalls.

T: Fully immerse yourself in seeing the beauty of your IPOP, seeing, hearing, feeling, and using your sense of smell to imagine being there now, feeling safe and peaceful (pause). Now make an inner heartfelt call for your Inner Spiritual Goddess Self, or one of your guides to join you there, whoever would be most appropriate for today's session.
> Sensory integration and deepening of her experience in her IPOP.

C: It's Nabibaway (client had connected with this guide in previous sessions). She's an aspect of the Goddess…she has a timeless look…like she's in her thirties or forties. She's taking my hand…like she's going to show me…another lifetime.
> I am unsure of the exact spelling, and unfamiliar with the name of this guide.

T: Client is guided using Ascension Technique above the clouds.

T: When I count to ten, I would like to you descend into another time and place, in
> Guiding and pacing client into another lifetime.

T: (cont.) another body, in whatever lifetime is highest and best for you to see and heal today. When I get to ten, your feet will be touching down on a particular surface. Ready…(slow count) one…two…three…descending into another lifetime…four…another time and place…five…whatever lifetime is most important for your healing…six…feel Nabibaway's loving protective presence … seven…eight…almost there now…nine… your feet will be resting on a particular surface when I get to…ten (pause). Now look down at your feet and tell me what you are wearing on your feet?

C: I'm wearing leather sandals…around ten or eleven years old. I'm too tall for my little dress…I'm feeling awkward. (pause) There's water on one side…like a lake…or river…I'm in a city with old looking narrow buildings made of stone or brick…with tenements and narrow streets…it feels like Scandinavia. I'm getting the sense that I'm in Denmark. There is a farmer's market nearby.

T: Where are your parents?

C: My father's at work…and my mother is home cooking…she sent me to the market to get something.

T: Do you have siblings?

C: I have an older sister in her late teens… she's either working or in school…and a younger brother.

T: Do you recognize your parents or siblings as anyone you know in your current life?

C: No, not that I can tell. It doesn't feel like I've know any of them before.

C: It's in the late 1930s or early 40s…my parents are concerned about the Nazis… because we're Jewish, even though they have not been to Denmark…they're rounding up people…so my parents put me on a train… with my younger brother…we went to the

C: (cont.) country...to a farm house...
somebody my father knew through work...
who's not Jewish. We stayed there a couple
of years...both of us...me and my brother. It
was boring and frightening...they kept us at
home...so we would be safe...they felt like
strangers.

T: Can you see them now?

C: Yes.

T: Are they anyone you have known in this
lifetime?

C: My parents never made contact with us
when we were there. I was around thirteen
or fourteen...a teenager...and restless...
and my brother was around ten. We felt
we wanted to go back. They didn't want to
send us back...but we insisted. We wanted
to go home for the Jewish High Holidays...
Rosh Hashanah. So they tried to contact
our parents...they sent a telegram...but
there was no response (pause). We took
the train back to visit our parents...when I
got off the train...we had to show our ID
papers. We had some ID papers we had to
carry...they said we were Jewish. (pause)
We were taken in a big truck...with slats
on the sides...with a few other people who
came off the train. I knew we were in big
trouble...they were Nazis. It was very quiet
in the streets...they'd only come a few
days before...planning to round up Jews
in the temple for Rosh Hashanah. A lot of
Danish people who were not Jewish helped
thousands of Jews to escape by sea. The
Nazis were really disappointed and angry.
My family...my parents and older sister...
were evacuated...they were saved. My
brother and I didn't escape. They took us to
a big police station...their headquarters...
they took my brother away. (client cries
gently) I never saw him again...

T: What happened next?

Client ignores the query about whether she
recognizes the people who took care of her and
her brother. Since it is not critically important
to know the answer to this, I allowed her to
proceed with her own process.

C: They've separated the males and females in that truck. They put me in with some other teenage girls...all healthy young women...nobody really old. They put us in kind of like a boxcar...sending us someplace...it was awful...dark, dirty, crowded, and smelly. We traveled for about two to three...a few days. I think we got a little bit of food, but not enough to sustain us. So we were all weak and dizzy. They let us wash a little...they gave us uniforms and a tattoo of a number on us. Then they put me in an infirmary...like hospital barracks...(pause). I've been chosen for some medical experiments...because I'm pretty young and healthy. I have a sense of...helplessness, it's worse than fear...not being able to escape...it's overwhelming.

T: Just take a moment to breathe deeply and relax now. Remember, your spirit will only guide you to remember what you are ready to emotionally handle.

Reminding client that she will only be shown that which she is emotionally strong enough to handle helps to allow her to bring into conscious awareness what is held in her unconscious mind.

C: I get a sense of being tied to a bed...like on a hospital bed. That made me even more crazy...just as helpless and powerless as you could possibly be. If I yelled, they gagged me...so I stopped screaming. I was literally out of my mind with terror and helplessness. The experiments had something to do with my left side...everything they did was a series of injections...of an experimental serum...in my left temple and my left hip. Afterwards, I felt woozy and dizzy. Everything looks red...my field of vision is blurred...I was vomiting (client has insight). My migraine symptoms in this life are in my left temple. The injection itself relates to the migraines. I felt so much helplessness and fear...there was no anesthesia...even when they did the tattoo...no numbing. The man was dressed like a doctor...in a white coat with a mask. He'd pinch and prod me...ask me questions...and take notes. I have a feeling I'm not getting up much...I'm getting weaker. It's been weeks strapped to this bed. They only feed me a little potato scraps and black bread.

Client continues to move forward without prompting.

Here, Diana has an insight into the past-life connection with her current life migraines.

Her language continues to suggest that she is dissociated watching what was occurring.

T: I'm going to count from one to three, and I would like you to move forward in time to the next significant event by the time I get to three. Take a deep breath with each count, and release the fear and helplessness…with each count. One…two…three…(pause). What is happening now?

Using focused intention with breathing facilitates the release of accumulated negative emotions.

C: This goes on for weeks…not months. It's causing damage to my brain…I'm in a woozy, dazed …red state…feeling sick. I'm beyond scared now…just sick, nauseous and dizzy. All I felt was pain, rage, fear and helplessness.

T: Ask Nabibaway if there is anything important to know about the serum you were injected with?

C: The cells in the left side of my brain died…I lost the verbal stuff…it's hard to track…I'm losing my verbal sequential abilities…feeling very frustrated…in a timeless place. The kind of feeling…that I couldn't articulate…I'm losing the ability to talk…my situation, I'm feeling…it's getting worse and worse… (pause).

Notice her less connected speech congruent with loss of verbal sequential abilities.

T: Now…what happens next?

C: I'm looking down at myself on the bed… I'm really thin…she's lethally thin…I've got all bed sores…very weak…the guy with the white coat…gives me another injection…in my left temporal frontal area…I'm floating in a sea of pain…I feel this injection…and I died very quickly…from a brain aneurysm.

T: How old were you when you died?

C: I was fourteen…I'm looking down feeling grief for the child…from the perspective of passing out of the body. She lived with that pain and shame and guilt…and fear, terror, and helplessness.

T: Are any of those emotions still being held in your body?

Finding the location of residual negative emotions from that lifetime.

C: There's pain...definitely in my left temporal and frontal area...where I get my migraines...and in my left hip. I have a kind of weakness in this body. Sometimes I get dizzy from orthostatic hypotension. A physiological psychologist friend in California said they have new equipment that shows it has to do with the temporal blood flow...also, sometimes I get a sharp pain in my left occipital region...and have to hold my head.

T: Now, take a deep breath and shift your attention to reconnect with Nabibaway. Ask her how to best heal these physical pain symptoms...and release the negative emotions.

C: She says I need to clear the karma...I was to a certain extent responsible for my brother... If I look for him and find him in this life... his name was Hans...it will help release the guilt. This is only part of the healing that will need to be done. It's important to have a sense on a cellular level that...that was then...in a past life...and I can transcend being a victim. I need to remember this is a whole new state...I have all the "credit" so to speak, that I needed to be a wounded healer. I know it doesn't serve me now. I wasn't responsible for my own death and that of millions of others...

T: Are there any additional suggestions from Nabibaway to heal yourself on physical, emotional, mental and spiritual levels?

C: She says that running the violet flame would be very good...and balancing my energy bodies using the three fold flame so I can love and forgive myself...see with the eyes of wisdom...and get my power and energy back. She also says to listen to the cellular healing tape that I have by Orin. Using the spiritual alignment techniques and adding affirmations and decrees that I forgive myself and I ask that they forgive me...for the roles we played.

Here are more direct parallels to her current symptoms in this life as connected with the past life.

This client had done prior past life regressions revealing the multi-layered causal roots of her depression and migraines.

T: Are there any other assignments or messages related to healing the guilt, which is related to your depression and migraines?

C: Nabibaway says that I need to go over old lifetimes...one around forty thousand years ago...when I was in a "catch 22" ...another one in which I was an Egyptian slave...a priestess of Ishtar, and a medieval lifetime... when I was French...and burned at the stake as a witch...to release the pain, suffering and guilt from those lifetimes.

T: Okay, we can do more past life healing on those lifetimes in future sessions. Just breathe out any residual negative energies on the physical level from your left side... especially your left temple...and on the emotional level...releasing guilt and depression...mentally accepting your soul's choice to experience victim and perpetrator roles through your incarnational stream and spiritually choosing to come from your Inner Goddess and higher compassionate Self-loving, forgiving, releasing and healing that lifetime during the Holocaust. (pause)

Integrating the release on physical, emotional, mental and spiritual levels.

T: Will you commit to completing the homework assignments from Nabibaway?

C: Yes. I will do the visualizations and meditations and decrees...and listen to the cellular healing tape.

Obviously, this was a very difficult lifetime for the client to re-experience. As previously mentioned, she had multiple past lives related to her problems with depression and migraine headaches some of which she had seen in prior QTH sessions. Subsequent sessions were focused on doing additional healing work on this lifetime, as well as some additional past lives, to further reduce her depression and migraines.

Handling Strong Catharses or Abreactions in Clients During Past Life QTH Sessions

Deeply accessing repressed memories of strong negative or traumatic experiences such as from physical abuse, torture, sex abuse, rape, and murder can lead to catharsis or abreactions expressed as intense crying, screaming, moaning, gasping for air, choking, shaking, kicking, flinching, body stiffening, etc.

As in all therapeutic situations, it is very important for the therapist to refrain, as much as possible, from going into anxiety or fear over the client's emotional catharsis, or carrying judgment regarding the content of the material the client is expressing. This emotional neutrality and non-judgmental stance can only be developed through experience - either from the therapist's own personal healing of similar issues or assisting clients with similar issues in this or other lifetimes. Traumatic events such as violent physical abuse, rape, torture, dismemberment, etc. are content areas that tend to evoke strong feelings in therapists who have not previously worked through similar events in their own personal life, or past lives, or encountered and assisted clients working through such traumatic experiences. In that sense, there is no substitution for experience! As therapists, we must strive to cultivate an attitude of acceptance and non-judgment from viewing the depth and breath of the range of human experiences on the victim – perpetrator continuum.

When the therapist vicariously re-experiences the client reliving disturbing content that the therapist is unfamiliar with, the therapist should actively focus on expressing caring and concerned detachment, and strive to minimize any signs of discomfort in vocal tone, wording, facial expression or body language, which will greatly assist the client in continuing to successfully relive and process through the trauma. Negative emotional or thought patterns emanating from the therapist will be sensed or felt by the client in the interactive therapeutic process, and can result in the client shutting down or becoming blocked as a result of the therapist's anxiety, fear or judgment (conveyed either verbally or non-verbally). When the therapist experiences some mild discomfort, anxiety, fear, etc. triggered by the client's abreaction of trauma, she can still continue to compassionately and gently guide the client through the reliving and releasing process. If you as the therapist are unclear, clear yourself! Physician heal thy self! Be very self-aware and strive to embrace all intense emotional material presented by your clients with unconditional love, compassion and forgiveness. It is also recommended for the therapist to clear herself using the golden white light (spiritual alignment) and violet light (transmutation) meditation prior to the session, or during the session if needed, to clear any negative emotions and release any negative thoughts of mental judgment.

Differential Diagnosis of Multiple Personality Disorder (MPD) vs. Past Life Personalities

On a clinical diagnostic note, I would like to address the topic of differentiating between multiple personality disorder (MPD) and past life personality emergence.

From a theoretical perspective, MPD represents significant disintegration or dissociation and "splitting" or fragmentation of the psyche. MPD is typically the result of severe, and often recurrent abuse or trauma, which leads to the inability to subconsciously, consciously and superconsciously integrate the traumatic experience. MPD is specifically defined (DSM IV-R, 1994) as having at least two (or more) personalities that are not aware of the existence of each other.

In contrast, persons may show distinct expressions of different social roles, ego states, or even "sub" personalities within the normal range of human personality, on a continuum of increasing disintegration, or dissociation, albeit not significant enough to constitute MPD. Similarly, the flow through of soul awareness representing greater integration of the superconscious into conscious awareness, may give the appearance of another distinctly different human personality self with thoughts, feelings, strengths, weaknesses, preferences, and behavior patterns from another lifetime, as an expression of a past life aspect of the self.

Multiple Personality Disorder represents significant psychopathology and a lack of integration of unconscious material. Past Life personalities on the other hand, are consciously remembered as distinctly different persons from other lifetimes. If the person is aware of another "subpersonality" or ego state that appears as a result of a past life emergence, by virtue of his conscious awareness, it cannot by definition be MPD. Past life memory emerges only when the person has accessed the superconscious, I/H Self.

Toward a Unified, Multidimensional Understanding of Past/Parallel/Future Lives and Reincarnational Theory

Here is a graphical representation of the three main density levels and spiritual laws as they pertain to understanding past/parallel/future lives and the theory of reincarnation.

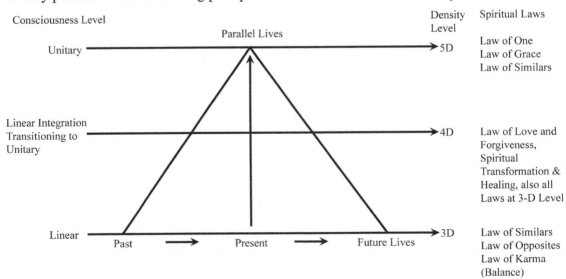

In 3rd density there is the most experience and perception of polarity or duality of good vs. evil, and gender opposites of male and female, and the Law of Opposites (attraction of opposites) is the most pronounced. This is the level of consciousness where sin (from a Christian perception), or karma (the Buddhist or Hindu equivalent) exists. We also perceive time as linear (past → present → future) and hence as past or future lives. The 5-D equivalent is called parallel lives.

In 4th density, the Heart Chakra opens to experience greater love and the 3rd eye chakra opens to experience greater nonjudgment. Christ Consciousness integration occurs in 4th density. This is where one also experiences healing of this and other lifetimes (consciously or unconsciously) with forgiveness of self and others for errors in thought, word or deed. The majority of the human population on planet Earth is currently transitioning from 3rd to 4th density consciousness.

In a unitary consciousness (5-D) state, we perceive simultaneous overlapping or interwoven lifetimes as "parallel lives" and the reason for reincarnation is simply to achieve a balancing out of experiences. For example, if someone was a neglectful parent in one lifetime, they will in some other lifetime reincarnate as a child who is neglected by its parents. Or, if a person betrays and murders his friend in one lifetime, he will similarly experience the opposite equivalent in another life.

In 5-D consciousness, there are no judgments or experiences of "good" vs. "evil," all experiences are simply expressions within a unified field of consciousness. In 5th density, the Law of Grace prevails. This is where spontaneous healing takes place in a unified coherent consciousness field. There is no perception of gender polarities (female vs. male) as all beings are evolved to a state of androgyny (with high levels of both positive female and male traits).

CHAPTER 9
Spirit Release

Aloa Starr in *Prisoners of Earth* (1993), differentiates between two main categories of attached spirits - discarnate astral spirits of deceased humans, and demons, which are energized thought form creations.

Some astral spirits of persons who have died do not leave the earth plane at the time of death, due to particular attachment to the place they lived prior to dying, or attachment to a person. Frequently, spirits of deceased family members may choose to remain on the earth plane to comfort and assist their grieving loved ones. Helping the guilt-stricken person understand that the spirit is eternal, and that the deceased loved one can be contacted through prayers, and is "only a thought away," can assist him or her to work through feelings of depression and any unresolved issues regarding the loss of the loved one. Then, the spirit of the deceased will not sense the need to remain on the astral plane of the earth, and will transcend to a higher plane.

However, at other times, astral spirits are unrelated or unknown to the host or hostess, and may attach and cause physical or emotional symptoms in that person. Many of these spirits, when queried, arc not aware they are dead, and once they are made aware of this fact they will usually readily be released to a higher plane and return to God (Source) to continue their spiritual evolution.

Next, I will discuss the 2nd category of spirit attachment and possession, that of demonic spirits, including a brief historical review of the belief in demonic possession.

Historical Review of the Belief in Spirit Possession

Throughout history, many people and cultures have believed in the existence of spirits, which is termed animism. The early writings of the Chinese, Egyptians, Hebrews, and Greeks reflected their understanding that most sickness, both physical and mental, was caused by evil spirits or demons.

According to Rollo May (*Love and Will*, 2007), the word demon originated from the ancient Greek "daimon," and referred to a divine spirit, divinity or manifestation of divine power, either good or evil. It represented a combination of both creative and destructive energies and was used interchangeably with the word "theos," meaning God. A daimonic person was one who was inspired by a daimon, an indwelling spirit or genius. Poets and artists such as Blake, Yeats, and Picasso directly attributed their creative inspiration to daimons. Later, the form was changed to daemon (Latin) and referred to influence or possession by only evil spirits, which reflects the popular usage up to the present time. The taming or integration of one's daimons results in happiness or "eudaimonism" in the Greek. Daimon is also curiously similar to the word diamond, or clear crystalline light, which is often associated with the highest and clearest light emanations of the Divine/Source/Creator energies. I believe the hidden meaning encoded within the word Diamond is "Divine I Am MONaD, which refers to the individualized Divine I AM spark or DIA – Monad at the time of creation. This spark of diamond light, which is in the heart chamber of all human beings, exists also in the "darkest" of demonic spirits, as this very spark of light is the link that connects them to Source or God/dess, and allows for their return to and reintegration with the undifferentiated *pure* light of All That Is for further purification and evolution. Truly, darkness is only the absence of light, as scientifically darkness per se cannot be measured, only the degree of presence of light (photon) particles. In *Remarkable Healings* (1997), Shakuntala Modi describes in detail an archetypal and beautiful representative example of the release of a demonic spirit. The spirit release involved expansion of the light "spark" within the entity, empowered by healing angels and brilliant white light. The demonic spirit actually saw this very spark or "star" of light expanded within itself and the light transformed and absorbed all of its darkness.

Ken Page in *The Hidden Side of the Soul* (1991) located over forty-two references in the Bible, primarily in Matthew, Mark and Luke, of the exorcism of demonic spirits by Jesus the Christ. His primary method was to raise the lower vibrational energy into greater love through the power of the spoken word (logos), transmuting it into a higher vibration.

Although the majority of references to the battle over human souls by the Archangelic and angelic legions of Light and Darkness, led respectively by Archangels Michael and Lucifer, were removed by the Catholic Church at the Second Council of Nicaea in the 6th Century A.D., *The Book of Enoch* makes reference to the war in the heavens that ensued after Archangel Lucifer and one-third of the heavenly host were cast out of heaven by Archangel Michael. *The Book of Enoch* was believed to have been written in the 2nd Century B.C. and originally appeared written in a Semitic language, probably Aramaic. It was popular for around five hundred years, and copies of manuscripts were translated into Greek and Ethiopian. A recent discovery of the book was found among the Dead Sea Scrolls in Qumran (Prophet, 1984).

Belief that mental or physical disease conditions were caused by negative spirit attachment or possession has since waxed and waned throughout history. During the Middle Ages, primarily from 500 A.D. to 1500 A.D., but extending into the 1700s, there was a resurgence of belief in spirit possession which has, for the most part, since fallen out of favor (Baldwin, 2002).

Interestingly, though, William James, one of the great psychological minds of the late 19th century, believed in demoniacal possession and stated:

"The refusal of modern enlightenment to treat possession as a hypothesis to be spoken of as even possible, in spite of the massive human tradition based on concrete experience in its favor, has always seemed to me a curious example of the power of fashion in things scientific. That the demon-theory will have its innings again is to my mind absolutely certain" (James, 1996).

To wit, several modern psychologists have made significant contributions to our understanding of spirit possession and release. Edith Fiore, Ph.D., previously mentioned in chapter eight as a psychologist who does past life regression therapy, also authored The *Unquiet Dead: A Psychologist Treats Spirit Possession* (1995). I would also like to highlight two other outstanding authors in the field of the treatment of spirit possession: Shakuntala Modi, M.D., a psychiatrist and author of *Remarkable Healings* (1997) and William Baldwin, D.D.S., Ph.D., a dentist turned psychologist and author of *Spirit Releasement Therapy* (2002). Both books are voluminous and provide a wealth of information on the causes, symptoms, manifestations, and subcategories of various types of spirit influence, attachment and possession. Both books include a broad array of verbatim transcripts and case studies highlighting the techniques and nuances of spirit release therapy. I would highly recommend these two tomes to the reader interested in more in-depth study on this topic. The following is a summary of some of Dr. Modi's and Dr. Baldwin's findings.

In *Remarkable Healings* (1997), Dr. Modi systematically analyzed a sample of 100 cases out of hundreds of patients she had treated with spirit releasement, as well as soul integration and past life regression therapies. She categorized clients based on presenting primary and secondary psychological symptoms, as well as physical symptoms. Depression, generalized anxiety disorder, panic attacks, psychotic features, manic-depression, fears and phobias were the most common psychological problems. The most common physical symptoms were headaches, neck and back pain, general aches and pains, allergies, weight problems, PMS, and gastro-intestinal symptoms. She found that about eighty percent of the primary and thirty percent of the secondary symptoms were caused by possessing spirits and soul fragmentation. Her average percentage of cure of treated primary and secondary symptoms was an astounding ninety-two percent, based on an average of three spirit release sessions per patient.

Similarly, in a sample of clients from Dr. Baldwin's transpersonally oriented clinical practice, more than eighty percent showed signs of spirit attachment. After the spirit releasement procedures, seventy percent reported improvements via reduction of their original presenting problems or symptoms (*Spirit Releasement Therapy*, 2002).

Dr. Modi's and Dr. Baldwin's results, although not controlled clinical studies, strongly support the value of doing spirit release work of attached spirits as part of a total treatment approach, and as an effective form of treatment for a wide range of common acute and chronic psychological and physical (somatic) ailments.

Additionally, the international spiritual organization Sukyo Mahikari, originating in Japan, believes that approximately eighty percent of physical, emotional, mental and spiritual dis-ease symptoms are related to spirit attachment (Tebecis, 2000). Persons can receive light at a Mahikari center to facilitate purification and spirit release.

How and Why Spirit Attachment Occurs

Attached spirits can range in influence from partial or intermittent attachment (moving in and out of the person's physical body and aura) to full attachment and one hundred percent possession. Nonetheless, they are often "invisible" to that person or others due to the absence of any overt symptoms.

Spirit attachment takes place under a variety of circumstances. It can occur when there is weakness, illness, and/or holes in one's auric field and or subtle energy bodies. Our subtle bodies are in a weakened or vulnerable state when we are experiencing directly or witnessing any form of abuse, or while in a state of fear or shock, such as at the scene of a death (when the spirit of another person is released from the body). During episodes of physical abuse or sexual abuse, the intense physical and/or emotional pain leads to one's spirit leaving their physical body. This phenomena is often reported by victims of painful sexual abuse or rape, when they describe "leaving their body," or "floating above their body and watching," because the pain is too much to bear. This leaves their physical body open to intrusion and attachment by the same type of angry, abusive spirit that is often transferred from the perpetrator to the victim of abuse.

Spirit attachment can even occur when there is movement in and out of the body cavities such as when eating food, having sex, or going to the bathroom, or during surgery or physical injury/accidents.

Spirit attachment can occur during the sleep state, since during sleep, everyone's spirit body leaves the physical body and travels on the astral or other planes. When one's spirit has temporarily travelled out of the physical body, discarnate astral or demonic spirits may attach or attack when a person is more vulnerable and less consciously aware during sleep and dreaming.

Finally, frequent or heavy use of alcohol or drugs creates a weakening of the etheric body, which can also leave people vulnerable to negative spirit attachment.

The Principle of "Like Attracts Like" or the Law of Similars

Strong negative emotional states of anger, greed, jealousy, envy, and lust can attract like-type discarnate spirits or demons, which can subsequently attach to the person who "matches" their vibrational frequency. If the person has significant core unresolved emotional-mental issues, these energetic patterns act to magnetically attract similar or "like type" energies, including other people as well as spirits. For example, a person with an alcohol addiction will attract other alcoholics who have similar thought, feeling and behavioral patterns, and likewise attract the same type of beings from the spirit realm.

A person with significant core unresolved anger and depression issues will attract and be comfortable with other similar people who are angry, depressed and like to indulge in expressions of anger, complaining, criticizing, etc. According to the same "Law of Similars" as Plato referred to it, they will attract discarnate spirits who are primarily angry and/or depressed, as well.

Conversely, discarnate spirits may also spontaneously detach themselves from their human hosts, if the underlying energetic "resonance" patterns do not sufficiently match to sustain attachment. That is why it is important (and often necessary) to heal and release the core unresolved issue (anger, low-self-esteem, depression, etc.) that allowed for the possession to occur in the first place, and permitted the attachment to continue to persist over time. Otherwise, if a spirit release is done first, the weakness in the physical, emotional, mental and/or spiritual bodies of the person who had an attached spirit will usually attract the same or a similar spirit entity, once again.

Baldwin (2002) has found that in approximately half of the cases he has treated, there is no "personal" connection with the host/ess, and the attachment is a random event that occurs when there is a weakening or opening in the physical or subtle energy bodies of the individual. He also believes, as I do, that almost all people will have some form of spirit influence or attachment at some time.

Manifestations of Influence, Attachment or Possession by Demonic Spirits

If one has a possessing demonic spirit, it will usually be present and manifest itself frequently or periodically within the person's thoughts, feelings and behavior, such as with obsessive/compulsive/addictive issues with food, smoking, alcohol, drugs, sex, gambling or shopping. The negative or demonic spirit is generally responsible for the strong urges or insatiable cravings for a particular physical/material substance or experience to induce the "high" or an extremely pleasurable state.

After demonic entities are released, the person will typically notice he is not "driven", although he may still have some of the same thoughts of indulging in the habit or addiction. However, the left over energy is notably minus the drive, intensity or craving to perform the desired behavior. This makes it much easier for the person to develop self-control and further reduce the unwanted thought, feeling and behavior patterns.

Extreme anger and rage, with acts of verbal abuse, physical violence or sexual abuse/incest/rape are also often manifestations of negative spirit influence or possession, usually of demonic spirits. In schizophrenia, schizoaffective disorder and bipolar disorder with psychotic features, where there are auditory hallucinations in which the person is hearing voices that are usually persecutory or grandiose (associated with manic states), this typically indicates a strong negative, often demonic spirit attachment.

Due to the fact that the vibrational frequencies of the earth and all its inhabitants are continuously speeding up, it is now easier to "spot" attached discarnate entities or demonic spirits, because the higher frequencies of light literally illuminate all of one's shadow aspects, including attached spirits, and bring them into the light of awareness. As such, it is increasingly easier for more healers with inner sense abilities to elicit and facilitate spirit release.

Command Exorcism vs. Compassionate Spirit Release

The traditional and most well known form of exorcism or spirit release can be described as "command" exorcism. This is when a priest, minister, shaman, healer or the person afflicted calls in the power of their own spirit (by whatever names), God and/or other higher Spirit energies to command out the attached or possessing "evil spirit." M. Scott Peck, in his book *People of the Lie* (2006) describes this type of exorcism from the Catholic perspective. The ritual of exorcism as traditionally practiced by the Roman Catholic Church is premised on an attitude of judgment and condemnation of the demonic or negative entity and consists of overpowering it with the forces of God, Jesus or other beings of Light, to forcibly drive out the demon, without recognizing the Divine (daemonic) spark within them, and returning them to the Light of God. Such traditional exorcistic practices do not abide by the Cosmic Laws of Love and Free Will for all beings (including spirits), and therefore are not based on the highest spiritual principles.

Let's take a closer look at this type of exorcistic method, and the spiritual principles (or lack thereof) it expresses. Command exorcism is premised on the principle of "might makes right," which is overpowering the forces of darkness with the forces of light. The analogy I have repeatedly been given to illustrate this point is that of the playground bully. If one is being harassed by a playground bully (analogous to a negative attached spirit) and calls in his friends to beat up or overpower and drive out the bully (analogous to calling in and aligning with the forces of light), this represents a misuse of power and violation of the free will of the spirit.

Although the exorcism may be successful, what are the principles that have been utilized? The use of sheer force of the power of Light (even in the name of God) for it's own sake, is premised on viewing the process as a battle (or war) between the forces of good and evil. By using this approach to exorcism, we are utilizing a method that promotes benevolent misuse of power. At the highest level of God/dess consciousness, embodying the principles of Love and Free Will for all beings, there is no war, and there is no battle with the forces of darkness. There is only love, compassion, and assistance to return discarnate or demonic entities back to Source.

The modern Spirit Release techniques of other practitioners such as Baldwin, Modi, and Fiore are based on love and compassion toward the demonic spirit, and are premised on the understanding of the commonality and frequency of spirit attachment and possession phenomena, along with the broad range of possible effects or symptoms. Strictly speaking, the therapist or client does not have to believe in the existence of discarnate astral or demonic spirits per se, but simply follow the recommended QTH guided imagery (or hypnosis) process to open dialogue with the spirit. Then, the therapist can facilitate the spirit's understanding of truth that it is either 1) lost or confused (as with discarnate spirits), or 2) deluded (demonics), and then release the spirit back to Source.

Techniques and Approaches to Releasing Attached Spirits

William Baldwin, D.D.S., Ph.D., in his comprehensive and thorough book *Spirit Releasement Therapy: A Technique Manual* (2002), outlines six steps of Spirit Releasement Therapy for spirits of deceased (earthbound) humans:

1. Discovering and identification of any attached discarnate spirits or entities,
2. Differential diagnosis of the spirit – as an earth bound discarnate, demonic (satanic), or other non-physical being,
3. Dialogue with the spirit,

4. Release of the Spirit into the Light,
5. Sealing Light Meditation,
6. Ongoing Therapy.

He states that the purpose of dialoguing with the spirit is fourfold:

1. To resolve any physical needs or emotional issues that have kept the discarnate astral spirit trapped on the earth plane,
2. To discover the particular details of circumstances, such as when and how the spirit became attached to the client,
3. To uncover the client's susceptibility or weakness (unresolved issues) that allowed the original attachment,
4. To determine the specific effects of or influence the attached spirit has had on the client.

Spirits of discarnate humans are relatively easy to release, once they understand that (1) they are deceased (which they are usually unaware of) , and (2) they realize that it is necessary for their spiritual evolution (and that of the host) to detach and return to the light (Creator Source).

Discarnate astral spirits of deceased humans often retain the memory of details of their former life such as gender, age at the time of their death, etc. They can impart similar physical or emotional problems, and mental judgments or belief systems, as well as preferences, habits or addictions on their human host.

From his extensive work in spirit releasement therapy, Baldwin lists three primary deceptions of dark, demonic spirits, which are used by their superiors (Lucifer, Beelzebub, Satan, etc.) to force them into absolute obedience and control.

1. They are told there is nothing in them but darkness (instead of the truth that they contain a spark of God (light) within them).
2. They are threatened with annihilation or destruction if they defect to the Light.
3. They are told to fear the light, that it burns and they should stay away from it.

It is therefore important to re-educate demonic spirits that all beings or spirits were created by God, with an individualized spark of light within them. Light (and love) is literally the magnetic energy at a quantum physics level that results in sufficient coherence (particle integration) to create an individuated spirit or a separate, distinct entity. Since at their core, they are light, letting them know this in a calm, loving manner and that all spirits are eventually returned to the Source (pure diamond white light) from whence they came, helps to correct their prior (deceptive) programming.

Next, I will discuss some important topics pertaining to therapist requirements for doing spirit release work.

Therapist Requirements for Doing Spirit Release Work: Releasing Disbelief

Just as in traditional forms of psychotherapy, as one evolves as a therapist and continues to hear increasingly dramatic or horrendous stories of physical and sexual abuse, rape, mutilations and violence during war, etc., the therapist is challenged to accept (often without any validation or proof) the client's narrative as real and valid and release his/her own sense of disbelief or incredulity. Psychologically speaking, it is not necessary to have proof or establish the validity of the content of the client's story, but only to understand that this is a real and valid expression of their own psyche. Just as the content of dreams is a product and expression of the unconscious (but may not necessarily be "real" or factual); the dreaming is nonetheless a real and valid expression of the unworked through personal content manifesting through fears, or desires, etc., and psychological templates or archetypal themes of that person's psyche.

Therapist Requirements for Spirit Release Work: Releasing Fear and Judgment

The therapist engaging in spirit release work must abide by the professional and ethical standards of integrity, confidentiality, personal and professional boundaries, and must be an open-minded unbiased non-critical observer of what appears and unfolds in the session. Training and experience in hypnosis or guided imagery work, which are essentially the same on physiological (increased relaxation) and neuro-physiological levels (increased alpha, theta and/or delta brainwaves), is a desired (and some would argue a necessary) pre-requisite for doing spirit release work.

If the therapist experiences any negative emotional responses such as fear, revulsion, anger, etc., or on the mental level, disbelief or judgment, it is a signal that the therapist has additional work to do. What is indicated is the need for self-introspection, and acceptance of that particular type of human/spirit expression or experience, or perhaps one's own self-healing of the same or a similar problem or issue, whether or not it is related directly to spirit attachment.

Therapist Requirements for Spirit Release Work: Treating Demonic Spirits

More than any other category of Quantum Transformational Healing, doing spirit release work, especially with demonic spirits, requires a firm foundation and anchoring at higher levels of Light, unconditional love, and non-judgment based on a deep, inner experiential knowingness of the truth that God created all beings and spirits and loves all equally.

A test of readiness to do release of powerful dark demonic spirits is whether one can know and *feel* the truth that God loves Archangel Michael as much as Lucifer or, to use a human level example of extremes of polarity, that God loves Hitler as much as Mother Theresa. If in your heart, you do not resonate with these levels of truth, I would not recommend attempting spirit release work with dark demonics or other very evil entities.

When the therapist encounters a demonic spirit in the course of doing QTH, she needs to access and hold the aforementioned state of God/dess consciousness of unconditional love and non-judgment before proceeding. This can be accomplished by doing a meditation (along with the client), such as steps one through four from the *Spiritual Alignment, Christ Integration, Transmutation and Protection* process, outlined in chapter two on spiritual self development.

Language Patterns that Facilitate Spirit Emergence

Oftentimes, the client or therapist may not necessarily believe in the existence of spirits. Or, actual identification of the source of a particular problem as related to spirit attachment may be disturbing to the client. In these cases it is best to use a term acceptable to the client and congruent with his/her current belief system. I frequently use the word "part" instead of the term "spirit" to refer to specific aspects of what the client identifies as the problem or issue. For example, the therapist can say "I'd like to talk to the part of you that (refer to client's description of the symptom) gets you to drink, gives you migraine headaches, causes you to have angry, violent outbursts, take drugs, etc." Use of the term "part" is a wonderfully non-specific term and can allow for the emergence of whatever aspect of the person's psyche needs expression.

If the part is in fact an aspect of their own soul, spirit, or human self, then instead of being released, it will automatically become integrated into their Hu-man personality self. As previously mentioned in chapter five on QTH, aspects that are part of the person's unique soul, spirit, or human personality self can include unhealed childhood or adult issues, past parallel/future lives, and they can be any specific physical, emotional, mental, or spiritual issue that is part of his/her unique soul template. Ask the part: "Are you a part of _____ (name of person's) soul?" If it is not the case, they almost invariably will admit that they are a separate spirit. Further questioning can determine the type of distinct spirit: "Are you the spirit of a deceased human (another human being who died), a demonic spirit, or another type of non-physical entity?" This is an example of another language pattern that can be used to identify the particular type of spirit/entity.

"Parts" that are <u>not</u> an aspect of that person's soul or spirit include discarnate spirits, demonic spirits, or other entities, and also spiritual implants, which will be addressed in chapter ten. In sum, (1) Parts that belong to the soul/spirit of the person are healed and *integrated*; (2) Parts <u>not</u> belonging to the unique soul of that individual are healed and *released*.

Treat Spirits Like People

During spirit release work, one of the principles is "treat spirits like people." Just as if you are introduced to a new person who may be fearful, angry, or refusing to talk with you, it is important to first and foremost express on nonverbal and energetic levels an attitude of welcoming, loving, unconditional acceptance and respect. Any discomfort, fear or judgment on the part of the therapist will telepathically be picked up by the spirit, and interfere or block communication and release of the attached entity.

Here are two preparatory healing techniques that can be used to literally "lighten up," integrate and heal dark entities (DEs).

#1 Integration of Polarities Technique:

If you are dealing with a "Dark" entity (DE) or demon of the male polarity, pick a "Light" female polarity being *at the same or preferably a higher power level* (vibrational frequency) to do the integration (and vice versa – for a female DE, use a male Light being). This creates integration of 2 polarities/dualities simultaneously, i.e. dark and light, male and female (which heals the original split from the time of creation into dualities).

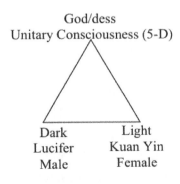

Figure 9-1

In the example above, since Lucifer is a "Dark" Archangel, I used Kuan Yin, who is a female on the Karmic Board. You could also use a female Archangel (called Archaei), Elohim or Cosmic Master for integration. Pick a Light Being you have a close connection or alignment with. Align with your own Divine "I AM" self, then

A.   (1) <u>If the DE is an aspect of your own soul</u> (i.e. – a past/parallel/future life aspect), integrate the Light Being *within* you. (2) Call forth the DE out in front of you and send love (pink light) or Unconditional Love (magenta light) energetically by visualizing pink or magenta flowing from your heart, extending love, mercy and forgiveness to the DE. Do this for as long as and as often (Ex: fifteen minutes per day for four weeks) as you receive inner guidance to repeat this process.

B.   (1) <u>If the DE is NOT an aspect of your own soul</u>, call forth the Light Being *in front of or above you* and the DE across from (or below) it. Send the love and light from the Light Being to the DE, as in Step number two from A above.

This and all healing processes should be done only if you *get permission from the Higher Self or God Self aspect of the DE*. Otherwise, you are violating the Law of Free Will and may suffer consequences, such as attack or "negative" energy manifestations. The lower (dark) levels of intention and purpose of Dark, unhealed energy aspects are to create fear, disempower us, kill us, etc. The highest levels of intention and purpose are to <u>get our attention</u> so they can be healed with Love, the greatest healing force in the Universe. All Lightworkers who are called to do healing work with very powerful Dark entities need to be strongly integrated with their own Divine "I AM" Self and Light Beings for their own protection. Dark entities will feed on fear and all other negative emotions (anger, aggressive retaliatory impulses, etc.) and the healer needs to clear her/ himself of all negative emotions or thought patterns before proceeding with the above process.

Very dark entities are filled with incredible self-hatred and loathing as a result of their actions and need to be reconnected with Divine Love since they have chosen to "play out" a "Dark" role separate from God/dess (Love). Remember, there is always a core of Light within the Dark, since all energies/entities were created from source (God/ dess), which is Unitary Consciousness that contains within it both the Light and Dark.

Here are the steps to the 2nd technique I use to work with DEs.

#2 Color Ray Healing for Integration of Christ Consciousness, Activation of the Divine "I AM" Self, and Ascension

1. Align with your Divine "I AM" Self,
2. Call forth the DE to be healed in front of you,
3. Visualize a sphere of clear white or golden-white (GW) light around the DE (for Divine Alignment),
4. Visualize violet light (for transmutation) around the DE within the white (or golden white) light sphere,
5. Visualize the Three-Fold-Flame in the heart of the DE and expand it to about five inches,
6. Then, visualize the Ascension Flame (pink and gold combined) encompassing the DE, and expand it outward. The Ascension Flame increases the Divine Love and Wisdom rays, and this reduces the likelihood that the DE will further misuse power, (since its blue power ray is already in excess of its love and wisdom),
7. Ask permission of the DE to integrate its Divine "I AM Self." If granted, then call for the integration of the Divine "I AM" self of the DE and visualize a tube of white light around the DE going up to Source (God/dess).

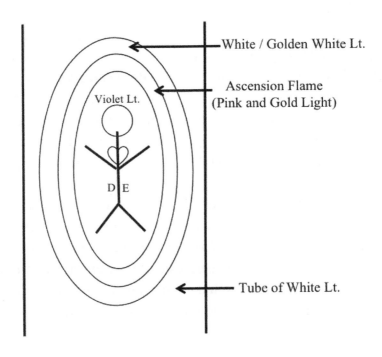

Figure 9-2

These 2 techniques effectively create 3 levels of Integration, with their corresponding integration triangles depicted below:

1. Human (male and female)

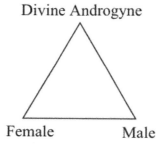

2. Christ Consciousness (Balanced: Love, Wisdom & Power)

3. God/dess Consciousness

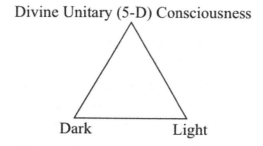

Figure 9-3

Next, I would like to present the basic summary and script for doing spirit release work, which can be used in conjunction with the standard QTH model.

Spirit Release: Basic Summary and Script

1. Do steps one through three from the *Spiritual Alignment, Christ Integration, Transmutation and Protection Meditation* in chapter two. This maximizes the likelihood of a successful spirit release, because it brings more light, love, and transmutation into and around the body of the person and "lightens" up the attached spirit in preparation for release. The light also tends to agitate the spirit so it can be more easily sensed (seen, heard, and felt) by the person to whom it is attached.

2. Make sure that you and any other person helping you with the spirit release are strongly aligned with their Inner/Higher Self and/or Spiritual Guides. All fear, hate, judgment, or resistance will block communication with and release of the spirit. These negative emotions must be replaced by love, compassion, and often an understanding of the "hidden positive function" of the spirit. Try to ascertain the spirit's power level and the level of attachment, from infrequent influence to the extreme of full, one hundred percent possession. If you have a very powerful dark or demonic spirit, you will most likely need to effectively call in Archangel Michael and other beings at the Ascended Master, Archangel, Elohim or Cosmic Master level for assistance to match or exceed the power of darkness and anchor more love and light. Also, you may call for "human reinforcements," i.e. have other Lightworkers present to "hold the field," to assist in strengthening the focus of love and light to create a successful spirit release.

3. Now, call forth the attached spirit in the name of your Inner/Higher Self or Divine "I AM" Self and/or spiritual guides. Say "In the name of my I/HS/Divine I AM Self and/or name all spirit helpers present, I call forth in love and light the spirit that _____ (name function/effects of spirit)." Attached negative spirits typically create compulsions or addictions to sex, food, alcohol, drugs, cigarettes, material things, gambling, etc. They need to attach to a human host to experience the vicarious pleasure through the host's body, since they no longer have a physical body. Send love energetically to the spirit and/or visualize surrounding it in pink light (Divine Love). Pink and gold light (the Ascension Flame) and/or violet light (for transmutation) can also be used. Keep sending love to the spirit and ask it if it will talk with you (telepathically). Continue to embrace it with love and compassion, understanding that you made an agreement

with it, and recognizing it has assisted you in some positive, albeit hidden way. Ask the attached spirit "What do you want?" If the answer is not positive, ask "What do you want at your highest level of intention and purpose?" Optional questions "When did you first attach to me?" "What are some of the ways you have influenced me throughout my life?" etc. Inform the spirit that it is dead, and you are two separate souls (if it does not know this), and that you have decided to change agreements with it - and assist it in a journey to the Light, to return to God (Source), so that both of you may evolve separately. Ask the spirit "Who can help you to get what you want?" Then ask your I/HS or Spirit helper to go any where in the universe to give the attached spirit what it wants.

4. After you have asked any questions of the attached spirit, ask it if it is now ready to return to the light. If not, ask it what else it would want (or need) to be ready to be released. Note: Powerful, dark and demonic attached spirits may want to more fully tell their story, and may wish to receive more love and acknowledgment for being masters at whatever their main role(s) and function(s) were. Also, they may frequently give the host/ess homework assignments to take more spiritual responsibility for him/herself, before they will leave. Often the positive helping function of the attached spirit needs to be reassigned to either the I/HS of the person, or another positive Spiritual Guide, Angel, etc., before the attaching spirit will agree to be released.

5. After all the requirements of the attaching spirit are fulfilled, which may take several weeks or months of "homework assignments," and multiple therapy sessions, ask if it is now ready to be released into the Light. If it is ready, then imagine a tunnel of light, going up to Source, with a brilliant white light at the end of the tunnel (this is a bridge from the 3rd to 5th density). Thank your attached spirit for assisting you with _____ (name the hidden positive function), and say goodbye to it. Wait and observe if it actually moves into and up through the tunnel of light. Ask it if it needs an angel, Archangel, or other spiritual being to accompany it as it travels up the light tunnel and returns to Source. Check if you can see, hear or feel that the spirit has actually left and ascended through the tunnel of light back to Source.

6. Due to a void being left by the release of the attached spirit, check your body and energy field (aura) for holes, and surround yourself with bright golden white or crystalline, diamond white light, to seal off your body and aura, and prevent other unwanted negative energies or spirits from entering.

Next, I will present three case studies of spirit release work.

Spirit Release Session 9-1

Alice had been in therapy for several months prior to this session. She had originally sought help to reduce her chronic low-grade depression (dysthymia), slightly overweight condition, obsessive thinking patterns about food and her appearance, and relationship problems with her husband. This session uncovers and releases an unexpected demonic spirit that was underlying her low self-esteem, self-criticism, and depression.

T: Spiritual Alignment, Open Inner Sight and Hearing, Locate IPOP.

C: It's on a hill. There's a bunch of grass that leads to a huge riverbank. I'm on a porch that overhangs the river.

T: Now I'd like you to call forth your Inner Self, Full Potential Self, or one of your Spiritual Guides.

C: She's my Full Potential Self." (FPS)

T: What is she like?

C: She's thin, wearing a hat…a sheik little hat that matches her outfit. She's on a cell phone (client cries). She's very successful, she's not as lonely and she's happier…she looks intimidating, more distant.

Generally a person's FPS would not be intimidating or distant. This is a projection of her unhealed human self who would currently be intimidated and keep her distance from more successful women.

T: Ask your FPS what is the most beneficial problem or issue to work on today?

C: She says it's that I didn't feel emotionally secure even when I was thin. (client says she feels her body going backwards.) She (FPS) says to write about it.

When someone experiences spontaneous sensations of their body moving in space (ex. spinning) or in this case, going backwards, it usually represents a corresponding shift or movement in consciousness, akin to somatic and perceptual alterations in kundalini awakening.

T: Ask your FPS to help you find where in your body you're feeling the emotional insecurity.

C: It starts in my head…my criticalness of my nose, my arms, my stomach, my inner thighs…

T: What does it look like?

C: It's black…deformed…kind of a round shape…like a demon…it screams at me and makes me feel ugly and disgusting.

If someone who is unfamiliar with seeing attached spirits (as she was) says, "It looks like a demon," it probably is.

T: How long has this been with you?

C: It's been in my head since I started hiding from my father…in my closet…in the 7th grade. It tells me, "You're fat, you're stupid, you're a slob."

This suggests that the demon attached to her when she was in the 7th grade, in a fear state hiding from her father's critical remarks in her closet.

T: What does it want?

C: It wants me to be miserable, never to succeed or be happy…or lead my own life. It makes me look in the mirror 20x a night. (pause) It's teasing me… (client has realization) I got sucked into or tricked into believing in someone or being someone I'm not…it's my punishment.

The lowest, or negative intentions of the entity/energy.

T: What does this part want at its highest level of intention and purpose for you?

C: It wants me to keep striving…working toward what I want. It wants me to work hard to become something wonderful. But somehow that feels selfish…it won't be easy. It's too old and set in it's ways…like my father.

Here she has the insight that her fear (false expectations appearing real) led her to taking on an energy complex of limiting beliefs about herself.
Another suggestion that this energy/entity originated from her father.

T: Can your FPS or someone else help it to get what it really wants?

C: It doesn't want help. It's not going to talk anymore.

T: Send it love from your heart. Embrace the black round shape in your head with love. If you like, visualize pink light which represents love and forgiveness enfolding it, embracing it so that it feels it's safe to talk.

A good example of the power of love to melt resistance using focused intention and color healing (pink light representing love, compassion, and forgiveness).

C: Client sends love as instructed.

T: (waits) Will it talk with you now?

C: No, it won't.

T: Send more love, just keep sending it love. (repeats two more times)

C: It's like light from my soul came from my eyes and went around it to secure and embrace it.

Her own more loving spiritual (soul) aspect becomes activated by continuing to focus on sending love from her heart.

C: The more love I put in it, the more black gets pushed out.

The black getting "pushed out" is evidence that the transformation is already beginning, simply from sending love.

T: That's great! Is it willing to receive help now?

C: Yes, it's more open now.

This is a good example of how one needs to continue to send love until the resistance is dissolved.

T: Can your FPS or someone else go anywhere in the universe now to find what it needs so it can get what it really wants, it's positive intention? What would that look like?

C: I see a bright light…white and shiny."

Although we do not know or query who or what the bright white light is, it is more than likely a spirit appearing as a ball of light.

T: What shape is it?

C: The same…like a circle.

T: Is the black round shape in your head willing to receive help from the bright white light?

C: Yes.

T: Is the bright white light willing to help the black round shape?"

C: Yes it is.

T: Then see the white light moving into your head and absorbing all the black energy.

C: Client visualizes integration.

In a typical spirit release, a helper spirit escorts the attached spirit back to God. This has probably occurred, although it was not described by the client or directed by me as part of the guided transformational process.

T: Now, breathe the white light up and down, through your whole body. What does this transformation look like?	Physical integration
C: It doesn't look evil anymore…All the black is gone…	In saying "all the black is gone," the release of the attached evil or demon energy is very likely complete.
T: What does it feel like?	
C: It feels clean…not as heavy.	Emotional integration
T: Does your FPS have any messages or assignments for you?	Mental integration
C: It tells me not to give up. To do the things I enjoy and the other things will come in time…and to be patient.	Doing things that she enjoys is a way of nurturing herself and literally bringing in more joy so she will be more open to accept greater success and happiness in her life in the future.

This QTH session was a breakthrough for Alice, and she began to feel less critical and depressed, and more self – loving, and hopeful about her future after the session.

Spirit Release Session 9-2

Christopher was a spiritual older gentleman, who had been seen for help with depression and relationship problems. In this QTH session, he spontaneously accessed two "carnal" or sexual entities or spirits. One was completely released and the second one was not able to be released that day. This session illustrates how having one attached spirit opens the door for "like type" spirits to attach, and become "nested" even in unexpected, less vulnerable circumstances.

One of the carnal spirits, which was probably demonic, attached to him when he was sexually abused by an older woman as a very young boy. The second attachment was a discarnate astral spirit of a teenage boy who was killed in a car accident, and who attached to the client when he was at the scene of the accident. Notice the relatively benign desire of this boy's spirit, who wanted to attach to a human body so he could vicariously experience and "get good at sex".

T: Client is guided to his IPOP and asked to connect with his I/H Self or Guide(s).

C: I'm feeling something shift in my spine. It's making me feel more grounded and centered. Now I'm seeing a blue light...it's turning into a blue man.

Although I did not query further about the blue man, he clairsentiently felt positive to me, congruent with the client's feeling grounded and centered. It's a good idea to ask, when in doubt, although spirits will usually reveal themselves in their words and functions later as helpers or guides, vs. shadow aspects that need to be released.

T: Send a feeling of love and gratitude to the blue man, and ask him what his name is.

C: Now I'm getting sexual images interfering. He's a sexual being, he's thinking about leaving...He's a red man...he's exposing himself, says he can't get any action.

T: What does he want?

C: He's got an insatiable sexual appetite. A sexual terror. He likes cunnilingus...a real compulsive sexual driver. He's been patiently waiting for me to get some sex. (client has not had sex with a woman for many years) He's a miserable little fucker. Doesn't give a shit about nobody or nothing. Likes things "screwed up." He just wants to get the goods sexually.

The fact that the red man exposed himself and has an "insatiable" sexual appetite, are suggestive of a demonic spirit.

This is his human self-expressing in a judgmental way, comments about the carnal entity.

T: What does he want at his highest level of intention and purpose?

C: He wants to go back to God, not to have to suffer and be so sexually frustrated.

T: When did this "red man" become attached to you?

C: When I was three or four...I was roughed up by a lady...in her house and yard. She was possessed...hysterical, crazy (client has realization of connection to his behavior). That's when I started looking at Esquire Magazine...at nude pictures. Now I'm seeing a teenager...a blonde guy...he was hit by a car...and killed...He was at the peak of his sexuality...he wanted to get good at it. He had just started having sex right before he was killed.

Carnal spirits usually become attached to a human body when the person is in a state of fear or other strong negative emotion, such as when being sexually molested or assaulted.

At this point, we do not have any idea what the blond guy relates to.

T: Does the blonde guy who was killed have anything to do with the red man?

C: They both think I'm boring – because I've had no (sexual) relationships. They want big time thrills. They want novelty thrills. I'm not the big time. And the blonde guy is inept... he's trying to get good at it.

T: Is the blonde guy a separate attached spirit?

C: Yes...it's because when I was twelve, I was at the scene of the accident when he was killed. He wanted to live...so he could get good at sex.

T: What does the blond guy want at his highest level of intention?

C: He wants to have a body...so he can get good at sex.

T: Can you tell him he's a separate soul, and that he needs to go back to God...back up to the light...and then he can come back in another body...so he can get what he wants?

C: Now the blue man's chanting Hare Krishna. The red man doesn't like sound therapy... not those squeaky crazy sounds. (Client is referring to the Sound Energy Research tape he has been using). He's laughing... a nervous laugh. The blue man told him (the red man) to wear a cross around his neck.

T: Are the red man and the blonde guy ready to go back to God?

C: The blonde guy is...but not the red man... he will probably leave later. The blonde guy wants a full life exploring sexuality. He was a young soul...he wants to learn and explore. He was mad when he was killed.

T: Is the blonde guy ready to go back to the light now?

C: Yes.

A logical question to attempt to clarify the relation and function of these two spirit beings.

Most likely, the state of fear activated by seeing a dead body, blood, etc. following a car accident, allowed the blond guy's spirit to attach to this client, since he had another like-type energy/entity already attached.

Client doesn't answer question because of distraction from activity of the red man receiving help (chanting and suggestion from the blue man).

This is another way of asking which spirit(s) are ready to be released.

Returned to earlier question that wasn't answered.

T: Then imagine a tunnel filled with bright white light – going back to God...back to Source. Just allow the blonde guy to be released into the light of the tunnel and go back to God. (pause for approximately one minute).

C: He's gone...He's gone up through the tunnel.

T: Now surround yourself with brilliant golden white light...thanking the blue man for his help and the red man for making himself known and open to receiving help. Remember to continue to assist the red man to be free by chanting, doing your meditation and spiritual practices, and using your sound therapy tapes. This will help the red man to be released in the future by raising your vibrational rate and balancing your four energy bodies.

The actual spirit release was relatively quick in this case because the spirit of the blonde guy was very ready to be released.

I reiterate the suggestions from the blue man to facilitate future release of the red (carnal) entity.

Due to lack of time in this particular session, further integration on physical, emotional, mental, and spiritual levels was not able to be accomplished. However, there was a sense of surety that the release or exorcism of the "blonde guy" spirit was complete. If the therapist has any doubt, she can always re-check with the I/H Self or Guide in a future session.

Notice that the initial attachment of the stronger, darker spirit occurred earlier (age three or four), and is very likely demonic based on the client describing it as exhibiting "an insatiable sexual appetite," and being "a sexual terror" and a "compulsive sexual driver." Again, if there are intense strong cravings, compulsions or addictions to an activity or substance, there are almost always one or more "demonic" spirits.

Spirit Release Session 9-3

This next session was Leilani's first experience with QTH. She was an extremely bright graduate student, spiritually gifted and an active Buddhist practitioner. On an interpersonal level, she had problems with creating dependencies with others by being an excessive "giver," but she was also was very outspoken and strongly opinionated.

T: Spiritual Alignment, Open Inner Vision and Hearing, Locate IPOP.

C: I'm seeing what looks like mud...brown or grey, fine particles at my crown. Above the top of my head there's a dark cloud...grey-black, (D_1) that's lighter in density. It's softer and more permeable.

As sometimes happens at the beginning of a QTH session, the client accesses an unhealed "dark" energy complex prior to accessing a clear source of guidance and healing (I/H self or guide).

T: Just allow these images to fade and focus now on finding your IPOP. A place where you can feel safe and peaceful, seeing the colors, hearing the sounds and feeling the energies in that IPOP. When you find the IPOP that you are most comfortable in, let me know where you are and what you're experiencing.

So, I go back to guiding her to find an IPOP.

C: I'm in Yosemite Valley. There are streams and flowers...I'm in a meadow.

T: Allow yourself to see the beauty of nature all around you. Use your inner vision to focus in...just like you're zooming in with a camera...to see the flowers...and the flowing stream. Hear the sounds of nature...and feel the deep peace and tranquility there. Take a deep breath, and imagine inhaling the scents of the plants and flowers around you. (pause) Now, I'd like you to relax your inner vision and focus in your heart center. I'd like you to open your mind and heart to the possibility of connecting with your I/H Self or one of your guides, whichever is most appropriate today. Relax your inner vision and let go of any expectations...just allowing whatever you see, or don't see... to be okay. Make a heartfelt call to your I/H Self or guides to connect with a source of clear inner guidance and healing. Look into the near distance and just allow...whatever images...perhaps unclear...or fuzzy to take shape...(pause) Do you see your I/H Self or one of your guides now?

A good example of a more detailed language pattern to guide the client into a deeper, richer inner sensory experience of her IPOP.

An example of more detailed wording to access one's I/H self or guide(s).

C: Yes, I'm seeing my grandmother... "Nana," she's one of my paternal female ancestors... now she's gesturing and introducing me to someone else...she looks like a Fairy Godmother...her name is Eva...she's

C: (cont.) beautiful…with luminous light all around her.

T: What color(s) do you see around her?

C: There's golden-white…a light blue…and turquoise.

The description of a "luminous light" and golden-white, blue and turquoise colors suggest that this is a higher clearer guide, not an unhealed energy (usually brown, grey, or black).

T: I'd like you to look in Eva's eyes… connecting to her on a soul level…and ask her if she will talk with you.

C: She says I have to help myself…I have to stop taking care of others…she says it's because I don't accept or like myself enough… that's why I don't take care of myself.

T: Where in your body is the energy of not wanting to take care of yourself located?

C: I'm not sure…

T: Just imagine being able to see into and scan your body…like x-ray vision…Ask your guide Eva to help you look within…to find where that energy is located and what color and shape it has.

Suggesting the client have "x-ray vision" is an often effective method to facilitate inner vision.

C: It's in my upper chest…I have a feeling of sadness. It's a dark brown-black color…a kind of rounded shape. (D_2).

T: Ask that brown-black roundish energy what it wants …at its highest level of intention and purpose?

C: It wants me to be healthy and happy… and to have more companionship and right relationships…and more income.

T: Can you ask Eva which energy is most important to heal first, the dark energy cloud on top of your head (D_1), or the dark energy in your upper chest (D_2)?

C: The energy on top of my head. Eva says if I take better care of myself...the dark cloud in my head (D_1) will be filled with a great golden white light...the top tier...is about uncertainty...cloudiness of purpose and lack of clarity. The bottom tier is about anger...it provides energy. She says I need clarity...so I don't run rough shod over people...related to misuse of the throat...(pause). Now Eva says we have to clear the throat...(exclaims) I feel hands around my throat! It's strangling me...it's a demon (D_3) ...screaming "Shut Up!" It reminds me of my mother's hatred for me...It wants to shut me up...It's silencing me...to keep me out of trouble with authority figures...

A third unhealed energy complex is revealed. The demon expresses its "lowest" level of intention and purpose.

T: What does the demon want at it's highest level of intention and purpose?

C: It wants me to speak with love...instead of critique.

T: Ask the demon who can assist it to get what it wants at its highest level of intention and purpose (HLIP).

C: It says Eva can help...but now he's screaming at me...he's giving me hell for all the times I've screwed up...when I don't listen to him...like when I had a confrontation with the chief judge...I can be severely critical... and obnoxious.

Here the client is referring to her work as a interpreter in the courtroom.

T: Is there anything else the demon needs to tell you?

C: No.

T: Then ask the demon if he is ready to receive help from Eva now...

C: I felt the pressure off my neck...he took his hands off.

C: Yes...Eva is telling me...she says I know how to do the Buddhist practice of chanting for the happiness of the person I'm critiquing...

C: (cont.) and to send myself love...because in my head I'm telling myself...I'm better than you...to the people I criticize...it's really an inferiority compensation...that's why she says to send love to myself.

Here, client has insight into the psychological issue underlying her criticism of others, which is always self-criticism and judgment!

T: Are there any other messages or assignments to release the demon?

C: Eva says I should write these down:
  1. To spend at least five minutes every day sending love to myself,
  2. To make it a priority to work on the issue of changing to a more positive way of speaking the truth with love,
  3. To change my attitude about the person and send love and appreciation to them,
  4. Ask for forgiveness for those I've offended through chanting and doing my Buddhist practice.

These are wonderful suggestions for anyone who is overly self-critical, and critical of others!

T: Ask the demon if he will be ready to be released after you've done the homework assignments and integrated new attitudes about yourself and others, and ask if you are able to speak your truth with love, instead of criticism?

Reiteration and summary of issues client previously described.

C: Yes.

T: Will you agree to do all 4 homework assignments?

C: Yes.

Client expresses agreement to follow guidance leading to physical emotional, mental, and spiritual integration.

T: And what will happen to the other two energy complexes you mentioned at the beginning of the session...the dark above your head (D_1) and the dark brown-black energy in your upper chest (D_2)?

Checking on potential impact of clearing and healing on two previously mentioned unhealed energies she located.

C: They'll get a little lighter...because they're related to sadness from how I was treated as a child...and how I use my intellect to protect myself from not feeling good about myself. But I still need to work on healing issues from

C: (cont.) my mother…and my father…who couldn't stand to hear me cry…in order to heal those issues.

T: Okay, is there anything else we need to know or do prior to completing this session?

C: No, I just need to do my Buddhist practice more and the assignments Eva gave me.

Common Problems and Solutions during Spirit Release using QTH

Spirits who attach to humans do not typically occupy their body or reside in their auric field one hundred percent of the time, but move in and out and may only be present or enter their body when an opportune time arises. For example, a spirit that craves alcohol or drugs may only merge with the person when they are mentally or emotionally thinking about and desiring to drink or use drugs, or once they have already done so, and may create an insatiable drive for more. Or a carnal sexual spirit entity may create the desire for sexual arousal and release intermittently.

Therefore, with persons who are affected by a spirit only intermittently or in certain situations that are difficult or impossible to recreate in the therapeutic setting, the therapist may have difficulty eliciting or "calling forth" the spirit into the therapeutic session to initiate communication with it. However, the spirit usually responds by calling it forth with the words "I'd like to talk to the spirit that _____ (state a specific characteristic/problem or known fact about the spirit). For example "I'd like to talk to the spirit that craves alcohol…gets you to masturbate excessively…causes you to lose your temper," etc.

Once discovered by the therapist, attached spirits may express fear or resistance to being released due largely to fear of the unknown or change.

Discarnate astrals of deceased humans typically do not know they are dead and need to be educated about the fact that they have died, and their spirit has not left the earth plane. They often may need to be reminded that their spiritual progress is thwarted or "on hold" if they remain earthbound, attached to another human. Informing them that they can go back to a higher plane in the Light, or God/Source, which is a place of great peace and comfort, to rest and prepare for their next lifetime is often all that is needed to facilitate their release.

Also, just as with humans, it is important to take time to develop rapport and trust with the attached spirit, which may require several sessions. It may also take weeks or months for the person to complete his "homework assignments" sufficiently to complete the healing of unresolved core issues related to the attachment, or increase his "light quotient" as a prerequisite to, and often part of the "hidden positive function" of the attached spirit.

Powerful, dark and/or demonic spirits often need to be recognized and acknowledged for the level of power or control they have had over that person. They need to be given the necessary time to describe in detail the breath and scope of areas they have influenced that person's life. Often as a preliminary step prior to the actual release of the spirit, gratitude and appreciation needs to be expressed by the host/ess for the "hidden positive function" of the "negative" spirit.

Common "Hidden Positive Functions" of Attached Spirits

One of the "hidden positive functions" of attached spirits, especially for more spiritually aware persons or advanced lightworkers, is to become aware of the fact that almost all humans have one or more attached spirits, and to take responsibility for and become educated and empowered to be able to effectively release said spirit(s) from oneself, as well as potentially educating and assisting others in the future. The more discarnate astrals or demonics that are released from the earth plane, the clearer the physical plane, and the clearer the lower and upper astral realms of earth will be! So doing spirit release work with oneself or others is a privilege and a service to humanity.

Another hidden positive function of attached spirits is to bring into the person's awareness the unresolved issues that created the "resonance" of "like attracts like," and the underlying issue that needs to be at least partially healed for the spirit to be released. If the underlying core issue is not sufficiently healed, spirit release may nonetheless occur, but often another similar spirit with the same "like type" predominant addiction, negative emotion, etc. may be drawn to and become attached to the same person.

A frequently encountered common hidden positive function is to block or prevent the person from expression of her personal will, power, or a strength. The hidden positive function is to prevent the person from misusing power and creating new karma. Focusing on integrating the Three-Fold Flame of Love, Wisdom, and Power in perfect balance, and agreeing to abide by the two Cosmic Laws of Love and Free Will are useful techniques to ultimately prevent misuse of power and avoid karma creation.

A Note Regarding Schizophrenia and Related Psychotic Disorders

The Diagnostic & Statistical Manual of Mental Disorders (DSM-IV-TR 2000) used by psychiatrists, psychologists and other mental health professionals, is the diagnostic "Bible" used for the definition and classification of mental disorders. In the DSM-IV-TR, the diagnosis of schizophrenia is defined as a psychotic disturbance that has lasted for six months or longer and includes at least one month of two or more of the following active symptoms: delusions (false beliefs about external reality), hallucinations (false sensory perceptions of external stimuli i.e., auditory, visual, tactile, etc.), disorganized speech, grossly disorganized or catatonic behavior, and other negative symptoms such as flattened affect, alogia (non-logical or irrational speech), avolition (lack of will), and social/occupational dysfunction. Auditory hallucinations (most typically hearing "negative" voices that are not the client's own inner self-talk), are frequently related to the presence of attached or possessing spirits and can lead to accompanying delusory, persecutory, or paranoid beliefs.

Typically, these clients are usually clairvoyant, clairaudient and/or clairsentient, and they are actually hearing a voice inside or outside of their head, and feeling or seeing the presence of one or more negative spirits, typically a demon. Use of spirit release therapy is therefore indicated to effectively release the source of the auditory hallucinations, and often related delusional, paranoid symptoms.

In actual clinical practice, underlying issues of self-esteem and core unresolved child or adult abuse issues must be significantly healed prior to embarking on communicating with and releasing any attached discarnate or demonic spirits. Issues of readiness to change, secondary gain, and a willingness to learn (and integrate) new social and life skills may also need to be addressed, especially in cases of chronic long term mental illness in which the client is "attached" to a lower level of interpersonal functioning. He/she may not have worked for years due to the disabling effects of hearing voices on a continuous or intermittent basis. If the attached spirit is demonic, the client must also become involved in a regular spiritual practice to increase their light quotient (such as meditation, receiving healing light, etc.) in order to successfully release and prevent further attachment of other demonic spirits.

CHAPTER 10
Spiritual Implant Removal

The implants I am referring to in this chapter are non-physical, etheric implants that primarily originated in other lifetimes, but are carried over in the subtle bodies from one lifetime to the next (similar to some attached spirits). Much of the activity involving use of spiritual or etheric implants occurred during a period of intergalactic history called the Orion Wars, which was hundreds of thousands of years ago (Nidle, 2005) and involved much fierce and prolonged warfare between various extraterrestrial civilizations. The Star Wars movies and the Star Trek series are fictionalized depictions of that period of intergalactic wars.

As such, understanding the more "esoteric" topic of spiritual (etheric) implants is predicated on both the acceptance of 1) reincarnation and the soul memory that is carried over from one incarnation to another; and 2) belief in extraterrestrial civilizations.

I have previously provided information to substantiate the belief in reincarnation and past/parallel/future lifetimes in chapter eight. The validity of extraterrestrial visitation by various off planet groups has garnered increasing validation and support in the past two decades. Perhaps one of the foremost ET researchers is Dr. Steven Greer, M.D., former medical doctor, who is the founder of the Center for the Study of Extraterrestrial Intelligence (CSETI). In his book *Disclosure* (2001) he reveals the testimonies of over 60 top secret military, government intelligence and corporate witnesses who reveal the truth about the government's involvement with various extraterrestrial species. He describes the reasons for 50 years of government and corporate suppression of the benevolent extraterrestrials' advanced technologies, which will enable humanity to reverse environmental pollution and restore the environment, provide an end to war and poverty, as well as provide free energy and advanced propulsion systems as a solution to our current over-dependence on fossil fuels. Dr. Greer estimates there are 200,000 distinct civilizations populating the cosmos of multiple known universes.

Sheldon Nidle, a scientist who has had face to face contact with various galactic beings since childhood, provides a detailed explanation of the history, culture, society and home worlds of twenty-two of the main extraterrestrial races, including the main humanoid races, the Pleiadians, Sirians, and Andromedans, as well as other non-humanoid races, in his book, *Your Galactic Neighbors* (2005). These benevolent,

Christed extraterrestrials and ultra-terrestrials greatly outnumber any of the "negative" alien races that have interacted with our planet.

All benevolent ET races abide by the Cosmic Laws of Love and Free Will. The so-called Prime Directive of Star Trek is a reiteration of the same principle of non-interference with the free will of a sentient species. The benevolent Christed extraterrestrials are here to assist us with their higher spiritual wisdom and advanced technologies.

Etheric implants are primarily spiritual limitation devices which have unique and specific characteristic that impose a blockage, limitation or external control program on the individual. There are many types, purposes and causes of etheric implants, or spiritual limitation devices, but they are basically designed to control and lower our consciousness and vibration, to keep humanity trapped in duality or polarity consciousness (Stahr, 1993). Implants, or spiritual limitations devices, are often seen as metallic objects in the body, and often (but not always) originate from one of three main extraterrestrial groups: the Zeta Reticuli ("Zetas"), Sirians, or Reptilians (including Dracos). Remember again, that since there are no victims in the universe each soul agreed to incarnate and experience this limitation. And the memory of the lifetime and agreement to experience the implant is stored in the unconscious memory of the individual.

Being implanted by an alien race is qualitatively similar or the same as to be taken advantage of, manipulated, and used or abused by another human being. It is seen as more strange or foreign due to the literal "alien" nature of the experience and the veil of unconsciousness that is often more difficult to break through and bring into conscious awareness.

In order of difficulty of integration, for example, it is easier to remember suppressed memories of neglect or abuse from childhood than past or parallel lifetimes in which there were traumatic or disturbing events. Accessing and releasing etheric implants is an even less frequently encountered occurrence, even for more advanced, spiritually evolved individuals.

Many higher level clairvoyant healers can detect the presence of/and remove spiritual implants. According to Stahr (1993), in *All About Implants and Spiritual Limitation Devices*, almost everyone incarnated on the planet has more than one etheric implant.

We do not necessarily have to be consciously aware of implants to release them using QTH, another method, or via an adept clairvoyant healer. As with the integration and healing of all shadow aspects, the good news is that as one's vibrational rate is raised, and one aligns and integrates the Christed Oversoul and Divine I Am Self, and chooses to abide by the Laws of Love and Free Will on the path to personal ascension, all aspects of the lower or shadow self, whether unhealed inner child or adult aspects, past/parallel/future life complexes, attached entities, or spiritual implants, will either be

1) integrated, or 2) released as one increases his/her light quotient. The QTH process is a tool to consciously facilitate the emergence and release of etheric implants, as one of the subtypes of energies or blocks that impede our personal spiritual evolution.

The elicitation of the location in the body of spiritual implants is accomplished using the standard QTH script. Implants stand out categorically due to their typically metallic nature, be they symbols, objects, or other metallic devices. Typically, they would go unnoticed by the QTH practitioner, and would naturally be released and/or transformed in the same format and pattern as any other unhealed, shadow aspect. It is important to remember that implants, as well as all shadow aspects, need to be transformed and released by connecting with a spiritual guide that is at a level of light or vibrational frequency that is higher than that of the implanted shadow aspect.

In his clinical hypnosis practice with clients, Dr. William Baldwin in his book *Spirit Releasement Therapy* (2002) describes his discovery of extraterrestrial probes, implants or testing devices used to send and receive information between species or to control and limit their free will and evolution. He encourages the therapist to suspend disbelief and work with the emergence of implants as if they were real.

The experience of being physically or etherically implanted is a very widespread phenomena according to evolved clairvoyant healers who can see and assist in the removal of implants, which may have originated in other lifetimes hundreds of thousands of years ago in linear time, but exist concurrently in our present, parallel reality.

Alexandria Stahr, author of *All About: Implants and Spiritual Limitation Devices* (1993), is one such clairvoyant healer who uses a spiritual guided imagery process for removal of etheric implants. She stresses the importance of the client's conscious participation in the implant removal process, in order to abide by the Cosmic Laws of Love and Free Will, and successfully release the implant after both parties agree to it.

Remember, a soul's evolution necessitates a broad spectrum of experiences on the victim - perpetrator polarity continuum. Thus, if a person experiences a sense of victimization in any extraterrestrial contact (including implantation), he has forgotten that in a superconscious (or subconscious state) his soul agreed to have this experience for its growth and evolution, to ultimately integrate and then transcend all polarities, including transcending all victim and perpetrator roles, which are based on fear and powerlessness, coupled with aggressive misuse of power, respectively. Enlightened understanding and seeing "the big picture" pave the way for acceptance, which then allows one to release the fear and judgment which blocks integration and healing.

The following three transcripts elucidate some interesting etheric implant removal sessions.

Spiritual Implant Removal Session 10-1

This was the first QTH session for Theresa, a spiritually enlightened woman who was seeking to find out the hidden cause for her bad headaches. She successfully uncovered two implants from the same extraterrestrial race, one which did end up being the cause of her headaches.

T: Deep Abdominal Breathing, Open the Heart, Open Inner Vision, Locate IPOP.

C: I'm someplace near the Sun,...there's lots of white clouds and rainbows all around.

T: Is your guide there?

C: He is a masculine angle...He has big features and long hair...with a long robe and wings.

T: What's his name?

C: Antario.

T: Is he your guide for today's session?

C: Yes.

T: Ask Antario what the most important problem or issue is today?

C: He says it's connected with my health... and removing protection of the heart.

T: Where is the problem located in your body?

C: It's in my solar plexus...and lower...and into my heart.

T: What does this energy that's protecting you look like...it's color and shape?

C: It's a thin copper shield (D_1)...shiny and pretty...with snaps so it can be removed when the work is done...not big...looks like about a 1 ½ ft. long and 1 foot high shield.

Implants are usually identified and seen as metallic objects in the physical body.

T: How long has this shield been with you?

C: It's timeless. It's been with me in all human form.

T: How did it originate?

C: It was placed there by the Gaglecians, a race I worked with...a "study group" from another planet. I wanted to protect my human self and learn as much as I could learn...

I have never heard or read of any race whose name resembles the Gaglecians...so the spelling of their name is approximate.

T: What was their role or purpose?

C: They were trying to help me learn what I could learn on Earth. The purpose of the shield was so they could monitor me and protect me...so I would not get too emotionally involved...so I could do my work.

T: What was the nature of the agreement with the Gaglecians?

C: The original agreement was to create a shield of light...white, blue and violet light to protect me on a daily basis...and that I can remove it at my free will.

The fact that the original agreement was based on her free will, and did not involve manipulation or control to limit or impose restriction on her power, implies that the Gaglecians are working on the "Light" side of the force...e.g. to assist in spiritual evolution, not constriction and de-evolution.

T: Are you ready to remove the shield now?

The fact that she had a choice about when to remove the shield and the Gaglecians honored her free will in the past suggests that we do not need to explicitly ask the Gaglecians or the shield if it is ready to be removed.

C: I'm calling in the light now...and the shield is being removed. I see pink skin underneath. Antario is assisting. The shield is being spun out ...and turned into a jillion light sparkles. I feel a heartbeat in my solar plexus.

The transformation begins! Implied also is that the client's Spiritual Self aspect is the healing/helper part, along with Antario. Here she gets visual and kinesthetic (feeling) evidence of the transformation.

C: My solar plexus feels tingly and my HS needs a pair of sunglasses (jokingly)...the light is so bright! I'm seeing fuchsia light dissolving into white and blue.

T: Breathe the light up through your head and down through your entire body to completely absorb any old energies related to the shield.

Integrating the transformation on the physical level.

C: The solar plexus wants reassurance that it...I won't go through the melodrama of extremes. It wants me to not get so involved emotionally...just focus on seeing the beauty of a flower and dwelling on that...instead of human emotional problems.

T: Will you agree to do that?

C: Yes! There'll be an adjustment period of 1 week and I'm to hold my emotional focus for 1 week.

T: Great! Is the process of removing the shield complete?

C: Yes...(pause)...there's something else though, there's a band around my head... head clamps (D_2). There are two strips... for stimulating of the neurons and balanced brain activation. But that's what is giving me the headaches, especially the last one. It was placed there by the same people... the Gaglecians. But it's antiquated now... it's purpose has been served...my brain is expanded and it's causing pressure on the band, and headaches.

T: Ask the band if it's ready to be removed?

C: Yes...and Antario is ready to help. I'm seeing the bolts unscrewing...and feeling the pressure releasing....they're spinning and going up into a vacuum of light...back to the planet!

T: Breathe it all out...and release the head clamps completely. Are they completely gone?

C: Yes...I don't see them anymore. My head feels lighter and more expanded.

T: Good, are there any other messages or assignments from Antario or anything else to complete the healing today?

C: No.

Here the client receives an assignment (emotional integration) to amplify and deepen the clearing.

Here, a 2nd implant is revealed.

Abiding by the Laws of Love and Free Will

Completing they physical release.

Emotional (feeling) integration and signpost of the release.

Mental Integration

After the session, Theresa reported that she was no longer getting any headaches, lending credence to the possibility that the etheric implant was most likely the (sole) cause.

Spiritual Implant Removal Session 10-2

In this second session Walter experienced the spontaneous emergence and release of a spiritual etheric implant that was blocking his spiritual growth. He also received beautiful words of comfort from Jesus to love and accept himself, and release his self-judgment about being gay.

T: Spiritual Alignment, Open Inner Vision & Hearing, Locate IPOP.

C: I'm in a place like the Parthenon...in a pavilion with rolling green hills in the background, and pretty trees and clouds. It's bright, not hot, and there's a lot of people around. It smells like sea air. There are several beings. I can't see their faces...just their feet. They're standing there waiting for me to talk to them. I feel I don't deserve to talk to them. That I'm not okay because of being gay. I feel transparent, seeing people looking and pointing...that's why I stay at home a lot.

T: Send love to the beings and ask who they are and if they're willing to talk with you?

C: One of them is Jesus. He doesn't know why I'd be troubled by this... he says it is my self-judgment. This judgment is not helpful. It's wasting time and energy. (pause) Jesus is talking to me...he's talked to me before about this...about being gay and not accepting myself. He says that in regard to sex that any act of love is of God. Jesus says I'm not supposed to believe what others say. He's sort of exasperated with me. He says that homosexuals are the next evolutionary leap. That is, it's not about gender or being male or female, it's about equal human rights, and that the trans-gendered ones will be involved in leadership roles. He says I'm already there... so I'm ahead of the game.

This term, "trans-gendered" I took to refer to mean those who are beyond or have transcended gender (not specifically cross-gendered), since the client himself was masculine in appearance and demeanor, and

C: (cont.) But I feel so out of context…He's saying something about that being trans-gendered is somehow not biological but spiritual. From being in that process comes greater acceptance due to social judgment. (pause) It's not an imperfection. (client starts crying deeply) It's not an imperfection.

C: Now other beings are coming in…Now Jesus is putting a golden vapor fog around me. He's embracing me energetically. He say's "Rejoice and know you are worthy." He's telling me I've been suffering at my own hand. Now he's pulling something out of my spine. It's got spikes on it…it looks like a stainless steel thing…(pause)…My spine is relaxed now. I thought I had to behave correctly. It had to do with rigidity.

T: What is the function or purpose of the implant?

C: It's got something to do with a communication process…emanation or vibration creating nervous energy. It was placed there in a previous lifetime…part of a method of controlling my behaviors from before…that's not necessary now. It's conflicting with me now. I want to know who put it there and why…

T: Then ask Jesus who put it there and why?

C: He says I'm not ready to know. It looks like steel though. Jesus is talking and saying other extraterrestrial populations did the implant that is symbolic of constriction.

T: Ask Jesus what the effect will be on your thoughts, feelings and behavior now that the implant is removed?

C: He says that an increased energy flow has been opened. There was an energy flow restriction because of the constriction that resulted in judgment related to my relationship with my mother.I had to be the same way she was to be accepted by her. I wanted her love and acceptance so I mimicked her. I'll

not physically transgendered.

Here client does not hear as "clearly" because he is in resistance to the message.

I sensed that the metallic nature suggested an implant.

Here, he would have corrected me if this term was incorrect.

It is not necessary to know the who, what, or why…just continue facilitating the transformational healing process.

C: (cont.) be more free flowing now...
(pause)...The implant also prevented
unwanted energies from coming in.

T: What was the positive function of the
implant?

C: It protected me from unwanted energies
coming in because the absence of love in my
heart would have been filled by something
negative if the implant had not been there.
Jesus is reminding me of my genuineness...
because I wasn't sure it would be received,
I've been restraining it. Now I see in my
heart...three colors of pink, gold and blue.

This was a completely spontaneous revelation
received by client of the Three-Fold Flame
from Jesus!

T: Yes, that's the Three-Fold Flame of Christ
consciousness' integration: pink for Divine
love, gold for Divine wisdom, and blue for
Divine power! Breathe into this flame and call
for perfect balance of the Divine attributes of
love, wisdom, and power. Expand the Three-
Fold Flame until it fills your entire chest.

C: The sensation I get is that I am connected
with spirit. I shouldn't worry if I'm meditating
correctly or not.

T: Are there any other messages from your
spirit?

C: Yes...to expand to others more. But I want
to know my specific mission.

T: Ask Jesus if more of what your mission
entails can be revealed to you?

C: Jesus won't tell me. I get the impression
I'm not ready.

T: Ask what your next steps to prepare for
completion of your mission are.

C: He says my preparation is completed.
And he's reminding me to be patient. What I
continue to be told is that I no longer find it
useful to make judgments about people. My
mother's been an example of how to not be

C: (cont.) judgmental…because it's been her undoing. I'm not to withhold love from her. Now I'm more deserving, but that's not a judgment.

T: Ask Jesus if the implant has been completely removed.

C: Yes it has. There's just golden light where it was in my spine.

The void has been filled!

T: Do you notice any changes in your thoughts and feelings as a result of the implant being removed?

Checking for emotional and mental integration.

C: Being gay is not an issue of unworthiness for me now.

T: Good!…Now breathe the golden light through your entire body to clear and release any judgment, especially about being gay, then ask Jesus if there are any messages, assignments or anything else we need to do to complete the session for today?

Physical integration and asking about additional mental and behavioral integration.

C: The essential thing is to check that I'm clear about my vision of the future…which has to do with the order of things in the so-called civilized world, for them to move towards peaceful co-existence. Jesus says the end result of the process is inevitable… but the timing is of it's own accord. He says don't add friction by trying to control it. That the consciousness of humanity is elevating… (pause)…Apparently I've been being trained in my sleep state for years and haven't been aware of it. (client's eyes begin to tear up). It seems like some kind of an imposition.

In fact, our spiritual guides and teachers do work with us in our sleep state, which bypasses our ego (fear and desire) and is not consciously remembered by most people.

T: Ask Jesus if there has been an imposition?

C: He says that I already volunteered. It's like the equivalent of being hooked up to a kidney dialysis machine and being cleansed. I'm being told something about dimensions…I'm being taken through…that I'm in position and "on hold." My physical body is in a position that can be utilized. There will be a network emanating from me…from which everything will be manifested.

Confirmation that the forces of Light and Christ consciousness will only act when given permission, and do not use manipulation, control, or force.

T: Can you more consciously release your resistance and accept that you have volunteered and are being prepared for your mission, primarily in your sleep state, and that everything is in Divine order?

Checking for spiritual integration of accepting his mission.

C: I know the connection with Jesus has always been there. I pretend to not notice. I'm embarrassed to say I've put a smokescreen between myself and Jesus, not feeling worthy before spiritually. But I have no resistance now.

T: Then ask Jesus if there is anything else we need to do to complete this session for today?

C: It's complete.

Spiritual Implant Removal Session 10-3

Athena was spiritually and psychologically very advanced and familiar with the QTH process from prior sessions. She had previously made contact with many other spiritual guides at the Ascended Master to Intergalactic levels. This first session provides a context of independent validation of reincarnation and for understanding the origins of the implant, which was revealed several weeks later in the 2nd session.

T: Spiritual Alignment and Locate IPOP.

C: I'm in a void...in a state of bliss... Archangel Michael is here...I'm feeling resistant and nervous. I feel a dark energy over my back...arching over me.

The client was very experienced with QTH and was spiritually and psychically very well developed. She regularly went into the void as her IPOP.

T: What does the energy look like?

C: It looks like a lizard...or dragon. It feels betrayed by what I'm doing here...I agreed to not send it away...

T: Ask the lizard what it's name is?

C: His name is Falgar...(exclaims "Oh my gosh!") He says he's been with me a very long time...before coming to the planet. He says

C: (cont.) he's a Draco...there's a family connection...it almost feels like a father. He says, "You're betraying your family" ...(pause)...He says he's a blood relative from time immemorial. I agreed to stay connected. I'm seeing lots of other Dracos now...from the past...(pause)...they were real intense over me. I was a female Draco. They were different levels of Dragons or Draco energies. Some were angels...like in the Luciferian rebellion...some became Draconian or Dracos...they were the heavies.

T: So you were a female Draco and Falgar was a relative, and he's here to remind you of your origin?

C: Yes.

T: What does Falgar want at his highest level of intention and purpose?

C: He wants to be able to surrender to this... losing what he knows...his power and being separate. He's avoiding the agreement to merge back with his original source...of Divine Oneness. He's afraid to hear what Archangel Michael has to say...Michael is using himself as an example...He's telling Falgar that he's in the Light...and with a lot of power. Falgar is agreeing to join with Archangel Michael...He gets to be a soldier...in the legions with Michael...with the understanding that he needs to study on the Inner Planes with Archangel Michael.

T: How long will the process of Falgar being released take to complete?

C: It may take sometime...I still feel a little attachment...Falgar is still hanging on...He can move very quickly...as soon as those two main thoughts about fear of loss of his power and being separated are dealt with...he wants more proof that he'll like it...(pause)... Archangel Michael says to check back in two weeks with Falgar to see how he's progressing. He also says visualize violet, pink and gold light around myself before I go to bed...to

The Dracos (from the constellation Draco, meaning Dragon), were one of the races of upright Reptilians who were an immensely powerful dark group of beings who waged intergalactic warfare and were the ultimate warriors - conquerors, controllers and manipulators of other Galactic Federation planets and species (Nidle, 2005).

Key hallmarks of dark energies are attachment to separation and misuse of power. And here we have a beautiful expression of the spiritual truth that all beings (regardless of the level of darkness) will return to Source! This is a prototypical pattern as all beings in human and spirit bodies progress in their spiritual evolution by studying with an advanced spiritual teacher on the Inner (or Outer) plane!

C: (cont.) protect from Falgar's energies. He's trying to hold me back...but then he secretly resents me.

T: Are there any other messages or assignments to complete in today's session?

C: No.

Since all humans have a primitive reptilian brain, her QTH session invites all of us to integrate and heal the fear-based and controlling, aggressive energies and lifetimes woven throughout our incarnational stream.

Here is the 2nd follow-up session with Athena

Several weeks later (per Archangel Michael's instructions), an etheric implant from the Draconian lifetime was spontaneously removed by Archangel Michael.

T: Spiritual Alignment, Locate IPOP.

C: I'm in the ocean...swimming on another plane. It's clear and calm...the light is softly moving and playing...making patterns in the water.

T: What does it feel and sound like to be there?

C: It's peaceful...safe...and joyful. I hear the sound of the ocean...the birds and a waterfall.

T: Open your heart to make an inner call to have our own Inner Goddess Self or one of your guides join you in your IPOP in order to connect with a source of clear inner guidance.

C: I see Michael the Archangel. I sense his beingness...there are other angels...in armor...I can't get their names. Now it feels like Michael has entered into my body... (pause)...He went into my lower three chakras, now he's removed an implant. It has a machine type of appearance...like a car part. It was filling up my 1st to 3rd chakras, the bottom is rectangular and the top...looks like a skyscraper...now there is a lot of light

Spontaneous "merger" of her guide Archangel Michael with the physical body, and initiation of the removal of the implant.

C: (cont.) inside...white with a tinge of gold...it's very bright. Now he is giving me a retrospective of my past...A long time ago... from when it began till now. I did not always have earth lifetimes. It seems like it was a con, an experimental process. Like a blueprint, so I would go through darkness into light. It affected my perception on a deep level, with core issues of survival, creation, and sexuality. It distorted the truth...so that I could play my role. It's like a long-term experiment to see how a being will handle this type of distortion over many lifetimes...(pause)...It was more of an observation than a type of experiment... in moving into the experience of darkness and limitation. This distortion kept me confused... this goes into many lifetimes.

The two great mysteries (i.e. Death and Sex).

T: What group or race was responsible for the use of those implants?

C: (pause)...I can't quite get the name...it's like Dragonoids.

T: Is it the Dracos?

C: Yes...There's a wide assortment of this type of implant. There was a specific group of them that designed the implant...or somehow, they had their hand in it.

Here, I hazard a guess since the Dracos are dragonoid (upright reptilian) in appearance, and from her previous session with Falgar, who was a Draco family member.

T: Is there anything else important to know about the implant...the purpose and history of its effects?

C: The process has helped me to become more humble. The being I was expressing at that time was full of pride and overconfidence... in a kind of simplistic way. In that lifetime, I had a lot of power...and the consciousness of limitlessness. The long process and the thing I didn't do right brought me to a place of humility. Understanding the diversity of energy...of choices...of the infinite...so I have a fuller appreciation of the roles, the possibilities and choices...and outcomes of those choices.

T: Is there a particular lifetime?

C: I'm seeing myself as a golden being of light...a bit more masculine...but androgynous...I was part of a legion...a band of angels...then I made this choice to go into the experiment...I thought I could overcome any limitation...I expected to come out of it earlier...for the project to end. I couldn't believe it would take lifetimes to overcome.

This is reminiscent of the story of the angel trapped and implanted in the *El-An-Ra* book by Solara (1991), which is based on the Orion Intergalactic Wars.

T: What is the higher intention and purpose of this implant?

C: It's anchoring awareness of the power of choice. Integrating the importance of choices...every single choice is important... to bring it fully into my consciousness. With every breath...and every choice...there's an outcome. It has a ripple effect...(pause)...It's time for me to be fully conscious; aware that every choice I make has an effect on me and everyone around me...(pause)...It's a new level of awareness...There's a heaviness still. But I feel like I'm ready, so there's no reason for me to fear it. I've already put safeguards in place so I won't misuse power. I'm minimizing my tendency to rush forward, the overconfidence that blinds me to the myriad of possibilities that I could create.

A beautiful description of the God level of creative consciousness where whatever you put your attention or think about instantly manifests.

A very important "step" prior to the effective release of an implant is choosing to change agreements, making new choices usually to not misuse power.

T: Let's reconnect now with your Guide, Archangel Michael.

Here, I re-focus the client on her Guide in order to make sure we are on track dealing with the most important issue.

C: He says there is a particular area to pay attention to in my consciousness...

It's staying awake...not losing myself... moving into fantasy...He says I'm also bringing too much energy out of my body... pretending I'm not on the physical plane. Being awake in my body...and being responsible at all times...these are my lessons. (pause)

The issue of not wanting to be in a physical body was a highly significant and superordinate issue for this client.

C: I'm being given a reminder about judgment...the importance of not judging one level or dimension as better than others... embracing ALL the dimensions I'm operating on...(pause)...now I'm being reminded that I do want to be here...to be fully present and give the most to it...being here.

A universal truth reflecting the need for acceptance of the truth about and validation of multiple simultaneous dimensions or frequency levels.

T: Are there any other specific lessons or issues for you to learn or integrate?

C: Living a balanced life, a moderate, healthy and full physical life. First, not judging it as bad. To embrace the physical (3D) plane. As I do that I'll accept being here. Before…I'd pop out of my body as soon as I felt uncomfortable…(pause)…I need to get grounded so I can accomplish more. I'll feel more productive and integrate my spiritual awareness into my body.

More revelations of basic spiritual universal truths.

T: Ask Archangel Michael if there are any ways that you can specifically integrate more acceptance and balance in your life on physical, emotional, mental and spiritual levels?

Asking for more specifics on how to create more integration in the four body system.

C: He says, "not judging sex and sexual energy." I'm being encouraged to spend time with my 1st and 2nd chakras…to make friends with my 1st and 2nd chakras. I'm supposed to focus energy on them…feeling them and letting any emotions and impressions come to the surface and following my inspiration; letting the energy flow…and not turn my back on sexuality.

The client was aware of lifetimes as both a victim of sexual abuse and as a perpetrator of sexual abuse, hence the fear and judgment and avoidance of chakras one and two.

T: On a scale of zero to one hundred, where 100 is one hundred percent ready to focus on feeling your 1st and 2nd chakras, how would you rate your readiness?

Here, I used a rating scale to check the level of (any) resistance to following her guidance above.

C: I'm one hundred percent…I'm also feeling a lot of the expressions will come in speaking and writing…It will happen spontaneously… it's better for me to look at the short term… there is a fear and blockage…of speaking my truth…in my throat…I'm questioning whether a certain person or group of people are ready for information…or if I will be hurt for bringing out the information.

From past experience these comments suggest that the client experienced, either in this or another lifetime, negative consequences of disclosing certain information.

T: Let's reconnect with your guide, Archangel Michael. Is the fear energy in your throat chakra or somewhere else?

C: It's in my throat.

T: Then focus on the energy in your throat.

C: I'm seeing a light...coming into the throat...on the left side...there's a past life wound...a battle axe cut that part of the throat...(pause)...the light is going in...it's lifting the trauma out and balancing it.

Another beautiful example of a spontaneously expressed transformational healing with light.

T: What does this healing feel like?

Emotional integration

C: I feel a tingling...a subtle energy coming into my throat...it's a little bit warmer. (pause) Now something else is going on... I'm seeing fingers of light...making more of an opening...removing energy restrictions. There's soft violet blue fingers of light going into my throat...

T: Are there any messages or assignments from Archangel Michael to assist you in integrating the healing today?

Mental integration

C: I need to integrate my superconscious, conscious, and subconscious parts.

T: Who can help you to integrate your superconscious, conscious, and subconscious selves?

C: Archangel Michael. But the way I get information is to type it on the computer. This will help me stay on track to help me in my process of healing and expanding.

T: Then will you go to your computer and ask to receive more specific guidance from Archangel Michael about how you can integrate your three levels of consciousness?

C: Yes.

T: Is there anything else that you can do, to be able to speak your truth, and to complete the healing session today?

C: Archangel Michael says to "Be alert...Be aware of your choices."

This session exemplified how self-discovery of an implant is one aspect of remembering, or putting the "members," or parts of our soul and psyche back together to restore greater wholeness and create healing through integration of our superconscious, conscious and subconscious selves.

CHAPTER 11
Spontaneous Spiritual Healing

During the course of utilizing QTH in my practice, another "subcategory" would randomly and occasionally occur, marked by a more intensified, prolonged experience of the client being surrounded and "bathed" in one or more colored light rays (frequencies). These sessions typically resulted in a spontaneous transformation, often without much content, i.e. information about the specific problems or issues being healed.

These "color ray" types of QTH sessions necessitate that both the therapist and client let go of the mind's or intellectual ego's need to know what was occurring in the client's process. When a spontaneous unitary spiritual healing occurs during a QTH session, the benevolent and loving presence of often multiple higher vibrational spiritual or angelic beings is usually strongly felt, both by the client as well as the therapist.

Here are the inner sensory characteristics – visual, auditory and kinesthetic – of these types of sessions.

Although they may not be visible in a human or angelic form, the guides are often seen in their "light body" form as ovals or spheres of color, from a more opaque to clear diamond white, and the entire rainbow spectrum of white infused color. Or, there may only be fields of colored light(s) present. From the auditory inner sense ability (clairaudience), there is virtually no (or minimal) inner dialogue with the healing spirits or guides. Often there is very little specific information in the session. For example, we may not be able to receive the names of the spiritual helpers present, or the problems or issues that are being spontaneously healed, transformed and released. The combined presence of multiple spiritual beings is frequently felt as a current running through the body, which feels pleasant or ecstatic and even blissful. Often, clients describe sensations of a higher vibrational energy, almost like a low-grade electrical current is running through their body.

Spontaneous Spiritual Healing Session 11-1

Robert had been seen for several prior sessions of QTH and was familiar with the process. He was having current life problems dealing with divorce adjustment, imminent career change, and confusion about what to pursue next. He was also struggling with depression from an injury at his place of work. In the following session, unlike previous "content laden" sessions, which involved clearing multiple past lives, Robert experienced a very powerful spontaneous healing with many dramatic visual, kinesthetic and proprioceptive experiences, while being immersed in changing fields of colored lights.

T: Spiritual Alignment, Locate IPOP.

C: I'm in a void…it's all black…(long pause)…Now I see violet…with purple light swirling around.

A very high vibrational energy presence was sensed by me, which increased and was sustained for about thirty minutes.

T: Ask the violet/purple light if it has a name?

C: A name just popped in…Romulus. The violet light is still swirling.

T: Just continue to hold your focus on relaxing and absorbing the transmutational energy of the violet light, which is the most powerful healing color ray in our visible spectrum, and call for the highest and deepest possible healing of whatever issue is most important for you to heal today. I'm visualizing and holding the focus of violet light with you now.

It is recommended that the therapist assist the client in visualizing the colored light rays that spontaneously appear, to "hold the field" and amplify the healing taking place.

C: I'm feeling energy lifting and floating…I keep seeing the word "love" …love, love… it's infusing and replacing the rage.

T: Can you connect with Romulus…and ask him if that is the issue that's being cleared?

C: Yes…(client is in a very altered state judging from his voice and manner). Now I'm feeling upside down being pulled at 3 or 4 G's… about at a 60-degree angle banking right… there's a feeling like a very fine vibration… like a hum…touching a motor. I'm calling for all my anger…that's sabotaging me…to be transmuted. (Pause) Now there's violet and red all around me. When the violet light started earlier, I felt a tremendous pain in my right shoulder…it was so hot.

The red is most likely him viewing his own angry thought forms, mixed with, and being transmuted by, the violet light.

His right shoulder was where he had sustained a severe injury at work and was still having a lot of pain.

C: Now there's a muddy tan…fades to deep fuchsia. I feel warming and buzzing in my feet…It feels warm and vibrating like putting

Muddied colors reflect just that…less than clear, pure colors and tones representing unhealed energies.

C: (cont.) my groin against a lawnmower. Sounds like bumblebees. It's a fine but strong vibration.

C: The vibration is moving from my feet... going up to my knees...and up my back and neck. The energy in my neck is dark, muddy green...(pause)...I'm starting to feel blissful. Now there's green and white light... with blue...and dark violet light. A feeling of love...now it's turning blue-violet and green. I'm feeling a vibration in my right hand and right foot. I give myself permission to be whole and healed...and have the body that I did in high school.

The process at this point had already lasted about 30 minutes...as there were long periods of both the client and myself in silence focusing on accepting, maintaining and amplifying the powerful light healing that was occurring.

Client here affirms and accepts the deep healing that is occurring (mental integration).

C: The greatest change occurs with the gentle blowing of a breeze on a back porch...this is like that. (pause) I know the wisdom of this... it's expanding...I give myself permission to be my ex-wife's friend...to be a good father...successful, an actor, self-confident, a good student...to be a go-getter and be a good friend and receive good friendships. (Client starts crying) I feel happy...I say, "You deserve it." (pause) Now I feel pressure in my third eye, it's opening.

A beautiful, poetic analogy!

Here, he spontaneously affirms acceptance of traits and qualities indicating emotional and behavioral integration of the 5th density process of healing.

T: Can you ask the energy and guides orchestrating the powerful healing that you are receiving today if the healing is complete for today?

C: Yes...I have an assignment...to remember and focus on how I thought and felt when I was a lineman on the football team...my sophomore year in high school...so I can feel more confident, successful...(Client starts crying softly again) I am blessed.

This assignment will enhance the future integration of the session.

T: That's right! You are blessed...and breathe the knowingness of just how blessed you are into every cell and atom in your body, amplifying and integrating the depth of the cellular healing you have experienced today, and give thanks to the unknown healing presences that have transmitted this transmutational and transformational healing process!

Spontaneous Spiritual Healing Session 11-2

This next session was with a young woman named Linda. In her current life, she was having some relatively mild marital and life adjustment problems. This session provides another good example of several common features of more powerful spiritual healings that occur using QTH. Linda experienced a continuous and rapid flow of new experiences of seeing changing colors, and she also received spontaneous insights as to the meaning and nature of her experiences as she was going through them.

C: I'm on top of a mountain…it feels like I'm in Greece. I can smell the sun…there is a very bright light everywhere…it's holding me in its embrace. It says "I am peace."

The source of the bright white light was unknown but a strong sense of peace and calm came over the client so we know it feels positive.

T: What color is the light?

C: It's white… (then suddenly client exclaims) Now I'm seeing a gray cloud starting at my head…it's like a shield…blocking everything out.

A sense of almost "panic" overcomes the client, so I guide her to connect with her "light" positive guides(s).

T: Just breathe deeply and relax. Make a heartfelt call to your clear spiritual guides to come in and assist you in aligning with your own Spiritual or I/H Self.

C: I can't see the (white) light anymore. I'm being blocked by the gray energy all around me.

Client focuses…but cannot resume seeing the white light or sense a positive spiritual presence.

T: Ok, I'd like you to focus on visualizing a violet sphere above your head. Allow the bright violet light to send rays of transmutation down through the top of your head, filling your head with violet light. Then allow the sphere to descend through the center of your body. Let the violet sphere slowly descend, into the neck…filling the neck with violet light, then allow the violet sphere to move down into the chest…radiating violet light down through the arms…through the solar plexus…navel…root chakra (perineal area)…and down both legs. Then let the violet sphere rest below your feet. Next, spiral the violet sphere around your body in a counterclockwise rotation, absorbing the grey energy and clearing and transmuting it

Her inability to have sensory experience of the light of her guides led me to use a color healing visualization to transmute any unseen blockages using violet light, in order to clear her physical and subtle (emotional, mental and spiritual) bodies.

Counter clockwise rotation will tend to match and "unhook" or detach negative energy.

C: (cont.) into pure energy. Spiral the violet light from your feet, all the way up to above your head. Then let the violet sphere spiral from right to left in a clockwise direction around and down through you body to absorb and clear the grey energy in your auric field. Imagine a grounding cord from each foot now extending all the way down into the earth, going deeper and deeper until it reaches the center of the earth. When you have completed this, just say "now."

C: Now.

T: How does the grey cloud look now?

C: It's mostly gone…except around my heart.

T: Ask the grey energy in your heart what it wants?

C: It says it wants my power…it wants to take my energy…the love…in my heart. It's been there for many lifetimes.

T: What does it want at its highest intention and purpose?

C: It wants to protect me from being hurt…by others. But it wants all my energy and love. (In shock) It just went in me…it's cold and angry (client starts to cry).

T: Okay, let's call for all of your spiritual guides and helpers, calling for divine spiritual assistance to bring in more love and light to give the grey energy in your heart the highest light frequencies and loving energy, which is what it is wanting at its highest level of intention and purpose.

C: (Exclaims) Now, I'm seeing a light around me…it's light green…now it's changing to white.

T: Is the green or white light a specific guide?

C: It's rippling in and around me, spiraling… energy and brightness from right to left…

Then, always follow with the clockwise rotation (positive) of light visualization. The use of violet light allowed the client to clear her field of the grey cloud, which made its presence visible in order to be seen and cleared. Remember, all energies at their highest level of intention and purpose desire to transcend limitation and re-unite with the pure Light of God/dess Source energy.

Typical of partial clearing through use of the violet light for (spontaneous)transmutation.

Here, I get the sense that the grey energy is another distinct spirit.

Green is the lower octave color of the heart chakra.

Client is experiencing a powerful spiraling of light around her, and ignores my question.

T: Great! Just allow the white light to spiral around you and absorb all the grey energy.

C: I am letting go and letting the light spiral around me, (exclaims excitedly). Now, something is picking me up...and putting me down. It's filling me up vertically instead of horizontally!

Here, I could hear in her voice some slight anxiety and resistance.

T: Just breathe and relax, allowing the highest and most powerful clearing and healing to occur today.

Focusing client on relaxing since she understandably expressed some fear and tension due to having the sensation of being lifted up and down.

C: Now I see a face in front of me... (exclaims) It's me! I'm being framed with my hands (client spontaneously moves her hands around her head and then above her head) I'm healing myself! (says excitedly)

C: The light is very bright. Now it's turning a neon pink in my hands. I'm pushing it down through my whole body (client spontaneously moves both hands progressively down about twelve inches out from her body...from her torso and around her legs.)

Client is being shown an out-of-body picture of herself. Then she gradually started moving her hands from her head down through her torso past her knees. This took approximately twenty minutes. I simultaneously focused on "holding the field" of light and also witnessed the light turn bright pink.

T: What's happening now?

C: The dark has become much smaller. It's hardly there...(long pause)...now it's gone! It was very, very heavy!

T: Now, ask your Spiritual Self and your guides if there is anything we need to do to complete the session for today.

C: No...but I'm having an awareness that I was a healer in a past life. And I can do healing work again...on myself...and others.

T: Great! How do you feel about that awareness?

C: I don't know...(drifts off). It doesn't feel comfortable...or safe...it feels like it's from a past life. I don't feel safe...(in a weak voice)

A feeling of fear permeated the room.

T: That's ok. Just breathe in more of the pink light, which is the color of love, all through your body. Are there any homework assignments to help you integrate this session on physical, emotional, mental or spiritual levels?

C: I'm getting a feeling I should try to see that past life (tentatively)…some time in the future.

T: Okay. Now thank yourself for allowing yourself to heal yourself, and all of your unseen spiritual helpers for their assistance in facilitating the powerful healing that you received today.

In subsequent QTH sessions, Linda uncovered a past life in which she was killed (burned at the stake) as a healer in the Middle Ages, which is why she did not feel "safe" re-claiming her healing gifts.

The appearance of the bright white light when her I/H Self or Guides was called for, is a prototypical color of a clear, healing energy/entity, just as grey is a typical color of unhealed energy.

I frequently utilize the violet light to transmute any unclear or blocking energy in QTH sessions, whether it is thought or emotional forms, attached spirits, or any unhealed shadow aspect. Usually violet light will create a partial clearing of unhealed energies, preparing the way for later transformation, and more complete healing and transcension.

Atypically, due to the continuous rapid flow of expression of her inner experiences, I did not check for the names of the energies/guides that were creating or emanating the healing color rays of bright white light green and neon pink. Also, there was no specific content about the source of the grey energy that was present, except that it was coming from a past life.

The colors of light green and neon pink (that came in later) both pertain to the heart chakra, represent healing (green) and pink (love). These color rays directly correspond to her statement that the grey energy wanted to take the love energy from her heart. Her perceptions of the light spiraling around her, and her body being raised, and then lowered, are fairly unusual.

Finally, she experienced a wonderful activation of her ability to heal herself. In subsequent sessions, we were able to locate and clear the lifetime in which she was a healer in the Middle Ages who had been killed, freeing her to continue to utilize her healing abilities with herself and others.

Spontaneous Spiritual Healing Session 11-3

In this final session, Sandra had a very rich, prolonged experience of seeing many colors, with rapidly changing colors, fields and forms. After approximately twenty minutes of being bathed and immersed in this "color bath," she appeared to be in a blissful state and had difficulty getting access to the name of her guide (or much content other than colors) for nearly forty-five minutes.

As I surrendered to her process and just flowed with her experience of seeing colors while she shared some quixotic phrases (without any context of what was being healed or the names of the guides or energies present), eventually Sandra was able to express the name of one of her guides. At one point she was able to share that the main issue being healed was her feeling of powerlessness. She was eventually able to get good descriptive content of how she experienced her lack of power, and how she would look, sound and be different when she integrated her power in a variety of ways. A future pacing (progression) was incorporated to have Sandra view her more integrated, empowered future self.

T: Spiritual Alignment, Open Inner Seeing and Hearing, Locate IPOP.

C: Just on a hill...overlooking lots of other hills...by myself, next to a tree.

T: I'd like you now to open yourself to connect with your I/HS or Guide.

C: So far just colors...changing from purple to sometimes green...to a lighter green color... (pause)...It's dark purple again.

Purple (violet) is transmutational, and green is also associated with healing.

T: Great! Just allow yourself to see those colors. We call again for your I/HS or one of your Spiritual Guides, whomever would be most appropriate to heal whatever is the most important issue or problem to heal today. Just breathe and relax...(pause)...What is happening now?

C: Still colors.

T: Just send love from your heart to embrace those colored lights, inviting them to be with you. Do they a have certain shape?

C: Sometimes…sometimes just varying small circle shapes,…sometimes color that's just there, no shape. I'm seeing yellow…going to gray…then to more green…and then purple, then sometimes in a circle shape. Circles that sort of make concentric circles and spiral down. That's what I see now.

> This client is continuing to have a very rich inner experience of seeing various colors and shapes in an ever-changing panoply.

T: Where do you see those circles and concentric circles…in your body or around your body?

C: Just in my mind. At the bottom of purple they'll be green or vice versa. I see blue and deep, deep violet.

T: As you more deeply connect with those colors, then ask the energy that is creating these colors if it has a name or if it will talk with you?

> Trying again to establish a connection with her guides to obtain more specific guidance and direction.

C: Seems there's an "M" name but I can't place it.

T: It begins with an "M?"

C: Uh huh.

T: Just relax and take some deep breaths, and ask that spiritual presence to either tell you the name more clearly or perhaps print it out so you can see it in your mind's eye.

C: (long pause)…Okay, I don't see the name, I see colors still but there seems to be very definite lines where it looks like they're lightning…or like mountains in shape.

> She is continuing to experience a deep alpha-theta state, with slowing of her speech and the appearance of being in a deep, peaceful (trance) state.

T: With the same colors?

C: Uh huh.

T: It looks like lightning or mountains of the same colors?

C: Yeah, it's like black with the lines, but then there's color, but then it fades to orange where it's totally clear.

T: And again, you're seeing this in your mind's eye?

C: Yes.

T: Okay. Well, can we call this energy aspect "M?"

C: Sure.

T: Will "M" talk with you? Will you ask it?

C: (smiles) I'm not really sure if she's talking with me or not. Umm, I see grey and sort of fuzzy. I can't really make it out…it's just grey. Should I tell you what I heard in my mind, though? Umm…Don't tread on water that thickens…Don't bleed on shoulders that sing…I don't understand that…

Her inner vision sense (at least in this session) seems much easier for her to access than her auditory perception.

T: Don't tread on water that thickens…Don't bleed on shoulders that sing?

C: Yes.

I repeat her words, to make sure I heard her correctly. These were puzzling sayings without clear meaning, and without any prior context for interpretation.

T: Okay, just go within your heart and higher mind and ask yourself what does that mean for you? What is that message communicating?

C: I'm not sure. Umm…

Sandra is in a deep trance-like state.

T: Have you ever heard that before?

C: No. What came to my mind was the word "sword" or a "shield". That's what came to my mind.

T: To be a sword or a shield?

C: No, just the words came in…sword…and shield.

She is not able to get more auditory clarification. Although based on her later comments about needing to set limits on how she expends her energy, "sword" and "shield" suggest the need for integrating more self-protection.

T: Okay, can you still see all the different changing colored lights as before?

C: I see sort of green now…same…lines and purple back again.

T: Okay, ask M if there is a particular problem or issue that would be the most beneficial to work on today?

C: (long pause) I don't know...something that begins with a "B."

T: It begins with a "B?"

C: Yes.

T: Okay, just breathe deeply now and connect with your body. Imagine the purple and the green light coming in to locate where in your body you may be experiencing an issue or problem...to find where it's anchored in your body...and just breathe...and as you open your inner vision imagine shining a light of illumination and scanning your body seeing and feeling where an issue may be held in your body...(pause)...just let me know what you're experiencing.

This client's nervousness and tenuousness was possibly due to the fact that an observer was present videotaping the session.

C: Okay, it's still colors and possibly in this region (runs hand from navel to heart and back to navel).

T: Um hmm. From your upper chest all the way down to your navel? Okay. Just do some deep breathing and call for your I/H Self to be present and help you see within...just checking where in your body would be the best place to do some clearing and healing today? (long pause)

C: Maybe my jaw.

The word "maybe" indicates uncertainty, and typically suggests the person thought of this rather than intuiting it from her own guides or guidance.

T: Okay, do you feel anything in your jaw right now?

C: Not really.

T: Okay, just check again. Be as relaxed and centered as you can. And if you want, breathe up the white light from the base of your spine to clear the energies...and breathe up and out through the center of your forehead to open your inner vision, calling for your HS and the colored lights to assist you. (pause) Okay,

Using white light visualization (since she was already seeing purple light) to clear the central channel in her body, and to open the third eye - to be able to locate the color and shape of the unhealed energy in her body.

T: (cont.) when you look inside your body now, what do you see? Can you sense or see anything? Is it in your jaw, is energy moving around?

C: I think energy is probably moving around. It's purple becoming blue and going back to purple again…and it's almost like a flower…a flower shape…but it changes rapidly. My body doesn't feel uncomfortable. I don't feel any specific tension in one place.

This client appears to be in a rather blissful state from her countenance after being given a "color bath" for the past twenty-five minutes.

T: Did you feel tension before?

C: Not particularly. I felt tension in my neck, but not right now. No…(pause) I see purple and green again.

T: And is this purple and green energy still the same energy that calls itself "M?" Can you ask it?

C: No, this energy is always here!

T: Oh…okay…Ask this new energy what its name is, or what it would like to be called?

A new energy/entity or spirit presence has entered the client's field of awareness.

C: This energy is different from "M."

T: Does it look different or feel different, or sound different?

Checking for visual, kinesthetic or auditory distinctions in order to identify the energy as a separate entity.

C: Well, the energy that I see and the colors that I see are usually present.

T: Is what you're seeing now your HS aspect?

C: I don't know. I just see the colors in concentric circles.

T: Okay. From your heart, send out some pink light to embrace with love, these other colors that you're seeing and ask this energy if it will please reveal what it represents or what purpose it's serving right now. (long pause waiting for reply)

Again, I am probing for more "content" because my intellectual mind is wanting to know more about the focus of what is being healed.

C: I believe the purpose is just clearing, relaxation, healing.

The client confirms that direct spiritual healing is occurring (5th density healing).

T: Okay, so what should we call this energy? Can we call them the "Colored Lights?"

C: Colored Lights is fine.

T: Okay, can you ask the Colored Lights energy what is being healed?

C: Mmmm...(takes a deep breath and pauses)...possibly feelings.

T: Okay...is there a certain specific feeling that is being healed? Certain emotions? Or is there a certain part of your body that you can sense being healed or that has already been healed today?

C: I think it's basically...I'm not sure what's being healed today. Powerlessness possibly...

T: Where in your body are you feeling that powerlessness?

C: I think at the base of my spine.

T: Okay, take a deep breath and breathe down at the base of your spine. Look carefully in that place at the base of your spine. If you could see a color and a shape, what would that look like?

Connecting physically with breath and intention to focus on clear inner vision.

C: You mean what would the powerlessness look like?

T: I'd like you to look down at the base of your spine, if the energy of powerlessness had a color or a shape, what would that look like or be like?

C: Pause...heavy sigh. "Um...I would say dissipating grey."

T: And is there a particular shape?

C: I'm not getting a shape right now.

T: So you see some grey energy dissipating there. And what does that grey energy at the base of the spine really want?

C: (Laughs) It wants to get out.

T: Do you see any other light around it that's creating the dissipation?

C: Orange...a little bit...and violet.

T: Is the orange and violet light helping the grey feeling of powerlessness to be released?

C: Yes.

T: Great! And is there anything else that the grey energy that is gradually dissipating and clearing...anything else that it wants?

C: It wants its power back.

T: Okay, and who or what can give it its power back?

C: (breathes...laughs) That would have to be me.

T: Are you willing to give yourself your power back?

C: Definitely.

T: Okay, is that you as your human self or your HS aspect that can give you your full power back?

C: My HS aspect.

T: Okay, great! Can you see that happening right now? What would that look like or be like if you got your power back? Can your HS help that grey?

C: What would it be like if I got my power back?

T: Yes.

C: Freedom.

T: Okay, is that what that part really wants, freedom?

Confirmation that the transformational healing is occurring.

C: Yes, freedom to be myself and to be...well freedom to not be directed by other people's goals or motives.

T: Okay. And will the grey energy at the base of your spine accept help from your HS?

C: Yes.

T: Okay. And is your HS willing to give all the help that is needed to be your natural self and get your power back and not be directed by other people's wishes or intentions for you?

C: Yes.

T: Okay, so just imagine in whatever way, shape of form that might take place, whatever pictures or images come to mind...just imagine now, the HS merging energies with the grey energy at the base of your spine... and just watch what happens.

C: Okay, I see yellow light now.

Yellow corresponds to intellectual knowingness vs. gold, which represents wisdom.

T: At the base of your spine?

C: Mainly I see it in my mind.

T: Um hmm. If you look down at the base of your spine again, now could the H/S specifically help you to become more powerful, self-directed and natural?

C: (heavy exhale)

T: Perhaps you might ask for a homework assignment or message for the future...

Asking for mental and/or behavioral integration.

C: Basically...simplicity...and congruency with myself...my own life...thoughts, feelings...that my outer life represents my inner life as much as possible.

T: So your H/S is suggesting that you bring more simplicity and congruency between your outer and your inner spiritual self?

Reaffirming to client her own guidance.

C: Yes.

T: Does your H/S have any specific messages about how to do that?

C: I think I somewhat understand how to do that.

T: Can you see yourself in the future being more integrated with your H/S...and natural, free and powerful?

Checking for depth of integration by suggesting future projection.

C: Uh huh.

T: What does that feel like?

Querying for kinesthetic integration.

C: It feels like someone who understands people and understands things that go on are not always your lesson...are not always your stuff. And you'll be able to know what is and what's not. And also...(pause)...to release judgment about people and situations because there's no love in judgment. So it's not possible to have a clear picture of anything unless you're coming from a place of love first.

How true!!!

T: Right! Absolutely right! And are you willing in the future to make that commitment to yourself...and not personalize things that occur in your life, or blame yourself or judge yourself for them especially if they are other people's "stuff"?

C: Yes.

T: Okay.

C: That's an issue...it's a core issue.

T: Okay...And what does it feel like as you imagine yourself now being more powerful, more natural and loving...less judgmental?

C: It feels in my mind like...a butterfly...the ability to visit all kinds of opportunities and situations in life and still fly away happy from them...and explore...and do what I need to do without getting stuck...still being able to fly.

T: Uh huh. That sounds like more freedom and detachment, flying freely.

C: I think the M name that I told you earlier...I think it's Merria.

T: Merria...okay, is Merria still with you?

C: I think so.

T: Is Merria a H/S aspect or one of your guides?

C: Guide.

T: Okay...and is Merria also going to help you to achieve those goals and become more self-empowered...all the things you just mentioned?

C: Yes, she's gonna help me more when I get there.

T: How will you know when you get there?

C: I'll know when things in my life that happen don't disturb me as profoundly as they sometimes do now. And I can recognize what's happening without...on an emotional level experiencing everyone else's thwarted emotions projected towards me.

T: Uh huh. And will Merria help you to abide by the universal laws of love and free will for all beings?

Facilitating spiritual integration.

C: Yes.

T: Okay...are there any other messages or assignments from Merria or your H/S?

C: To find peace...and to share it with other people.

T: Anything else?

C: To bring forth beauty.

T: In what ways would you bring forth beauty?

C: One way is how you make other people feel when they're around you.

T: Or how you would model for them to feel...because they are responsible for their own feelings.

C: Right. That's what I mean. (laughs)

T: How would you be a model for them?

C: First by being clear myself...

T: Uh huh. Great. And is there anything else we need to do before we complete our session today?

C: No, just...just thank everyone for helping.

T: Yes...thank yourself...your H/S, and Merria for assisting you and all the unseen beings present today...completing some colored light healing and giving you some guidance and direction for your life.

Here, I reassign responsibility for feelings to the person generating them, since we cannot make or cause anyone to feel a particular emotion or feeling.

Perhaps Sandra was unable to articulate her inner experience and was rather tenuous and uncertain, because she was so deeply relaxed and in a state of spiritual consciousness that was "beyond words." Regardless, this particular session tested my patience, and I had to repeatedly let go of my desire to get more "content" about her guide(s), what was being healed, etc., and release my frustration with her frequently ambiguous or indeterminate answers. As I focused on acceptance of her process and became more patient and detached, she, too, became clearer and more able to articulate her inner process. Eventually, in the last third of the session, she could identify her guide Merria and what was being healed with greater conviction.

CHAPTER 12
Complex and Multi-Dimensional QTH Sessions

This chapter includes three examples of more complex and extended (one and a half to three hours) QTH sessions. In the first two transcripts, a multiplicity of unhealed issues are brought into conscious awareness with partial to complete levels of healing at the time of the session. A third session illustrates how QTH can be extrapolated and enhanced by expanding the personal healing that occurs to other levels – ancestral, racial, national, planetary, solar system, galactic, intergalactic, and cosmic consciousness.

Due to the complexity and length of these QTH sessions, after the transcript of each session, an analysis of the process is provided using the triangulation model illustrating the multiple I/H Self or Guide(s), the Disintegrated Unhealed Problems/Issues (D) and the Healing, Integrative Transformation (H). It's important to reiterate that even if the I/HS or guide indicate that there is a complete healing that day of the problem or issue, other facets or layers of the same unhealed complex may surface at a later date, since everyone is in a continuous process of clearing.

The following example is of a more complicated QTH session, which illustrates the process of the emergence of multiple unhealed dis-integrated energy complexes (labeled D_1 through D_5) in a single session of approximately one and a half hours.

Complex QTH Session 12-1

Paula was an advanced spiritual disciple who was familiar with the process of QTH, which accounts for the ease and rapid fluidity of the emergence of multiple problems and their healing solutions. Her QTH session is notable because of her beautiful and somewhat poetic descriptions of her inner sensory experience, and the number of unhealed (shadow) aspects that she was able to fully or partially resolve in a single session.

T: Spiritual Alignment, Locate IPOP.

C: I'm swinging on a hammock…of a crescent moon…surrounded by stars and moonlight…suspended in infinite space. It feels clear and bright…safe…warm, and loving.

C: I see a spiraling golden light with a bright blue center…it's Sananda.

Sananda is the Cosmic Christ…(whereas Jesus is the planetary Christ).

C: The most important issue is my confusion and indecision about being on the planet…the underlying issue…is to be fully present.

Here, she automatically identifies the most important issue since she is familiar with the QTH steps and process.

T: Where is the confusion located in your body?

C: It's in my brain (D_1)…the indecisiveness and lack of focus. I see sparks of light…and feel fragmented. It looks like zig-zag flashes…in the front of my field of vision…that inhibit my focus. They're bright orange with a tinge of red around the exterior…related to defense and fear mechanisms regarding the truth of my identity. The fear is like a shield. It's a fear of persecution…and not being accepted for who I really am as my higher self. Now the flashes are swirling gold and violet (pause to allow client to integrate violet and gold).

The changes in color suggests spontaneous transmutational healing (violet) and integration of wisdom (gold) of the insight she just described and greater acceptance of her HS.

T: Has the swirling gold and violet (H_1) completely absorbed all the indecisiveness and lack of focus?

C: Yes, I feel clearer and more focused now…but there's still fear in my heart (D_2) …There's a vise-like clamp around my heart (D_2)…preventing it from pulsing…making me short of breath…and creating a feeling of heaviness.

Here, she has focused on the 2nd unhealed complex.

T: Did the vise around your heart originate before, during, or after your birth?

An optional, but useful question, which allows for pre-birth (Christian perspective) or past/parallel lifetimes (Buddhist or Hindu perspective) to emerge.

C: It originated before my birth. Sananda says it's not necessary to hold onto it. Its energy was put there by my sister Amy (in this life) who envied my role as a healer in a past

C: (cont.) life. We were in the temple of Isis together. I initiated her but she was jealous of me...I didn't let go of the heartbreak. In the lifetime with Jesus...as Martha, my sister envied my relationship with Jesus by being my (biological) sister in this life. She's helped me in triggering the remembrance of who I am...part of the lesson is learning to let go and love unconditionally.

The vise in my heart now changed to a crown of thorns...like a circle piercing the heart. Now it changed to a gold crown (H_2)...it cried or melted.

The spontaneous transformation of the vise to the image of a crown (H_2), is a sign that healing just occurred.

T: What does the vise that turned into a golden crown want?

C: It wants to release the loving energy... to turn into a river of gold...to flow freely. Now it's flowering into the heart and hand of Sananda. It's like a golden river of light.

T: Now, breathe the love from your heart through your entire body to melt the fear and feel the lightness, and all unwanted energies absorbed and healed by the love.

Deepening the integration on the physical level.

T: How does that integration feel?

Emotional integration

C: It feels like loving, total acceptance of myself.

T: Are there any messages or assignments from the golden river of light?

Mental Integration

C: To love myself...know I am perfect and not always condemn myself for not speaking my truth in love, humility, and kindness, and without criticism and judgment, and without the need to be the best or perfect...to forgive myself for having turned away from him (Sananda). I denied his presence and power because I was afraid of being hurt again. It's hard for me now...to accept a lowly lifetime...my arrogance and willfulness is not necessary. I'm releasing the ego...all aspects...to be so fluid...so free and clear to move with any assignments that I'm given. I

C: (cont.) can't be bound with attachments to status or material things...or other's approval. Part of the block is the need for Terry's (her daughter) approval. I have a fear of losing her...that she won't understand and will not want to be with me. I've got a resistance to that aspect of me.

T: Where is the attachment to wanting the approval of Terry, and other people, anchored in your body?

C: It's in my eyes and sinuses (D_3). I've been clearing my sinuses and it's clouding my 3rd eye.

T: What does the energy in your eyes and sinuses look like?

C: It looks like...a full field...of dark green... it's about betraying my daughter. I'm afraid I'll lose contact with her and she won't want to associate with me. Some of it's from Carl's (ex-husband) influence...but it's temporary.

T: What does the dark green energy want?

C: It wants me to hold a feeling of unconditional love for them...in preparation for other people's non-acceptance of what I'll be saying and doing...(pause)...Around age 23 Terry will be awakening to her mission... her own healing with others. She's healing herself now...

C: The dark green energy wants to be clear.

T: Who can help it to be clear?

C: My Higher Self...she's angelic and a gold color. Now the green is getting brighter... turning into an angelic form...she's waving her arms outward. The green is turning to cobalt blue...and gold (H_3).

T: Now, look at and feel the energy in your eyes and sinuses. What do you sense?

Here is the transformational healing of the 3rd problem/issue in this rapidly paced session!

C: My sinuses are clearer…it's integrated into my entire body now. The message and my assignment is to embrace my purpose… bring my talents together to assist others in the remembrance of their own Divinity… to be in the place of love and always move forward – just do it!

Since this client was familiar with QTH, she automatically proceeds with deepening the integration on physical, emotional, mental, and spiritual levels.

T: Now, project yourself into the future and imagine Terry not accepting you.

Here, I added a future projection to check for integration.

C: I'm feeling the sadness of the separation (client starts to cry).

T: Ask Sananda or your HS to comment on the illusion of separation.

C: Sananda says it's not really any different… it's a normal, natural process and it will be okay with her. Eventually she'll be working with me. I just need to focus on unconditional love and detachment.

T: What would be the worst possible scenario you can imagine of Terry not accepting or rejecting you?

This is a question I use to have a person enhance detachment by imagining and accepting the worst case scenario, or most negative possible outcome. In this case, the worst imaginable outcome is rejection/non-acceptance by her daughter.

C: I'm presenting at an event. She's in the audience, but she doesn't understand or accept what I'm talking about. (Client has realization). But we each have our own journey, and it's okay.

T: Now, check if the clearing of your fear of not being accepted by your daughter is complete.

C: It can't be completed now. I'm not having everything open because it would be too much to integrate all at once. I need to be patient and willing to work a step at a time towards healing and completing my spiritual mission. I don't feel perfectly comfortable charging money for healing work…Polarity and Reiki…but I could do it without payment, or on a love offering basis…but not the workshop. I have a fear of not being supported but I need to trust the universe.

T: Where in your body is the emotional energy of not trusting the universe being held? (D_4)

C: In my legs and knees. (D_4) It stems from a past life.

T: Ask one of your guides or your H/S if it's necessary to see what the source in a past life is.

C: It's not necessary.

When a past life is mentioned, it may or may not be necessary to view part of it. Check the client's source of guidance if the client appears to be blocked, or if unsure of the answer.

T: What does the energy in your legs and knees want?

C: It wants to be strong and purposeful, to have the ability to climb any height I wish to go...to not give out when I'm climbing. I need to connect my knees and legs with my HS...to open the circulation...

T: Who can help your legs and knees to get what they really want?

C: I'm seeing a tall, guilded greenish-gold being...he's my Andromedan teacher...his name is Xanath...(pause)...he's funny. Now I'm seeing Sananda on the side...brilliant violet light and pink is enveloping Xanath and me.

T: Ask Xanath what the solution to transforming and healing the energies in your knees and legs is?

The sudden appearance of healing light (especially violet and pink) suggests that transmutational healing (violet) and divine love (pink) energies are being applied to transmute negative energies and facilitate healing.

C: He's giving me messages. I need to maintain a sense of humor with myself...don't be so hard about going further faster...to rely on my own HS...trust and not doubt...follow my intuition without analyzing or questioning. And be more grateful...not complain about seemingly slow progress...understand that the workshops are a stepping-stone to completing my mission. The instability in my knees and legs comes from being disconnected... dislocated at the knees and hips. I need to open the circulation in them...

The fact that this client received assignments which she will need to integrate in the future on emotional and mental levels suggests that this unhealed energy complex can only be partially cleared today.

T: Are there any other messages or assignments from Xanath or your HS, or is the healing of your knees and legs complete for today?

C: My H/S says it's willing to open the circulation in my knees and hips. Now the light is changing to green...it's entering my 3rd eye...filling all the cells of my body from my front...to the back of my arms. It's glowing...scintillating bright green yellow. energy (H$_4$). It looks like a fish net...now it's changing to a dense field of light. My legs feel tingly...(pause)...I got a rush of energy. It's connecting at the base of the spine to the base of my skull. Now there's spiraling silver light from my coccyx to my skull and head... flying out my 3rd eye and crown. (H$_4$)

Another spontaneous wave of very powerful healing light in this case green (representing change, healing) and gold (wisdom) probably related to clearing out analytical mental tendencies blocking the client from seeing and understanding the bigger picture, and being too hard on herself, impatient with the progress towards moving ahead and completing her mission.

T: Now, let's check the energy of not being supported in the area of your knees and legs.

C: It feels clearer...Sananda says my homework for the next month is to do visualization of healing...to see the green and yellow light filling my entire body daily... and anytime fear or feelings of defeatism come up. And he says don't separate my work from the details of my mission. In my contact with the public...in a position of authority... authority to oversee many facets of the job... to be attuned to more subtle levels of energy... improve my presentation style, and sharpen my intuition to meet their needs and guide them. I have a fear of asking for money. But times have changed...money is another form of energy. Or I can do barter...(pause)...I'm getting to charge $88 for my workshops.

Here, client is referring to integrating her spiritual sensitivity and intuition in her regular work, an important integration for everyone, regardless of the nature of their job.

T: Is the clearing and healing of the issue of not trusting the universe and following your guidance you've received to clear the energy in your legs and knees as complete as possible for today?

C: Yes.

T: Then let's go back and ask your HS and/or Guides what, of the other problems and issues that have been brought into your awareness

T: (cont.) today, is the next most important or beneficial problem to clear or heal?

C: It's the feeling of loneliness (D_5). He says my attachment to being understood by my family...wanting to fit into the human scheme...but knowing you're not...not being understood...yearning to go back to my true family.

A common problem for many spiritual "Lightworkers" and Star People with remembrance of off-planetary lifetimes is the desire to reunite with one's true spiritual family.

C: Sananda says to remember I am no-thing and we have the potential to be everything... when you say, "I AM" ...you are limiting yourself. Be open, flexible and receptive to whatever the universe brings. Sananda says this was a pre-agreement. I agreed to accept the loneliness. I will connect with more key players doing the work. I am not alone. The loneliness stems from my (names past life) lifetime. I will have my partner to help. I am not alone...(pause)...Now...I'm more open to receiving help...and not my ego thinking I have to do it all myself.

T: Where is the loneliness being anchored in your body?

C: In my throat. (D_5) It looks like a ball or knot of white...

T: What does it sound and feel like?

C: It sounds like...a wail...an echoing wail... and feels like sadness...crying. It's like a void...the lack of presence of love.

T: What does it want?

Emotional Integration

C: It wants to turn the wail into a beautiful song of love. I hear high lyrical angelic sounds now...violin strings...like a chant. The ball or knot is loosening up...turning into strings of a musical instrument. There's light blue and white in my throat...the instrument looks like a harp. (H_5)

A beautiful music and color transformation of the creative block in her throat chakra!

T: Now breathe the angelic sounds of the harp through your entire body. Are there any messages or assignments from the harp?

Physical Integration

C: I will be healed by speaking my truth and doing my mission…it will bring the people to me…will bring the players into the void with committed detachment…to allow everyone the space to exist of their own free will, with unconditional love.

Mental Integration

T: Is there anything else we need to do to complete the healing session today?

C: It's complete.

Next is a summary and analysis of Paula's session using the triangulation model.

Analysis of Paula's Session

Commentary

1

Swirling gold and violet

H_1 - Healing transformation

Dark (D_1)
confusion & lack
of focus in brain
orange with red
flashes of light

Lt. (I/H Self or
Guide)
Sananda

Complete, rapid clearing
& transformation

2

Loving acceptance, golden crown turning into a
river of gold

H_2

Dark (D_2)
Fear in heart - vise-like
clamp representing
unforgiveness

Lt. (I/H Self or
Guide)
Sananda

Complete clearing &
transformation

Analysis of Paula's Session

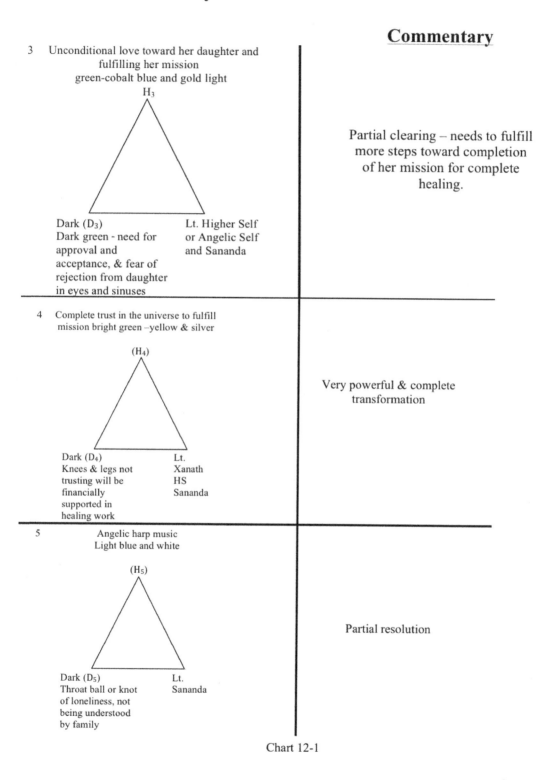

Commentary

3   Unconditional love toward her daughter and
fulfilling her mission
green-cobalt blue and gold light

H₃

Dark (D₃)
Dark green - need for
approval and
acceptance, & fear of
rejection from daughter
in eyes and sinuses

Lt. Higher Self
or Angelic Self
and Sananda

Partial clearing – needs to fulfill
more steps toward completion
of her mission for complete
healing.

4   Complete trust in the universe to fulfill
mission bright green –yellow & silver

(H₄)

Dark (D₄)
Knees & legs not
trusting will be
financially
supported in
healing work

Lt.
Xanath
HS
Sananda

Very powerful & complete
transformation

5   Angelic harp music
Light blue and white

(H₅)

Dark (D₅)
Throat ball or knot
of loneliness, not
being understood
by family

Lt.
Sananda

Partial resolution

Chart 12-1

Complex QTH Session 12-2

Victoria was a young woman who had no prior experience with QTH, and came in for the following extended session, which lasted approximately three hours. Since she was only visiting Hawaii for a brief stay, she was not able to return for a subsequent session. As such, there was only significant closure or healing of some of the disintegrated or unhealed aspects that emerged.

This QTH session is an excellent illustration of a very complex, psychologically difficult, extraordinarily multi-faceted session including revelations of multiple past/ parallel lives and unhealed shadow aspects; including dark Satanic energies, and multiple light guides/spirit helpers. A great deal of higher spiritual truth came through Victoria in her exceptionally free-flowing state allowing whatever "part" was seeking expression to speak through her. Additionally, a second therapist, Cynthia Chu (T2), co-participated in guiding the client and conducting the QTH session. Victoria interestingly revealed that she had been diagnosed by another psychologist as having multiple personality disorder (MPD). Since she was able to easily give a voice to these various parts and shift rapidly at times between parts each with distinct attitudes, beliefs, behaviors, and history, etc. it probably appeared to be distinctly separate personalities who had "split off" from her dominant personality, in line with the standard diagnostic criteria for MPD from a Western psychological perspective. However, although it was not possible to determine from a single session, it appeared very likely that she had conscious control and awareness over the expression of these parts, and they could be explained as past/ parallel life aspects. On that basis, Victoria would not be considered to have a true MPD according to the DSM IV-R. From my experience, past life personalities or attached spirits may appear as MPD to traditionally trained mental health professionals.

T: Spiritual Alignment, Clear Inner Vision and Hearing, Locate IPOP.

C: I'm up on a mountain, with a grassy meadow and lots of trees nearby.

T: Now call for your I/HS or spiritual guide to be with you in your IPOP.

C: She's a black bear – snuggled up around at my feet.

T: What's the bear's role?

C: She's my comforter (smiles). (Suddenly her face changes – client sits upright) Now I see a bird…it's fierce and big…not an earth bird. Before it flew straight to my mother… and tore out her eyes and then it tore out my father's heart. (look of anguish and distress) I made a commitment to not give a voice to these energies…

Spontaneous appearance of an unhealed aspect – judging by its fierce look and aggressive behavior - which we have no context for understanding.

T: Just relax. Let go of the pictures of the bird and go back to your IPOP. Call from your heart for your own guide(s) or helpers, whoever would be most appropriate for your healing session today.

When an unhealed energy or entity appears at the beginning of the session, we go back to the IPOP and connect with a clear source of guidance.

C: I'm seeing a green woman in a flowing gown…on my left…and another woman… who is white…to my right.

T: What are the names of these two beings?

C: One is Green Tara…and the other is White Tara. Green Tara is more expansive, flowing… her energy goes out and around and beyond. White Tara's energy is condensed…a focused energy that goes up and deep…(pause)… This information is difficult being said… unbelievable to this one who censored it up until now. (Suddenly, the clients whole body language and appearance changes now to look like an obstinate child) I don't want anybody to look at me. I want to be left alone (client doubles over and grabs her solar plexus… and gets a wide eyed distant look). I'm seeing scars on my ankles…I was in a UFO..they used drastic means…two beings from other realms interacting with us now. It's safer for all concerned to exchange energies on the ship. The first being is linked to the spiritual hierarchy. He doesn't usually take physical form. Most people would have their circuits blown (refers to being in the energy field). The second being abducted me. It was curious, fascinated with this physical form. They meant no harm…but have traumatized me greatly. Now my HS comes in…it's me…very beautiful and radiant…with a veil over my face.

These are two widely recognized aspects of Tara, the Tibetan Buddhist Goddess of love, compassion, mercy and forgiveness, and healing.

The speaker of this line is not known, but before I can ask who it is, she shifts again to yet another aspect.

This client moves and shifts between beings so rapidly when talking that it is difficult for the therapist to keep up with interpreting her process. However, I just allow her to go with her natural flow at this point.

Here, she uses language suggesting she is not in her body, but dissociated from it, when she says "this physical form."

T: Ask your H/S if the bird and the abduction experience are related in some way?

C: They're all linked. The bird is a warmer spirit…connected with my present…or rather a part who carries the energy of a past life in a Satanic cult. I was the one they sacrificed. My mother…they've driven her insane via the Catholic church…and my father is on the edge of breaking free…but stuck in the old patterns. The bird confirms that it's unhealthy to have any contact with them.

T: What does your HS have to say?

Presumably she is referring to her biological parents in her current lifetime.

C: It says "I as the pure being in spirit…I have not experienced the abduction and Satanic influence. Therefore my influence in bringing truth and clarity is limited…(pause)…I have a block…an unwillingness to accept reincarnation…and hence these things. I, in speaking in a childish way have transposed faces and events…the bird and E.T. energies have been mixed up.

Speaking from her HS aspect.

Client is speaking from her human (child) self now.

T: Connect with your HS and guides, Green Tara and White Tara to regain clarity of guidance.

Her rapid shifting is confusing and hard to follow. So I call in her HS and spiritual guides for clarity and direction.

C: They're here. The bird's name is Asha… she speaks bird language. My birdness is only what is perceived…(pause)…I'm seeing a body…it wakes up…there's a rebirth. (Now the client who was lying down with her eyes closed sits up abruptly, opens her eyes and defiantly addresses the group…consisting of two therapists and an observer). Those who are to stay…are those with no fear and who are not amused. If you think this is funny… you must leave. (client waits for response until 2nd therapist and observer shift out of the unwanted emotional states). My being is perceived as a bird because of my immense size and because I have a bird's eye now (makes bird sounds). I am not the bringer of the energy you call a downdraft…I am the liberator of it. The gatekeeper as you may call it. This being has the potential for resolution of that which has been termed evil…and the tendency of your kind to restrict that energy. In proceeding from here, I speak to you with all due respect and tell you if there is an opening …it will be taken advantage of…if you do not

Whose body she is referring to is unclear.

The client and I psychically picked up amusement in the observer and fear in the second therapist. The energies of loving acceptance must be present in order for this being to feel respected and honored.

"Downdraft" is a Holodynamic term referring to a negative, or unhealed aspect.

If a spirit energy claims to be working fully in alignment with the laws of the "Light" forces, it will not take advantage of an opening; therefore either the bird appears

C: (cont.) know what I speak of, you probably need to go.

(The second therapist, who had familiarity with her own "bird" aspect in a prior incarnation, now goes over to the client, embraces her, and speaks to her in tears of remembrance).

T2: By the Order of Ashtar and the Regal Elohim…we are no longer in the black box. The hawk has given it back. We are free again…you are the high priestess. (T2 apparently intuited that Victoria had a lifetime as a high priestess. Bringing this forth shifts her into a more positive Higher Self aspect for alignment with a lifetime in a "Light" role.)

The client curls up in a fetal position and the second therapist sings to her in bird language for approximately one minute. Client curls up in a fetal position again and then the second therapist sings to her again. Then the client sits up suddenly and sings in the bird language for thirty seconds and says, "I am the guardian bird and I will speak of the Satanic cult. The worst part was the baby was hung upside down by the feet and sliced repeatedly by a razor and put on a table to collect the blood. They raised my head and forced me repeatedly to stab the little baby. Then they cut pieces of the flesh to eat, and cut out the heart to eat that as well.

I was naked. It was underground and I was very cold…so freezing I would have done anything to get warm. Then they poured the blood over me and forced me to say I was a part of them and I belonged to what they called Satan. In my child state, the combination of warm blood and a warm blanket gave me pleasure. I led many ceremonies. I forgot who I was. I failed the test.

(Then client laughs a resigned laugh of sadness). And so did everyone else.

to have "mixed" energies of Light and Dark or she has two energies speaking thru her simultaneously.

Ashtar is a space commander of an intergalactic fleet of ships assisting in earth's evolution and ascension, and the Elohim are the Lords of Creation.

The observer and I are in awe and deeply moved, although the bird language spoken by the client and T2 is totally unintelligible but very clearly spoken and credible.

Client gives details of Satanic ritual sacrifice. As a general commentary, this brings to light the same distortion in various cultures, religions, and spiritual groups around sacrifice of animals or humans to "appease" or please their god(s). All like-type acts are not founded in alignment with spiritual guidance and the Cosmic Laws of Love and Free Will. Beings aligned with the Universal Laws of Love and Free Will would not request its followers to control and manipulate through fear to kill other beings.

This probably refers to the bird people succumbing to participate in sacrificial Satanic rituals.

T2: There is no failure. Only learning that can only come from experience. All have chosen dark and light roles through their various incarnations. We are all alike in that way. You can forgive yourself and come into your power as high priestess. It is the 3rd millennium.

C: (sits up straighter and appears to have accepted what was just spoken)

T2: I Am the Goddess Kwan Yin, and I bring you the forgiveness you seek. (T2 puts her right hand on client's heart and clients right hand over her heart – for transfer of energies (heart salutation) of love and forgiveness.) Child of Light, accept this healing of love to bring you into remembrance of the power of Light and goodness that you are.

C: (Client laughs wickedly as Satanic energy which is resisting the love and healing jumps in) You cannot release me! I will not leave! I am the force of de-evolution...the devil... energy in reverse motion. (client requests a paper and pen to write with...then spells perfectly the word motion backwards = "NOITOM."

T: Let's shift your focus back to your HS and Guides – Green & White Tara. We call now, in the name of the I AM THAT I AM from the Heart of the Presence, the Beloved Ascended Masters, Archangels and Elohim to anchor the Light forces of Love, Wisdom and Power within and around Victoria and all present here.

C: (Client visibly registers the change in alignment, with a peaceful expression on her face. She begins to name various spirit guides, some unknown to me.) As an acknowledgement of their presence, in speaking the name I honor the being: Asaak...(she begins singing other names and musical notes), Tara, and Kwan Yin. At the center of my being is my own soul...I bless myself. The male energy is behind me. The Gatekeeper is here...at my rear. I feel solid...I feel confused. An Archangel Nuit

This type of discourse about everyone playing roles of Light and Dark through various incarnations, I have found to be of great assistance in bringing the truth of "the big picture" to help get clients out of a state of debilitating guilt and self-recrimination/ loathing when they become conscious of lifetimes as perpetrators or participants in very "evil" actions.

T2, who mediates or "channels" Kwan Yin, brings thru the Chinese Goddess of Love and Compassion for healing and forgiveness.

This is reminiscent of saying that evil is the word "live" spelled backwards, i.e. anti-life or de-evolutionary.

When very powerful dark evil energies are present, it is imperative to call forth the forces of love and light at a combined power level that *matches* or *exceeds* the power of darkness!

At this time client's flow of speech is so rapid I do not interrupt her process for clarification since she was obviously connecting with some positive guides.

"Confused" represented a state of mental

C: (cont.) is here…also a Council member.

C: (She spontaneously resumes beautiful melodic singing and doing mudras). In this place…in this time…there comes the fulfillment.

C: Greetings…you may call me Adironaya… not for any need of mine. I am from the Council of Twelve, here to assist. I am speaking to the Dear One here. You have done well. Know you have found the ones on this plane you have been looking for. We've allowed you to use the process the therapist has chosen because your process was being drastically altered. Stay strong with your children; know they have chosen to come here. Stay strong with the man who was your husband; to not allow him entry on any level. Sometimes you have been unwilling to recognize the truth and accept your power in the Light. I do not like your energy spent in mere curiosity or doubt. I have a physical form and travel freely from it. I have worked with Cynthia and Ellara (T2 & T) and I will work with you.

Your mission is a fact-finding mission. The time of trial is over. You have built the shield for integration. Will you accept it? An integrated being is one whose subconscious (SC) is fully functioning. When the SC contains material that is limiting, it is out of necessity that the growth of the individual is limited. When the dilution is small enough so it can be passed safely, then healing can occur. The SC is one's best friend…it is the void, the place where anything is possible. It is most exciting when a being reaches the point where what has become its fear becomes its ally. All emotions are divine. They are universal elements of creation and when released, there is a tremendous amount of energy released, which can transform eons of karma in an instant.

A rule of thumb…If you have persistently wondered if it is true, it is! There are much crazier things to come. If one feels what they

reorganization; "solid" solidifying light energies coming in.

Mudra is a Sanskrit term referring to sacred hand gestures.

The Council member delivers specific messages to and through the client regarding her biological children and ex-husband.

Here, dilution probably refers to dilution of one's power, caused by the "shadow" or limiting aspect.

This truth is anchored in 5th density reality of unitary divinity, or the daimonic beyond the duality of good or evil.

C: (cont.) have seen is too bizarre, they will not go further.

Okay…the business at hand. I'll call it a "hanger-on"…this little hanger-on has threads or connections to a much bigger hanger-on. We can trace it and trace it…trace it all the way back to the Source. Ask Cynthia to help you trace it.	Adironaya from the Council of Twelve has now completed personal and spiritual delivery of general messages to the client and proceeds with healing the satanic entity via re-integration of the energy/entity at a universal level. "Hanger-on" suggests the attachment of the Satanic spirit entity.
T2: Go deep within now…to re-connect with the Satanic energies and remember all that is…at the time of Creation…(pause)…Take it seven layers deep. Bring forth that tear as a crystal glass…put that on your third eye… from the 7th level…and transform it to the 21st. As the veils drop off and truth re-emerges… all that remains is love.	Cynthia (T2) the co-therapist begins channeling guidance to facilitate multi-dimensional healing by taking the client beyond 5th density into higher and higher levels of Unitary Consciousness.
T2: The thread never leaves, the dream never ends, it just expands as it becomes aware of itself INFINITELY. It's about promises you've made to Satan…in that lifetime. Now you have the opportunity to change the contract…will you change your mind? Blood is only blood. (client starts crying deeply here).	If agreements have been made to align with the Dark Forces, these need to be changed, and the client's divinity and Light Body strongly re-anchored to consolidate the change.
T2: Call for the soul of the baby…to be completely healed.	Referring to the baby that was sacrificed.
C: I'm seeing this guy I met…George, who worked in a child abuse unit. He was one of the men doing the sacrifices…(pause)…	An interesting past/present life insight and revelation of how karma is being balanced. The previous Satanic child sexual abuser is now working in this lifetime to protect children from abuse!
C: I see my personality as my children. My task in the next level is to make a new personality. I understand! I see how I have been prepared and so I move back (in time) to console that part of myself that has finally broken through. There is more to the universe than she is presently perceiving.	Reflects client's unitary consciousness of the children she killed…being a part of her; in the same vein as we are all generally connected to everyone and everything. e.g. I AM THAT I AM & WE ARE ALL ONE.
C: I honor her (the baby) for that spark of myself that reached out and caused	Refers to honoring herself and her own inner child self (analogous to the baby she killed) to

C: (cont.) consciousness to dawn. I call you home. You have saved me. You have been a part of me, helping me by reclaiming the sacredness of my body...and the sacredness of my mind...and all of the wisdom agrees to align with the light!

C: (Suddenly, with an abrupt change in her facial expression and demeanor) I feel a band around my head, it's from shame...and guilt and fear. (D$_2$) The little girl in me feels shame. If people get close to me, they'll get hurt. My destiny is to get connected with the part of me that claims to be good but is part of the trap...

...I have a fear of leading people to hell.

T: Are there any other places beside your head that the fear and shame and guilt are anchored in your body?

C: It's where the spine meets the head and skull...and also in my shoulders and heart. (D$_2$)

C: (Now the client's inner child aspect emerges...visibly shaking) I took the path of fear.
My name is Missy (D$_3$), her little girl. She has brown hair...and is not too old, but almost old. I feel very old.

C: I built my house so carefully, thinking I was keeping something out...and finding I've been keeping myself in (pause). Missy is a gateway into the consciousness of me.

C: I've misunderstood...what clings to me or I to it...is a truer reality...and was my home. I thought if I died I would be free to go to my place...(drifts off)...I can't separate...I've been harming myself. I've been lied to...

C: ...I thought I was a member of the Dark! But all of it was false! I felt the purpose of existence was to...(drifts off and then starts crying and says in earnest) Is there free will?

express itself today.

As more light has been brought into the session from the unitary consciousness integration, she experiences seeing her wounded inner child self as parallel to the sacrificed baby.

Client speaks from the still unhealed, dark "Satanic" energy entity.

It's important to check for multiple sites of the unhealed energy, especially with multiple strong negative emotional complexes.

Client quickly shifts from being associated (when using "I" or "my" statements) to disassociated (when using "she" and "her" references) which often occurs especially when accessing intensely painful emotions/ memories.

I interpret this as a metaphoric way of saying she built her personality (ego strength) walls up for protection from external evil, but really it was internal- to keep her repressed emotional self in.

Although this was not particularly clear, I understood it to mean that the unhealed inner child aspect is the deeper home to truth.

Refers to the lying and brainwashing in the Satanic ritual sacrifice.

T: Yes we all have free will to change our agreements…to make new agreements and extend that truth into the past, present, and future simultaneously.

C: This piece (Satanic past life) has split off. I (referring to her Spiritual Self) am the salvation…but then she (referring to the wounded child aspect) has the truth…a piece of the truth that has been condensed and limited. I see the differentiation…and completion of the process of individuation. Standing in my own circle…connecting with my True Self…that is when I have the power…

The client is reflecting her somewhat confused identification with different parts/aspects of the self.

…Divinely ordained power to release that which is outside of the circle into the full potentiality of its energy. Standing in the circle…I know the limitlessness of my being and within me is all things.

Here, the client has connected with a higher, clear, unitary consciousness state, her own "True Self" reflected in her words as well as blissful countenance.

T2: Empty all so that thee can be completely filled infinitely and eternally. Bless yourself daily that you have created this with love, integrating infinitely into your future. Experience love within yourself. (Puts hands on client's heart to send love and help her integrate more love). All there is in truth is love.

C: (Begins singing and proclaims) In the power of this present moment and with the sword of my consciousness, I cut all ties with the past, I unhook all connections that are not conscious with any other being.

Referring to idea of separating from her dark shadow aspect of the past.

C: I claim the power of my choice. I claim the power of my will. I claim the power of this moment. I claim and remember the fullness of my being. Yes, it really is that simple!

C: The past only exists as we feed it!

Now client is in (5th density or higher) unitary consciousness state where there is no past and no evil.
Here, she appears to be referring to spiritual (vs. physical) nourishment.

C: I call home my own nourishment and feed myself. I commit to myself that others will be fed out of the overflowing natural abundance of my being! (pause)

C: Now I feel the Gatekeeper (D_4)...it's the embodiment of an archetype of a bird that eats carrion...It wants permission to leave.

Re-appearing in the light of the integration of her own I/H "I AM" Self, this shadow aspect comes in the light of her conscious awareness once again for the final release. If this had not spontaneously occurred, I would have needed to check with the Spirit helpers to see if it had been released (if a separate soul) or integrated (if an aspect of her own soul).

T: Who can give it assistance to leave?

C: I am...from within my own being I am to release it in the fullness of my being...in re-claiming my own power.

T: Are you ready to claim your power in the Light and release the Gatekeeper/Bird back to source?

C: Yes. But we need to create a matrix for it to be safe and leave my body.

T: What would that matrix be like?

C: We need to make an altar...and do a healing ritual for it to be released. (C, T, and T2 all build a beautiful altar of crystals and spiritual or sacred objects and call for the transformation of the bird and release all satanic energies associated with it).

T: Is the Bird feeling safe and ready to be released?

C: Yes, it's ready now.

T: Then see a tunnel or tube of light going back to Source...back to God. Bid farewell to the Bird...see it ascending in the tunnel of light. (H_4)

C: It is free. I am free! (she begins singing) That which is lame, can walk. That which is blind, can see. That which is deaf, can hear.

T: Check now, by looking in your head and skull, and your shoulders and heart, is the energy a clear bright color? (H_2)

C: Yes.

T: Ask your guides, Green and White Tara if
the healing process for today is complete?

C: We're complete. (End)   I return to check with the main guides for
                                             adequate completion.

Victoria's session was very intense, dynamic and powerfully emotionally evocative
for the two therapists and observer. It was also very challenging to conceptually organize
and analyze due to her very free flowing and rapidly changing stream of consciousness
and emergence of multiple, spontaneous guides and unhealed aspects or parts of her
psyche.

Nonetheless, here is a graphical triangulation analysis and commentary of her
session.

Analysis of Victoria's Session

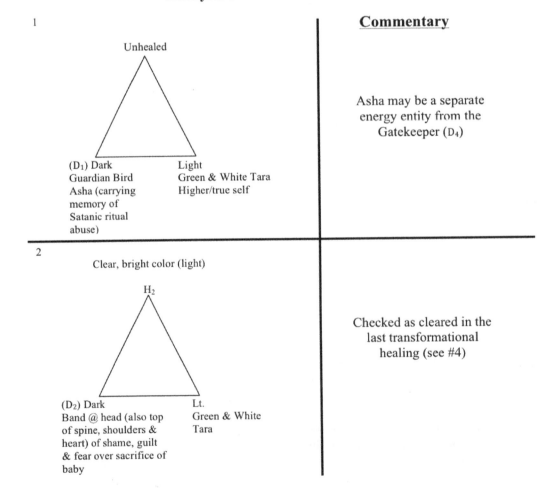

1

Unhealed

Commentary

Asha may be a separate
energy entity from the
Gatekeeper (D_4)

(D_1) Dark
Guardian Bird
Asha (carrying
memory of
Satanic ritual
abuse)

Light
Green & White Tara
Higher/true self

2

Clear, bright color (light)

H_2

Checked as cleared in the
last transformational
healing (see #4)

(D_2) Dark
Band @ head (also top
of spine, shoulders &
heart) of shame, guilt
& fear over sacrifice of
baby

Lt.
Green & White
Tara

Analysis of Victoria's Session

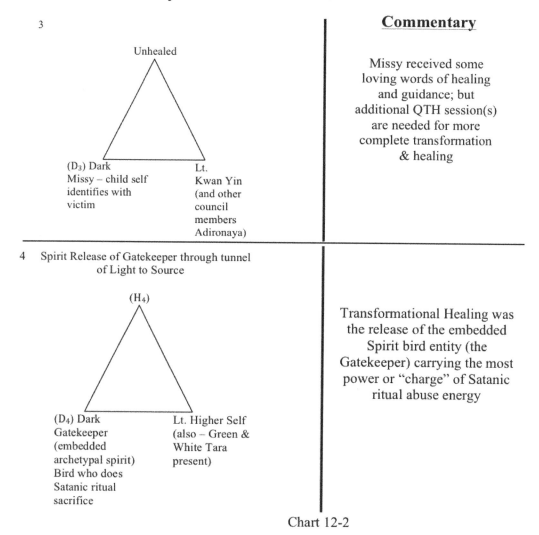

3

Unhealed

(D₃) Dark Missy – child self identifies with victim

Lt. Kwan Yin (and other council members Adironaya)

Commentary

Missy received some loving words of healing and guidance; but additional QTH session(s) are needed for more complete transformation & healing

4   Spirit Release of Gatekeeper through tunnel of Light to Source

(H₄)

(D₄) Dark Gatekeeper (embedded archetypal spirit) Bird who does Satanic ritual sacrifice

Lt. Higher Self (also – Green & White Tara present)

Transformational Healing was the release of the embedded Spirit bird entity (the Gatekeeper) carrying the most power or "charge" of Satanic ritual abuse energy

Chart 12-2

Polarity and Multi-Dimensional Integration Script

The following is a basic script that can be utilized to extend the transformational healing, integrating the polarities of dark/light, male/female, perpetrator/victim (as applicable), and extending the healing from personal to trans-personal levels – to the mineral, plant, animal, human, ancestral, racial, planetary, national, galactic, intergalactic and cosmic levels. The following script can be paraphrased and creatively improvised with sections repeated as necessary.

Here is the script:

Now, I'd like you to focus on the quantum transformational healing of (name of unhealed energy complex (D)), visualizing the same transformation (name the healing transformational symbol (H)) extended out to encompass with Divine understanding, acceptance, love, compassion, forgiveness, mercy and healing, integrating all the polarities of (name any applicable) good and evil, dark and light, male and female, perpetrator and victim into Divine Oneness.

Now extend this transformational healing exponentially to include all kingdoms and levels of creation, (input the following names of any you wish to include) – the mineral, plant, animal, human, ancestral, racial, national, planetary, galactic, intergalactic, and cosmic levels and dimensions. Continue to hold the focus of (name the healing transformational symbol (H)) integrating, transforming and healing (name the unhealed energy complex (D)), until the polarities of (name polarities) are balanced and transcended, and extending the healing multi-dimensionally to the (name the kingdoms or levels) until it is complete.

Multi-dimensional QTH Session 12-3

This last session is an example of how to extend QTH using polarity and multi-dimensional language integration from the personal to familial, ancestral, racial, national, planetary, intergalactic, and cosmic levels of healing. When we are anchored in Unitary God/dess Consciousness, we are At-One with all levels, species, kingdoms (mineral, plant, animal, human, angelic, extra-terrestrial etc.).

A deeper (female) and higher (male) connection to One's God-Self is typically more integrated into one's consciousness after the "peak" of the session, which is at the culmination of the personal transformational healing. Therefore, it is most appropriate to include a multi-dimensional integration QTH transcript at that time to demonstrate how to extend the healing as an act of compassionate service to all levels of creation.

Joel was a Jewish man in his late 30s with a past history of bipolar disorder and relationship problems. He was very bright, spiritually awakened, insightful, and experienced in doing the QTH process.

Here is the QTH transcript of Joel's session illustrating and example of the polarity and multi-dimensional integration language technique.

T: Spiritual Alignment, Open Inner Vision and Hearing, Locate IPOP.

C: I'm in a place that I've created …it's a cave in a big forest.

T: As you relax there in the cave, surrounded by the big forest, allow your inner vision to sharpen so you can see the colors and shapes more clearly. Hear the sounds of nature all around you and inhale the scents of the trees and plants…feel a deep sense of peace and tranquility as you relax in your IPOP… (pause)…Now, I'd like you to focus on your I/HS, or one of your spiritual guides. Open your inner vision and just allow whatever you see or don't see to be okay…relax your inner vision and de-focus your eyes. Just allow whatever impressions come to you.

Deepening of experience of IPOP.

C: I'm sensing a Christ Consciousness being. It looks like a bearded old man…(pause)… it's changing to an orange vertical eye…I don't know what it means…(pause)…it feels kind of evil.

T: That's okay. Let's create more spiritual alignment and healing by calling in the golden white light. Just visualize a golden white sun or sphere above your head. Allow it to descend from above your head to below your feet, filling you with golden-white light from head to toe. Then, spiral the golden white sun in a clockwise direction from your feet, back up to your head, filling your aura with golden-white light. Let me know when you are complete with that.

Here, I could also feel the presence of a darker "evil" energy enter the room. So I re-focused on strengthening his connection to a more powerful clear spiritual energy using golden white light (purity and wisdom) with violet (transmutational healing) ray.

C: I'm complete.

T: Now, I'd like you to focus visualizing a sphere of violet light in your heart. Breathe in the violet light, move it up through your head, and then let it descend and fill your entire body. Just say "now" when you have visualized violet light filling your entire body. Focus on the violet light transmuting any "dark" energies to pure light. And affirm that only energies in alignment with the Christ

T: (cont.) Consciousness (heart integration) will be allowed in your physical, emotional, mental, and spiritual bodies.

C: Now.

T: Next, I'd like you to check if the orange vertical eye is still there.

C: No, it's gone.

The "disappearance" of the orange vertical eye, which had a "negative" dark, ominous quality to it, probably was the result of the clearing of energies caused using the golden-white and violet light meditations.

T: Can you see the Christ Consciousness being now?

C: Yes.

T: Ask him what's the most important problem or issue to heal or clear today?

C: He says it's my heart chakra (D_1)…it needs opening. I'm being guided to pray directly to God. God is telling me that it originated earlier…before I came to earth.

Client had a rapid spontaneous connection to God based on his prior spiritual self-development. "God" is his second guide (H_2).

T: What does the energy in your heart chakra look like?

C: It's dark blue/purple liquid (D_1). My heart is shutdown. It's keeping everything out… (exclaims)…even love from God!

T: Okay, let's connect with the energy of God you experienced earlier.

C: He's here.

T: Great! Now reconnect with the dark blue/purple energy in your heart…ask it what it wants at its highest level of intention and purpose (HLIP)?

C: It wants love…and to open up.

T: Who can help the dark energy in your heart to open up and receive more love?

C: God can.

T: Is the dark energy willing to receive love from God now?

C: Yes…(excitedly)…now I'm seeing the dark bluish purple changing to a white circle with orange glowing around it (H_1)…it feels powerful.

A spontaneous transformation occurred, symbolized in the change in color and shape of the energies in his heart.

T: Now look in your heart chakra and notice if there is any dark blue or purple energy?

C: No, it's all gone.

T: Where did the dark energy that was just cleared originate from?

Checking source of energy.

C: It's my mother's holodyne. It's her cold dark energy that would just suck love from the room. I was aware of her sexual energy toward me…she'd be coquettish and press her body close to mine when I was a boy.

Client used the term "holodyne," meaning a "complex of energy" originally described by Vern Woolf, Ph.D. in his book, "*Holodynamics*"(1990).

T: Ask God if this energy is originating from your mother, or is it attached to you?

Here, I sensed a negative energy and suspected a spirit attachment due to the "parasitic" quality of the dark energy he described.

C: It's been attached to me since I was a little boy…I see an impish fearful Inner Child… he's bright and clever…he says, "leave me alone." It's an elfin aspect of myself when I was four or five years old. He's afraid of other people…and is keeping them at a distance. She (my mother) was very critical of me. By the time I was six or seven (in second grade) I formed a core belief of my "badness." By the third grade, I slacked off and got poor grades. It was because my sister was born… she's three years older than me. She was the "good" child…I was the bad boy.

T: Where is the core issue of the "bad boy" complex located in or around your body?

C: It's a grey blob over my face (D_2) that keeps me from breathing. I got it from my mother… when I was two or three. I'm seeing her…she had the same energy over the top of her head.

T: Did this energy originate from your mother?

Intuitive question

C: It goes past her parents...past my maternal grandmother...ten generations back.

Here we have an example of an ancestral holodyne, or energy complex.

T: What does the grey blob want?

C: It wants to make me suffer...it's punishment energy...it keeps me from breathing properly...so I can't feel comfortable. It keeps me from getting too carried away. It makes me wary of energies...and the bad things in life. It reminds me of my limitations...keeps me from growing and prospering...because I'd lose things...by getting hurt.

Generalized fear and distrust preventing client from taking risks and moving forward because of the fear he would get hurt.

C: The grey energy in front of my face (D$_2$) is controlled by something else...it's deep... on both sides of my family...a "Jewish" thing. It's a big black hole...a void...in my heart (D$_3$). It represents fear...fear of being persecuted...feeling hated...not wanting to be hurt...trying to survive...in a hostile environment.

A second deeper, darker energy is revealed in his heart.

T: What does the big black hole in your heart want at its highest level of intention and purpose?

C: It wants to know its safe...that it will be cared for...it feels insecurity...it needs to know God will take care of it at its highest level.

T: Is the black hole ready to receive help from God?

C: Yes.

T: Then allow God to clear and heal all of the energy of insecurity and fear of being persecuted...so it can feel safe, secure, lovable and worthy of being protected.

C: I'm seeing a row of people...with light flowers...opening up and blooming. The light is getting brighter. It's turning into a bright white light...(H$_3$)

T: Great! Let the bright white light absorb all of the black energy and fill the void in your heart (D_3) and around your head.(D_2)

C: (Excitedly)...Now the light is rising up...to the heavens. I see a new star being born in the space of the void. A new star...representing creation, fruition and healing...from Divine Inspiration and Integration! (H_2 & H_3)

T: That's wonderful! Now, would you like to extend the personal healing that you just experienced to others...since we are all connected as one?

C: Yes.

T: Okay, then...I'd like you to call for and visualize that the same energies of transformation releasing the victim (abused) role representing the energies of fear and insecurity, is sending understanding, acceptance, and forgiveness of the higher purpose and agreement that you chose to experience - the extremes in polarity (3-D Consciousness) - releasing attachment to the perpetrator (abuser) role not only for yourself, but for all beings on the planet. Connect with your I/H Self and visualize unconditional love (magenta and turquoise) flowing from Universal Source, from the victim to the persecutor, and from the persecutor to the victim.

T: Extend the focus of understanding, acceptance, forgiveness of self and others for their respective roles based on the Divine experiment of the split of Divine energy into the dualities of light and dark, good and evil, and the Divine plan for love to re-integrate all of the polarities, and transcend duality consciousness, returning to Divine Oneness.

Now, extend this transformation healing exponentially to include all persons, projecting this healing out to all of your ancestors, all Jewish people, all races, nations, and to the planet...and to the galactic realm...

Using language to encompass clearing of the last 2 unhealed energy complexes that came up in this session.

The birth of this "star" was suggestive of a higher order of multi-dimensional healing and a cosmic prototype from the microcosm and macrocosm of the healing of darkness (void) transformed to the light and the birth of a new star.

Here I added a linguistic description of a polarity integration technique, a multi-dimensional integration language pattern, and use of higher frequency magenta and turquoise rays of unconditional love.

T: (cont.) inter galactically…and all the way up to the cosmic levels.

Hold the focus of the bright diamond white light, balancing and healing all the fear and aggressive/abusive thoughts, feelings and behaviors for all beings on the planet and extend that to galactic, intergalactic and cosmic levels.

Here I could feel there was a perceptible increase in the higher vibratory frequencies in the room.

T: How does that feel?

C: It feels wonderful. I'm feeling tingling all throughout my body.

T: Now, I'd like you to check your heart area… to see if any of the dark bluish purple energy (D_1) or the black hole (D_3) is still there?

Always return to check for complete (or partial) clearing/healing of original unhealed issues.

C: No…it's only bright white light.

T: Good, now check the area in front of your face where you saw the grey blob (D_2). Do you see any greyness left?

Checking to see if the 2nd unhealed complex was cleared.

C: No. It's filled with a star.

T: Great! Then ask God if there are any other messages or assignments before we complete the session today?

C: The message from God is "Trust God."

T: Thank God for his Divine Guidance and Healing today, and choose to remember and integrate today's transformational healing on physical, emotional, mental, and spiritual levels.

Here is a graphical depiction of his QTH session:

Analysis of Joel's Session

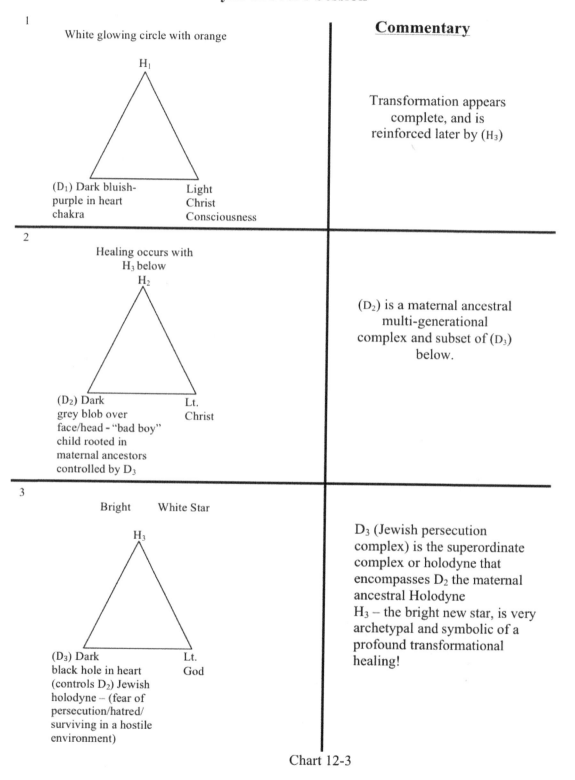

1

White glowing circle with orange

H_1

(D$_1$) Dark bluish-purple in heart chakra

Light Christ Consciousness

Commentary

Transformation appears complete, and is reinforced later by (H_3)

2

Healing occurs with H_3 below

H_2

(D$_2$) Dark grey blob over face/head – "bad boy" child rooted in maternal ancestors controlled by D$_3$

Lt. Christ

(D_2) is a maternal ancestral multi-generational complex and subset of (D_3) below.

3

Bright   White Star

H_3

(D$_3$) Dark black hole in heart (controls D$_2$) Jewish holodyne – (fear of persecution/hatred/surviving in a hostile environment)

Lt. God

D$_3$ (Jewish persecution complex) is the superordinate complex or holodyne that encompasses D$_2$ the maternal ancestral Holodyne
H$_3$ – the bright new star, is very archetypal and symbolic of a profound transformational healing!

Chart 12-3

CHAPTER 13

Clinical Diagnostic and Treatment Considerations in using QTH

Quantum Transformational Healing is an evolutionary guided imagery or hypnotherapeutic spiritual transformational healing process that accesses repressed unconscious aspects of the psyche. As such, it can initiate greater levels of inner psychic and spiritual self-awareness for those who have little or no actual experience of spiritual awakening. In addition, use of QTH may lead to additional opening, clearing and balancing of the chakras, and it can accelerate or expand kundalini awakening, which manifests in a multitude of physical, sensory, perceptual, emotional, mental, behavioral and spiritual changes, as discussed in chapter one.

Models of Psycho-Spiritual Integration & Transformation

Quantum Transformational Healing was developed to expand and deepen one's ability to potentially access and heal all "gestalts" or categories of unconscious, unhealed, or disintegrated "shadow aspects" or core complexes. *The Tripartite Consciousness Integration Model*, which integrates the three levels of the mind, or consciousness, from spiritual, psychological and Hawaiian systems described in chapter four, is a theoretical model of Psycho-Spiritual Integration. The primary categories of unhealed problems or issues previously treated in depth in chapters seven through ten include unresolved or unhealed childhood or adult problems, issues or traumas with symptoms manifesting as physical, emotional, mental or spiritual dis-ease patterns; and problems stemming from past life issues, attached spirits, and spiritual implants.

Another major contribution in the field of transpersonal psychology and psychiatry is the brilliant work of Stanislav and Christina Grof (1987, 1989). The term "Systems of Condensed Experience," or COEX system, has been coined by the Grofs to describe psychological complexes similar to a gestalt, which are core issues of significant and usually traumatic experiences from the past representing unresolved grief, angers, etc. and patterns of thinking, feeling and behavior. When a current life stressor or therapeutic process triggers a primary memory, the entire gestalt (or COEX system) may be recalled and cathartically released. This explains why a person in spiritual emergency may, for a while, regress to a more primitive state to resolve and integrate the emotional experience of the COEX system before evolving to a higher level of integrated functioning. Freud called this process "regression in service of the ego". This non-linear growth pattern can manifest as emotional outbursts, dramatic physical sensations, and other features congruent with the typical "psychic purging" during kundalini awakening.

Stanislav and Christina Grof (1989) identified six experiential patterns of spiritual emergence which may become spiritual crises if not handled by caring, experienced transpersonal therapists: 1) Kundalini awakening, 2) Shamanic journeying, 3) Psychological renewal through activation of the Central Archetype (Hero's Journey), 4) Psychic opening, 5) Emergence of a karmic pattern (aka seeing past/parallel/future lives) and 6) Spirit possession.

I have previously discussed all of Grof's categories save for the third topic, Psychological renewal through activation of the Central Archetype. Described by psychiatrist and Jungian analyst John Weir Perry (1976), individuals experience themselves as being in the center of the global or universal process, engaged in mythic rituals of death and rebirth with an archetypal conflict of forces of good and evil, in which the individual emerges victorious and raised to an exalted position of Savior, King, Queen, etc. This has also been described as the "Hero's Journey" by Joseph Campbell (2008), a world-renowned expert on cross-cultural comparative mythology and religious philosophy. The Hero's Journey is a cross- culturally identified mytheme of separation, initiation and return from the common reality to supernatural reality and back.

Psycho-Spiritual transformation and evolution necessarily results in the emergence of unconsciousness, repressed aspects of the self, which have been previously feared, judged or denied. These intense emotional upheavals and release are called catharses. The person moves from intense emotional release and a sense of overwhelm (non-coherent disorganization or chaos in quantum physics), to a return to a higher order (coherence and organization of functioning) when the catharsis is complete.

According to Ilya Prigogine, author of *Order Out of Chaos* (1984), increasing overwhelm or breakdown leads to entropy. The resulting disorder and chaos then reorganizes itself at a higher order of functioning and organization. When a person reaches a point of overwhelm of unconscious or repressed awareness coming to the forefront of conscious awareness, personal evolution can be facilitated by embracing, integrating, and healing the unhealed complexes or issues that are initially overwhelming, uncomfortable or disturbing.

By being in "at-one-ment," accepting and embracing our denied or repressed negative thoughts, feelings, etc., with our "witness" or "observer self," we can move through the feelings of being overwhelmed and go deeper into our awareness to "track" the false or limiting beliefs underlying dysfunctional patterns.

According to Grof and Grof (1989), spiritual crisis situations arise when the person is unable to integrate their spiritual experiences into their conceptual framework as acceptable and congruent with their self and world perceptions. When the psychic and spiritual phenomena are not understood, or when the person has a rigid model of human possibilities and lapses into judgment of his/her experience as strange, frightening, bizarre, and/or at worst pathological, the spiritual emergence becomes a spiritual emergency. Cognitive rigidity, as opposed to emotional and mental flexibility about accepting unusual experiences, acts as a barrier to insight and gaining of intuitive wisdom and understanding about the purpose and meaning of one's particular experiences. If the person fails to understand and integrate his spiritual experiences, he will probably deteriorate into a chronic state of confusion, or worse, long-term mental illness.

A differential diagnosis of a person engaged in spiritual transformation is ideally conducted by a mental health professional with a combination of traditional training in the diagnosis and treatment of mental disorders, coupled with direct experience or training in one or more spiritual paths, as well as a strong experiential base of personal spiritual transformation. The aforementioned prerequisites create a strong foundation for understanding the depth and breadth of spiritual transformational processes.

Differential Diagnostic Issues in Kundalini or Spiritual Awakening Crises

The following is a summary of signs of kundalini and/or spiritual awakening vs. the differential diagnosis of psychopathological symptom clusters, constructed especially for psychiatrists, psychologists and other mental health professionals trained in the diagnosis and treatment of mental disorders.

Signs of Kundalini / Spiritual Awakening vs. Symptoms of Psychopathology and Differential Diagnostic Considerations	
Signs of Kundalini or Spiritual Awakening as Symptom Clusters of Psychopathology	Differential Diagnostic Considerations to Rule Out
1. feeling depressed, crying episodes, lack of initiative, fatigue, loss of interest in usual activities, trouble concentrating, difficulty remembering or making decisions, increased irritability or anger, increase or decrease in appetite and/or weight, sleep problems or insomnia, passive or active suicidal ideation.	1. Major Depression

2. hyperactivity, increased psycho-motor agitation, expansive or elevated mood states with or without irritability, decreased need for sleep or insomnia, hypertalkative, inflated sense of self-esteem or exalted sense of self-worth, grandiosity.	2. Bipolar Disorder I or II. (aka Manic - Depression)

3. tense, fidgety, restless, irritable, trouble falling or staying asleep, headaches, numbness, aches or pains anywhere in body, twitching, spasms, epileptic-like (seizure) episodes, sweating, increased sensory acuity (of all five inner and outer sense abilities), specific fears or phobias, anxiety (panic) attacks, flashbacks, or intrusive negative memories of traumatic events from this or other lifetimes, psychic numbing or avoidance / hypervigilance when exposed to same or similar traumatic stimuli.	3. Generalized Anxiety Disorder
	  Hypochondriasis
	
	  Phobias, Panic Disorder
	  Post Traumatic Stress Disorder

4. appearance of distinctly different personalities or subpersonalities, ego states – related to 1) past life emergence or 2) attached spirits (discarnate astrals, demonics or other entities).	4. Multiple Personality Disorder (MPD) or Covert MPD
5. ideas of reference (interpreting external events as having personal significance or meaning), belief in paranormal or psychic abilities (Ex: telepathy, clairvoyance, healing, "magical" powers, etc.) unusual perceptual experiences, suspiciousness or paranoid thinking, increased social anxiety or withdrawal, inappropriate, constricted or blunted expression of feelings, odd or eccentric behavior.	5. Schizotypal Personality Disorder
6. delusions (false beliefs – persecutory, paranoid or grandiose), hallucinations (primarily auditory or visual but also kinesthetic, olfactory or gustatory), loss of reality contact, flattened affect, lack of volition, social/occupational dysfunction.	6. The Spectrum of Psychotic Disorders including: Brief Reactive Psychosis, Schizophreniform Disorder, Schizophrenia, Schizoaffective Disorder (schizophrenia and depressed or bipolar symptoms)

Chart 13-1

Whether the mental health professional based on evidence of sufficient clinical symptoms uses the standard psychopathological diagnostic labels or not, more important and critical is the integrated awareness and understanding that the client is actively undergoing a kundalini or other spiritual awakening process or transformational healing crisis, and that the symptoms are not seen as degenerative, but *pro-evolutionary*. The following figure illustrates the continuum of psycho-spiritual integration and transformation from normalcy to ascension. Increasing levels of psychological disintegration occur as we move from normalcy to neuroses, MPD and schizophrenia / psychosis. In spiritual awakening crises, psycho-spiritual dis-integration is temporary, and results in greater integration and positive personality transformation, all of which lead to a higher level of psychological functioning and spiritual evolution.

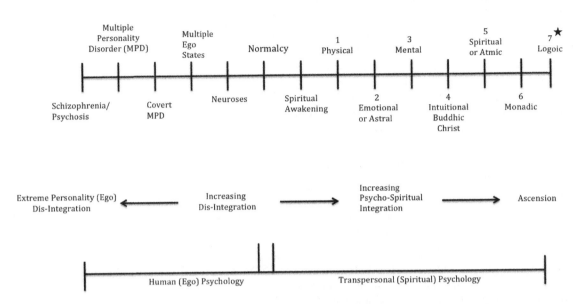

The Continuum of Psycho-Spiritual Integration & Transformation from Severe Psychopathology to Normalcy to Spiritual Awakening and Ascension
*The 7 Levels of Spiritual Initiation, excerpted from Beyond Ascension (Stone, 1995 pp. 1-12)

Figure 13-1

Contraindications in Facilitating Kundalini or Spiritual Awakening Processes

According to Grof and Grof (1989), the ability to see one's spiritual awakening as an inner psychological process and form an adequate working relationship with a health professional in order to flexibly adapt and integrate the new experiences is critical to preventing spiritual emergence from turning into spiritual emergency. This excludes persons with prior severe paranoid states, persecutory delusions and hallucinations, and those whose major defense mechanisms are denial, projection, exteriorization, and acting out.

As a general rule of thumb, use of meditation by individuals with borderline personality (Brown, 1981) or a history of schizophrenia, has been duly cautioned (Walsh and Roche, 1979). The borderline client, for example, may experience one-ness or unity with others or the cosmos, when they are actually experiencing fusion due to inadequate ego integrity and ego boundaries to differentiate self from others. From psychoanalytic subject-object relations theory, adequate ego integrity, ego strength and ego defense mechanisms must be present within a normal to neurotic individual to reduce the likelihood of ego disintegration or severe regression. It is critical to distinguish the presence of pre-existing borderline, narcissistic or other personality disorders, organic mental disorder, affective disorder, schizophrenic or other psychotic disorders, or a substance abuse problem, as they will interact with the spiritual transformational process. For example, psychological splitting- seeing persons as either good or evil, and other perceived hyperpolarizations resulting from unresolved early childhood or adult neglect, abuse, or trauma, may result in distorted projection of blame and responsibility on other people or situations, and perceptions of negative events as punishment. Individuals with borderline or narcissistic personalities (or with expressions of primitive defensive mechanisms such as projection, excessive blaming of others, splitting and/or disowning one's prior experience), are strongly advised to work through pre-existing childhood or adult abuse or trauma issues before embarking on meditation or other advanced spiritual practices. In cases of schizophrenia, Walsh and Roche (1979) cite several illustrative case examples, and they specifically suggest that the combination of intensive meditation retreats combined with fasting, sleep deprivation, a history of schizophrenia, and/or the discontinuation of maintenance doses of antipsychotic medications, may produce excessive stress and decompensation in individuals with a prior schizophrenic history. Close clinical supervision and monitoring is recommended under such circumstances to insure moderation is exercised and an excessive flood of unconscious psychic material beyond the capacity of the client to process is not produced. This can prevent a spiritual emergency and psychological decompensation. Treatment of persons in a spiritual emergency, especially with psychotic features, needs to be conducted in a loving, affirmative environment, or the patient will very likely become chronically mentally ill if they have bought in to the traditional psychopathological picture of their experiential journey.

If the person undergoing a spiritual crisis has a history of good psychosocial adjustment prior to the episode, the likelihood of having a positive outcome is enhanced. The availability of emotional support and interpretation of symptoms by an experienced friend or therapist is important to validate and assist in the integration of the spiritual or kundalini awakening as a positive, growth producing experience. If the person is not able to conceptually understand their experience as part of a deep, inner psychological process (Grof and Grof 1989), due to inadequate intellectual resources, and/or a significant, lengthy period of psychotic or schizophrenic illness, they will most likely return to their pre-morbid level of functioning after the acute phase of their spiritual emergency is passed, rather than integrate at a higher level of physical, emotional, mental, and spiritual functioning.

Treatment Considerations in Kundalini or Spiritual Awakening Crises

Bragdon (1988) has outlined eight basic steps (which I have amended slightly) to be used in the course of treating a person going through a spiritual awakening crisis:

1. Obtain a medical check-up to rule out organic causes. Altered perceptual, emotional, cognitive and physiological functioning may be due in whole or in part to a gross brain disorder from tumor or infectious degenerative brain disease. Some psychological or physiological symptoms may be the result of a physical disorder process. For example, depression may be the cause or effect of hypothyroidism, and frequent urination may be a symptom of diabetes, and not anxiety.

2. When possible, minimize the use of psychiatric drugs, which tend to block, distort or render inaccessible the client's inner process. Some psychotropic drugs, especially antipsychotics, make it difficult to access and integrate spiritual awakening experiences.

3. Provide a quiet, safe environment, preferably with natural lighting, soothing colors, quiet music, and simple furnishings.

4. Provide compassionate and knowledgeable companionship.

5. Establish a differential diagnosis of spiritual emergence from symptoms of a personality disorder, organic mental disorder, affective disorder or psychosis. Have the person be evaluated by a mental health professional educated and/or experienced in kundalini or spiritual awakening crises.

6. Educate the client about the spiritual emergence process using a description of signs of kundalini awakening, such as the developmental spectrum of consciousness model developed by Wilber (1980), the six experiential patterns of spiritual emergence developed by the Grofs (1989), and/or The Continuum of Psycho-Spiritual Integration and Transformation model as presented in Figure 13-1 in this chapter.

7. Help with grounding, centering, and/or catharsis to move the client from disoriented, labile or intense emotional states to ground or center themselves in their physical body by spending time in nature, or via bodywork such as massage, acupressure, or breath work, and engaging in cathartic release of feelings.

8. Refer the client to other persons or agencies providing 24-hour care, if needed.

Karen Bishop in *The Ascension Companion: A Book of Comfort for Challenging Times* (2006) suggests some additional techniques to remember when having physical or emotional discomfort symptoms associated with spiritual awakening and transformation.

Some of the most noteworthy suggestions include: listen to your own body, give it plenty of sleep, lots of healthy food, water, and exercise. Learn to "trust the process," and listen to your own spirit, or I/H self to guide you. Let go of the need to be in control so you can be attuned and receive inner guidance and be directed to the person, book, or situation that may provide you with the answers or solution you need. Take good care of yourself by doing activities you enjoy, or engaging in self nurturing activities such as taking epsom or sea salt baths, which aid in detoxification, and expressing your creativity (through writing, singing, art, dance, etc.).

Due to the importance of staying grounding and centered during spiritual transformation, I would like to further elaborate on this topic.

Grounding and Centering Techniques

Clients in spiritual crisis may swing rapidly from accessing unconscious material as they are working through unresolved past childhood, adult, or past life issues, to feeling at-one-ment with (and receiving direct communication from) one's spiritual I/HS or guides, as they integrate profound understandings on personal, global or cosmic levels. They may also become attached to staying in an ecstatic, blissful state but very detached from (or insufficiently in touch with) ordinary, mundane reality.

A person is considered ungrounded when he is not sufficiently identified with his body, or he is not sufficiently focused on taking care of basic bodily needs such as obtaining adequate food, water, sleep, etc. Other relatively ungrounded states may manifest as being out of touch with the earth, described euphemistically as being "up in the air" or living with one's "head in the clouds" instead of "having his/her feet on the ground." Some therapeutic techniques for people who are "spaced out" and feel disconnected to people and the physical world include: engaging them in eye contact, having them share emotions, or asking them to describe their immediate surroundings to get them in touch with concrete reality. Facilitating creative self-expression through painting, working with sand trays, dancing, music, or writing poetry may assist the person in communicating their experience when traditional verbal therapies are insufficient, as it is typical in spiritual experiences to find that reducing the profound and ineffable into words can be exceedingly difficult (Bragdon, 1988). Eating heavier foods such as meat and dairy products may assist others in grounding since both the denser vibration and the energy required for digestion draw more blood to the lower torso and away from the head and upper four chakras, which are typically the areas that undergo increased activation in spiritual awakening processes.

Using visualization techniques to foster reconnection with the earth is useful for individuals who are extraordinarily over-absorbed in their inner process. This is accomplished by imagining a line or cord going from the bottom of both feet and/or the base of the spine to the core of the earth, which is an excellent grounding visualization. Taking a walk in nature, preferably barefoot, also attunes one to the relatively slower rhythms of the earth. Bibliotherapy (reading books) is another important adjunctive strategy to assist persons in validating and understanding sometimes disturbing spiritual experiences. By reading books on the phenomenology of spiritual emergence, one gains comfort and reassurance about the parameters of normal transformational processes. Meditation may best be temporarily suspended or discontinued if the person is experiencing extended periods of being "spaced out" or seems to be excessively absorbed in his/her inner psychic processes.

Persons experiencing intense psychic opening and unitary consciousness states often feel hypersensitive, open and vulnerable to the negative emotional or mental energies of others. They can benefit from visualization exercises that affirm or create boundaries between self and others. In chapter two, the use of the spiritual protection meditation of visualizing blue - silver or silver light (in the "Spiritual Alignment, Christ Integration, Transmutation and Protection Meditation) is an excellent method, especially when combined with the affirmations to set protective energetic boundaries between oneself and outside energies. It is important to avoid persons or places felt to be overwhelmingly negative during intense periods of increased psychic sensitivity, especially when a person is experiencing enhanced telepathy, clairsentience, clairvoyance, etc.

Aspects of intense emotional experiences of feeling overwhelmed, overstimulated, victimized by the transformational process, frightened, disorientated, or out of touch with others, may persist for days or months. There may also be fluctuating levels of quiescence or plateauing followed by intense resumption of growth over periods of years. If one continues to be dedicated to ongoing personal spiritual evolution, the process of discovering and releasing ever more subtle layers of repressed, unconscious and super-conscious material stored in the deep recesses of the psyche and soma (body) (Lowen, 1994), is a never-ending lifelong quest for purification on physical, emotional, mental, and spiritual levels.

Finally, I would like to mention the recently published book *Rethinking Madness: Towards a Paradigm Shift in Our Understanding and Treatment of Psychosis* by Paris Williams (2012). Dr. Williams researched the outcomes of persons diagnosed with schizophrenia and other psychotic disorders in developed vs. undeveloped countries.

He found that the residents of undeveloped countries fared significantly better than in developed nations in the rate of recovery, and that the use of antipsychotic drugs to treat schizophrenia showed an *inverse* correlation with recovery rates. Furthermore, the Western view of schizophrenia as a "brain disease" and treatment focused on long-term administration of antipsychotic medication significantly increased the likelihood that an individual experiencing a kundalini (or spiritual) awakening, who is also diagnosed as being in the initial stages of a psychotic episode, will go on to develop a chronic psychotic condition (see also Breggin, 1994, 2007).

In contrast, persons experiencing a spiritual awakening crisis who are treated in individual psychotherapy or in residential treatment settings by spiritually aware, caring, empathic and experienced therapists, without the use of antipsychotic medication (Silverman, 1970; Perry 1976) had a much higher percentage of recovery and did not have any residual psychotic symptoms. Results of Williams case studies of persons who recovered from spiritual awakening with psychotic features showed that these individuals had undergone a profound transformation, with far more lasting benefits, including finding more hope and meaning in life, greater resilience, better connection with their own feelings and needs, an improved understanding of the importance of cultivating healthy relationships, a capacity to distance themselves from toxic relationships, a greater integration of the polarities of good and evil, and a strong desire to contribute to the well-being of others.

References

Aeoliah. (1992). Awakening Your Inner Light: Healing Self-Abuse and Reclaiming Your True Identity. Mt. Shasta, CA: Helios Rising Publications.

Aeoliah. (2000). Anchoring Your Light Body through the 8 Rays (CD). Mt. Shasta, CA: Oreade Music.

Ajaya, S. (1983). Psychotherapy East and West: A Unifying Paradigm. Honesdale, PA: The Himalayan International Institute of Yoga Science and Philosophy of the U.S.A.

American Psychiatric Association. (2000). Diagnostic and Statistical Manual of Mental Disorders (DSM-IV-TR) 4th edition. Washington, D.C.: APA.

Avinash, S. and Avinash, S. (1989). Boogie Busting: A "Light" Approach to Exorcism. Sedona, AZ: Earth Mission Publishing.

Baldwin, W.J. (2002). Spirit Releasement Therapy: A Technique Manual. Terra Alta, WV: Headline Books.

Bandler, R. (1988). Using Your Brain for a Change. Moab, UT: Real People Press.

Bem, S.L. (1976). Yes: Probing the Promise of Androgyny. In M.R. Walsh (ed.). The Psychology of Women: Ongoing Debates. New Haven, CT: Yale University Press.

Berman, M. (1990). Coming to Our Senses. New York: Bantam Books.

Besant, A. and Leadbeater, C.W. (1969). Thought Forms. Wheaton, IL: The Theosophical Publishing House.

Bishop, K. (2006). The Ascension Companion: A Book of Comfort for Challenging Times. Bradenton, FL: Booklocker.com Inc.

Bock, R. (2007). The Lost Years of Jesus (DVD). Narrated by Colbin, R. and Marshall, H. Tulsa, OK: VCI Entertainment.

Bohm, D. and Peat, F.D. (1987). Science, Order and Creativity. New York: Bantam Books.

Bradshaw, J. (1990). Homecoming. New York, NY: Bantam Books.

Bragdon, E. (1988). A Sourcebook for Helping People in Spiritual Emergency. Los Altos, CA: Lightening Up Press.

Breggin, P.R. (1994). Toxic Psychiatry: Why Therapy, Empathy and Love Must Replace the Drugs, Electroshock and Biochemical Theories of the "New Psychiatry". New York: St. Martin's Press.

Breggin, P.R. (2007). Brain – Disabling Treatments in Psychiatry: Drugs, Electroshock, and the Psychopharmaceutical Complex. New York: Springer Publishing Co., LLC.

Brown, D. (1977). A model for the levels of concentrative meditation. International Journal of Clinical and Experimental Hypnosis, 25, 236-273.

Brown, D. (1981). Personal communication. Buddhist and Western Psychology Conference, Claremont, CA.

Campbell, J. (2008). The Hero with a Thousand Faces (The Collected Works of Joseph Campbell). Novato,CA: New World Library.

Chopra, D. (1990). Quantum Healing: Exploring the Frontiers of Mind-Body Medicine. New York, NY: Bantam Books.

Chopra, D. (1994). The Seven Spiritual Laws of Success. San Rafael, CA: Amber-Allen Publishing.

DeArmond, G. (1990). Violet Flame and Other Meditations. Carson City, NV: America West Publishers.

Eisler, R.T. (1988). The Chalice and The Blade: Our History, Our Future. New York: Harper Collins.

Eliade, M. (2004). Shamanism: Archaic Techniques of Ecstasy. Princeton, NJ: (Bollingen Series) Princeton University Press.

Epstein, M. (2004). Thoughts Without A Thinker: Psychotherapy from a Buddhist Perspective. New York, NY: Basic Books.

Fiore, E. (1995). The Unquiet Dead: A Psychologist Treats Spirit Possession. NY: Ballantine Books.

Fiore, E. (2005). You Have Been Here Before: A Psychologist Looks at Past Lives. NY: Ballantine Books.

Frissell, B. (2009). Nothing in this Book is True, But It's Exactly How Things Are. Berkeley, CA: Frog Books.

Goldberg, B. (2009). Past Lives, Future Lives Revealed. Pompton Plains, NJ: Career Press.

Greenwell, B. (2002). Energies of Transformation: A Guide to the Kundalini Process. Saratoga, CA: Shakti River Press.

Greer, S. (2001). Disclosure: Military and Government Witnesses Reveal the Greatest Secrets in Modern History. Crozer, VA: Crossing Point Inc.

Grof, S. and Grof, C. (1987). The Adventure of Self Discovery. Albany, NY: State University of NY Press.

Grof, S. and Grof, C. Eds. (1989). Spiritual Emergency: When Personal Transformation Becomes a Crisis. New York, NY: Jeremy Tarcher/Putnam.

Grinder, J. and Bandler, R. (1981). Trance-formations. Moab, UT: Real People Press.

Hall, C.S. (1999). A Primer of Freudian Psychology. New York: Meridian.

Harner, M. (1980). The Way of the Shaman. New York, NY: Harper and Row.

Hoffman, E. (1981). Huna - A Beginner's Guide. Gloucester, MA: Para Research.

Howe Jr., Q. (1974). Reincarnation for the Christian. Santa Ana, CA: Westminster Press.

Hunt, R. (1981). The Seven Keys to Color Healing. New York: Harper Collins.

Hunt, V. (1996). Infinite Mind: Science of the Human Vibrations of Consciousness. Malibu, CA: Malibu Publications.

Hurtak, J.J. (2007) The Book of Knowledge: The Keys of Enoch. Los Gatos, CA: Academy for Future Science.

Ingerman, S. (1991). Soul Retrieval. San Francisco, CA: Harper.

James, W. (1996). In N. Fodor, Encyclopedia of Psychic Science (pp. 265-266). Secaucus, NJ: The Citadel Press.

James, W. (2001). Psychology: The Briefer Course. Mineola, NY: Dover Publications, Inc.

Joy, W.B. (1979). Joy's Way: A Map for the Transformational Journey. New York, NY: Tarcher/Putnam.

Joy, W.B. (1990). Avalanche: Heretical Reflections on the Dark and the Light. New York, NY: Ballantine Books.

Keyes, L.E. (1979). Toning: The Creative Power of the Voice. Marina Del Ray, CA: DeVorss & Co.

King, G.R. (1989). Unveiled Mysteries (Saint Germain Series – Vol. 1). Schaumberg, IL: St. Germain Press.

King, G.R. (1993). The Magic Presence (Saint Germain Series - Vol. 2). Schaumberg, IL: St. Germain Press.

Kornfield, J. (1979). Intensive insight meditation: A phenomenological study. Journal of Transpersonal Psychology, 11, 41-58.

Krisha, G. (1975). Kundalini: The Evolutionary Energy in Man. Boston, MA: Shambala Publications, Inc.

Kuhn, T.S. (2012). The Structure of Scientific Revolutions. Chicago, IL: University of Chicago Press.

Lake, G. (1995). The Extraterrestrial Vision. Livermore, CA: Oughten House.

Lawler, R. (1982). Sacred Geometry. London, UK: Thames and Hudson.

Lowen, A. (1994). Bioenergetics: The Revolutionary Therapy That Uses The Language of The Body to Heal The Problems of The Mind. New York, NY: Penguin Group.

Luk, A.D.K. (1996). Law of Life I. Pueblo, CO: A.D.K. Luk Publications.

Luk, A.D.K. (2003). Law of Life II. Pueblo, CO: A.D.K. Luk Publications.

Mahaney, T. (1991). Change Your Mind/Life. Sedona, AZ: Supertraining Press.

May, R. (2007). Love and Will. New York, NY: W.W. Norton & Co.

Melchizedek, D. (2000). The Ancient Secret of the Flower of Life, Vol. 2. Flagstaff, AZ: Light Technology Publishing.

Minto, W. (1976). Results Book. Salt Lake City, UT: Hawkes Publishing.

Modi, S. (1997). Remarkable Healings: A Psychiatrist Discovers Unsuspected Roots of Mental and Physical Illness. Charlottesville, VA: Hampton Roads Publishing Co.

Montgomery, B. (1993). The Thymus Chakra Handbook: Channeled from Kwan Yin & The Christ. Tollhouse, CA: Transformational Arts.

MSI. (1995). Ascension! An Analysis of the Art of Ascension as Taught by the Ishayas. Edmonds, WA: SFA Publications.

Muktananda, S., Chidvilasananda, S., Muller-Ortega, P. (2000). Play of Consciousness. South Fallsburg, NY: Siddha Yoga Publications.

Nidle, S. (2005). Your Galactic Neighbors. Pukalani, HI: Blue Lodge Press.

Notovich, N. (2008). The Unknown Life of Jesus Christ. Radford, VA: Wilder Publications.

Ouseley, G.J. (2005). The Gospel of the Holy Twelve. Gloucester, UK: Dodo Press.

Peck, M.S. (2006). People of the Lie. New York: Touchstone.

Page, K. (1991). The Hidden Side of the Soul. San Marcos, TX: Institute of Multidimensional Cellular Healing.

Pagels, E. (1989). The Gnostic Gospels. New York: Vintage Books.

Paulson, G.L. (1994). Kundalini & the Chakras. St. Paul, MN: Llewellyn Publications.

Perry, J.W. (1976). Roots of Renewal in Myth and Madness. San Francisco, CA: Jossey-Bass.

Prigogine, I. (1984). Order Out of Chaos. NY: Bantam Books.

Prophet, E.C. (1984). Forbidden Mysteries of Enoch. Malibu, CA: Summit University Press.

Prophet, E.C. (1997). Intermediate Studies of the Human Aura, by Djwal Kul. Livingston, MT: Summit University Press.

Prophet, E.C. (1976). The Great White Brotherhood in the Culture, History and Religion of America. Malibu, CA: Summit University Press.

Prophet, E.C. (1994). The Lost Teachings of Jesus 1: Missing Texts: Karma and Reincarnation. Livingston, MT: Summit University Press.

Prophet, E.C. (2000). The Lost Years of Jesus. Livingston, MT: Summit University Press.

Prophet, M.L. and Prophet, E.C. (2004). The Science of the Spoken Word. Corwin Springs, MT: Summit University Press.

Puryear, H. (1993). Why Jesus Taught Reincarnation. Miami, FL: New Paradigm Press.

Quigley, D. (1989). Alchemical Hypnotherapy. Redway, CA: Lost Coast Press.

Roerich, N. (1990). Heart of Asia: Memoirs from the Himalayas. Rochester, VT: Inner Traditions International.

Roerich, N. (2001). Altai-Himalaya: A Travel Diary. Kempton, IL: Adventures Unlimited Press.

Roman, S. (1989). Spiritual Growth: Being Your Higher Self. Tiburon, CA: H.J. Kramer Inc.

Royal, L. and Priest, K. (1989). The Prism of Lyra: An Exploration of Human Galactic Heritage. Phoenix, AZ: Royal Priest Research Press.

Sananda, S. (2004). The Narrow Path: Revelations in Advanced Spirituality. Claremore, OK: Living Spirit Press.

Sanders Jr., P.A. (1989). You Are Psychic! New York, NY: Fawcett.

Sannella, L. (1987). The Kundalini Experience: Psychosis or Transcendence. Lower Lake, CA: Integral Publishing.

Schlotterbeck, K. (2003). Living Your Past Lives: The Psychology of Past-Life Regression. Lincoln, NE: iUniverse.

Schucman, H. (2007). A Course in Miracles. Tiburon, CA: Foundation for Inner Peace.

Schultz, J.H. and Luthe, W. (1990). Autogenics. San Antonio, TX: Psychological Corp.

Scott, M. (1995). Kundalini in the Physical World. New York, NY: Penguin Group, Inc.

Selby, J. and Zelig, Z. (1992). Kundalini Awakening: A Gentle Guide to Chakra Activation and Spiritual Growth. New York, NY: Bantam Books.

Siegel, B.S. (1986). Love, Medicine and Miracles. New York: Harper & Row Publishers.

Silverman, J. (1970). Acute Schizophrenia: Disease or Dis-ease. Psychology Today, 4.

Small J. (1987). Transformers: Therapists of the Future. Camarillo, CA: Devorss & Company.

Solara. (1990). Invoking your Celestial Guardians. Mt. Shasta, CA: Star-Borne Unlimited.

Solara. (1991). El – An – Ra: The Healing of Orion. Whitefish, MT: Star-Borne Unlimited.

St. Germain Foundation. (1988). Purpose of the "I AM" Religious Activity. Schaumberg, IL: Saint Germain Press.

Stahr, A. (1993). All About: Implants and Spiritual Limitation Devices. San Pedro, CA: Star-Essenia, Inc.

Starr, A. (1993). Prisoners of Earth: Psychic Possession and Its Release. Sedona, AZ: Light Technology Publishing.

Stevens, J. and Warwick-Smith, S. (1988). The Michael Handbook: A Channeled System for Self Understanding. Easthampton, MA: Warwick Press.

Stevenson, I. (1980). Twenty Cases Suggestive of Reincarnation. Charlottesville, VA: University Press of Virginia.

Stone, H., and Winkelman, S. (1989). Embracing Ourselves. Marina Del Ray, CA: Devorss and Company.

Stone, J.D. (1995). Beyond Ascension. Flagstaff, AZ: Light Technology Publishing.

Stone, J.D. (1994b). Soul Psychology. Sedona, AZ: Light Technology Publishing.

Stone, J.D. (1994a). The Complete Ascension Manual. Sedona, AZ: Light Technology Publishing.

Stubbs, T. (2009). An Ascension Handbook. Lithia Springs, GA: World Tree Press.

Tachi-ren, T. (Channeling Archangel Ariel). (1995). What is Lightbody? Livermore, CA: Oughten House Publications.

Talbot, M. (1988). Beyond the Quantum. New York: Bantam Books.

Tart, C.T. (1983). Transpersonal Psychologies. El Cerrito, CA: Psychological Processes, Incorporated.

Tebecis, A. (2000). Mahikari: Thank God for the Answers at Last. Tokyo, Japan: L.H. Yoko Shuppan.

The Holy Bible (King James Version). (2010). New York: Oxford University Press.

Tuella (1985). Ashtar: A Tribute Compiled by Tuella. Salt Lake City, UT: Guardian Action International.

Two Disciples (1982). The Rainbow Bridge: First and Second Phases Link With the Soul Purification. Bel Air, CA: New Age Press.

Van Lysebeth, A. (1995). Tantra: Cult of the Feminine. York Beach, ME: Red Wheel/ Weiser, LLC.

Walker III, E. (2003). The Mystic Christ. Norman, OK: Devi Press.

Walsh, R., and Roche, L. (1979). Precipitation of acute psychotic episodes by intensive meditation in individuals with a history of schizophrenia. American Journal of Psychiatry, 136. 1085-1086.

Walsh, R., Elgin, D., Vaughn, F. and Wilber, K. (1981). Paradigms in Collision. In R.N. Walsh and R. Vaughan (Eds.). Beyond Ego: Transpersonal Dimensions in Psychology (pp. 36-53). Los Angeles, CA: J.P. Tarcher, Inc.

Wambach, H. (1984). Life Before Life. New York: Bantam Books.

Wambach, H. (2000). Reliving Past Lives: The Evidence Under Hypnosis. New York: Barnes and Noble Books.

Whiston, W. (translator) (1995). The Works of Flavius Josephus. Lafayette, IN: Associated Publications and Authors, Inc.

Whitfield, C. (1991). Co-Dependence: Healing the Human Condition. Deerfield Beach, FL: Health Communications, Inc.

Wilber, K. Ed. (1982). The Holographic Paradigm and Other Paradoxes. Boston, MA: Shambala Publication.

Williams, P. (2012). Rethinking Madness: Towards a Paradigm Shift in Our Understanding and Treatment of Psychosis. San Rafael, CA: Sky's Edge Publishing.

Wolf, F.A. (1990). Parallel Universes. New York: Simon and Schuster.

Woolf, V. V.(1990). Holodynamics. Tucson, AZ: Harbinger House.

Yogananda, P. (2007). The Yoga of Jesus: Understanding the Hidden Techniques of the Gospels. Los Angeles, CA: Self Realization Fellowship.

FREE RESOURCES AND INFORMATION

To receive FREE meditations, tips, tools and techniques to assist in your spiritual self-mastery and ascension; as well as information about the upcoming book *Quantum Transformational Healing – The 5-D Process*, and new future product releases, please go to:

www.DrLauraSturgis.com/resources

CPSIA information can be obtained at www.ICGtesting.com
Printed in the USA
LVOW03s1240281213

367220LV00003B/5/P

9 781478 719663